An MFA
For Your MBA

An MFA For Your MBA

Professional-Level Writing Advice for Mastering Communication and
Creativity in Business and in Your Career

Phillip Scott Mandel

atmosphere press

What do you think an artist is? An imbecile who has only eyes if he is a painter, ears if he's a musician, or a lyre in every chamber of his heart if he's a poet, or even, if he's a boxer, only some muscles? Quite the contrary, he is at the same time a political being constantly alert to the horrifying, the passionate or pleasing events of the world, shaping himself completely in their image ... No, painting is not made to decorate apartments. It's an offensive and defensive weapon against the enemy.

— Pablo Picasso[1]

CONTENTS

INTRODUCTION

Crises place heavy demands on leaders and managers, and it is easy to lose the already slim time we might have for reflection. But we won't see the big picture, let alone a shapeable picture of the future, unless we stand back and reflect. Most of the time in business we operate with our instinctual "fight-or-flight" nervous system that evolved to help us in high-pressure situations, like running from a predator. This system narrows our focus. But less emphasized is the parasympathetic, or "rest-and-digest" system, which evolved to manage mental and bodily operations when we are relaxed. We can imagine in hunter-gatherer days, the mental intensity of the hunt, followed by time back at home, reflecting on the day's stories, perhaps **imagining how to hunt better**.

— Martin Reeves and Jack Fuller, "We Need Imagination Now More Than Ever," *Harvard Business Review*, April 10, 2020[2] (my emphasis)

A Definition of Terms

MFA: Master of Fine Arts

MBA: Master of Business Administration

WHY I WROTE THIS BOOK

I once tried reading a book about creativity written by the CEO of an award-winning ad agency in Brooklyn. After the eleventh cliché I flung the book into the furnace, where it ignited with a satisfying *whoosh* and sent a gust of warm air back my way in suicidal gratitude. Okay, that's not *entirely* true—I don't have an open furnace in my office. But I did throw the book in the garbage.

The agency's website was also replete with clichés and marketing jargon, which saddened me because I was hoping these creative professionals would at least be proficient writers. After years of moldering in an enervating miasma of corporate banality, I'm always on the lookout for original and interesting language.

But I rarely find it. And as ever fewer college students major in the Humanities and study literature,[3] I have a hunch this will get worse. So I decided to write a book that draws on everything I know about putting words together to help people improve their writing, use fewer clichés, and make their overall business communication more effective—and, frankly, more bearable (to me).

WHY YOU SHOULD READ THIS BOOK

There's more to *An MFA for Your MBA* than annihilating cliché. The process of becoming a better writer will make you better at thinking, solving problems, and communicating your ideas and feelings. This will give your professional deportment the polish it deserves and help you make more money.

Also, these days you need to be able to write better than AI.

Reason 1: Hunting Better

The first lesson of the book is: don't skip quotes.

So now that you've gone back and read the quote at the

beginning of the Introduction, let's talk about "imagining how to hunt better."

How can you make more sales, retain more clients, keep your employees happy, and become more profitable? How can you survive economic downturns or disruptive events such as coronavirus? How do you come up with better solutions to common problems?

Imagining how to hunt better means thinking deeply. It means rejecting your first idea and reviewing a problem or issue again and again until a new, better idea comes up. It's why professional writers edit their work fifty times before it goes to print, filmmakers shoot ten takes of each scene, and gifted comics hone their set at countless nightclubs, refining the timing and punchline of each joke, before filming their standup special.

Unfortunately, this practice is vanishingly rare in everyday office life, no doubt due to a lack of time, motivation, or incentive. True, some people only put in minimal effort for eight hours (or fewer, if they can) each day, then stop working—and the rigors, lessons, and exercises demanded by this book probably won't appeal to them. But the rest of us are giving it our sincere best, and the modern corporate world seems to be evermore obstructing our process of deep thinking.

We're assaulted with messages and distractions nonstop, new plagues are appearing every day, our attention spans are being decimated, social media is a cesspool, our politics are increasingly fractured, and despite technological "progress," individual workers are expected to produce more work in fewer hours. Even the most high-performing employees are burning out, making mistakes, and deciding the game is no longer worth playing (at least, with the rules the way they are). In March 2022, the US Labor Market saw a record 4.5 million people quit their jobs—and it's not just about money. All these expectations and outside bullshit are over-saturating our brains. It's no wonder our collective writing and problem-solving skills have suffered. Something has to change.

Throughout this book, I will apply the lessons of a graduate-level creative writing degree to professional writing—an idea that might seem unconventional at first. Art and Business are supposed to be separate, right?

So we are taught to believe. But success often comes from the unconventional, and by the end of this book, you will be a stronger writer, a more creative problem solver, and a better communicator.

Reason 2: Money

From a purely practical, capitalist perspective, another reason to read this book is because *poor communication drains cash*. That's right. The money and time you spend on this book will save you money in the long term because this advice will make you and your company better at collaborating and sharing information, and thus more productive.

Don't believe me? Countless studies have shown how much money poor communication wastes every year, and it ain't pennies. David Grossman (2016) found that companies with 100K+ employees lost an average of $62.5 million each year due to crap communication.[4]

I know there's a lot of advice out there (see Figure 1), and I've read countless business books in my career. Some were good, many were drivel. You don't need yet another person to tell you to dare to be creative or make your bed in the morning or "how to get things done." Or "how to be f*cking great," or "how not to g*ve a sh*t about being f**king great," or whatever.

Maybe you don't *want* to be that great, or you like giving a f*ck.

The concepts in *this* book, however—avoiding cliché, the magic of shitty first drafts, particularity, revision, story arcs, showing up every day—will, if not wholly transform your life, at least get you to write better, think harder, and do business differently today. Remember: these days it's not *daring* to be creative; it's *necessary*.

Figure 1. So much f*cking advice for sale.

Reason 3: Speed and Efficiency

With deliberate practice and by learning the writing techniques in this book, you'll be able to communicate your ideas more quickly, effectively, and persuasively. Soon you'll write cogent and clear missives in five or ten minutes instead of thirty. This will make you more efficient with your time so you can get back to doing what you love.

See how efficiently I was able to communicate that point?

Reason 4: Perception Is Reality

Yes, this phrase is used so often it might feel like a cliché, but only because it's so true. I'll prove it using an optical illusion you may have seen before:

In Figure 2, Square "A" and Square "B" are the same color,

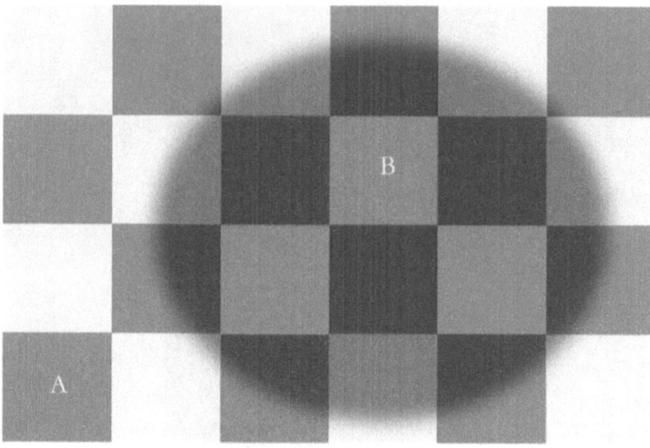

Figure 2. It's an illusion!

even though your eyes don't perceive it that way. I know it's true because I designed the image myself, but if you don't believe me, look at Figure 3:

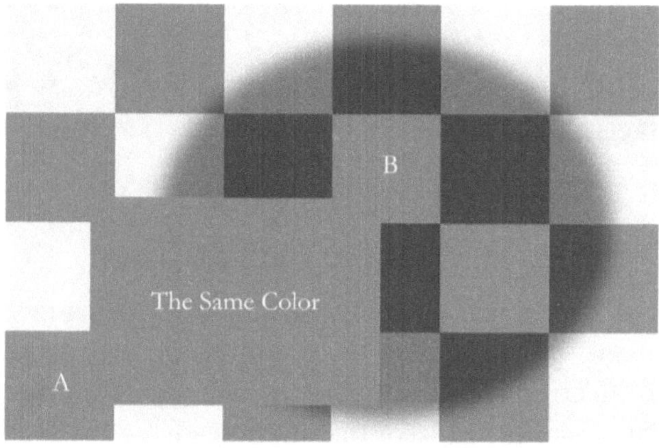

Figure 3. Told you!

This happens because human brains are subjective meaning-makers, not cold and objective calculating machines.

A software analyzing Figure 2 would identify the color of the pixels in boxes A and B as hexadecimal code #747474, regardless of any surrounding pixels. But humans make judgments, decisions, and meaning through relationships, comparison, and expectation. We see Box B as lighter than Box A because the boxes surrounding it are darker, and because our brains are telling us it should be lighter based on the pattern. But figure 3 shows us the reality that's been true the entire time.

Unfortunately, life doesn't offer a Figure 3.

This means that even if you are a brilliant logician, a shrewd negotiator, an inspiring manager, a natural leader, a skilled craftsman, or a genius architect, if your writing sucks, people will think you're an idiot. This is the truth, whether you like it or not; whether it's fair or not.

Maybe it isn't fair. But people's perception of you, professionally, is largely determined by the way you write and the words you use, especially when you are not around to demonstrate your talents, charm, and intelligence in person. If your writing is filled with typos, clichés, jargon, bad grammar, clutter, tedious details, and confusing argle-bargle, people will automatically assume—fairly or not—that you, too, are careless, pompous, boring, unreliable, irresponsible, and stupid.

Poor writing, in other words, is unprofessional.

But despair not. The lessons and exercises in this book will help you hone your writing into the sleek, sophisticated, poised, and polished craft worthy of your name.

Reason 5: Your Well-Being

If performing better in your career and saving money aren't enough to convince you why writing better is important, allow me one more persuasive argument: better communication will make you happier. Being able to effectively express what you think and how you feel at work will redound to your benefit at home, in your relationships, and with your family and friends. It will allow you to connect with people better.

And don't just take it from me. Take it from Thich Nhat Hanh, a Zen Buddhist monk who taught mindfulness for over seventy decades:

> Never in human history have we had so many means of communication—television, radio, telephone, fax, email, the

internet—yet we remain islands, with little real communication between us. When we cannot communicate, we suffer, and we spill our suffering on to other people. (*How To Fight*, 2017.)

We'll come back to this idea many times throughout this book.

Now, you're probably wondering who the hell am I to tell you how to write, think, or hunt better? I'm glad you asked...

WHO AM I?

If I existed 200 years ago, all the other farmers in my community would be like, That guy is worthless! He's sitting on a rock, jumping up like a frog, coming up with weird concepts and ideas, making faces, and combing his hair into a giant pastry. It's a good thing I was born in this century, when superfluous television seems to be part of the economy.

— Conan O'Brien

I always kind of figured that if/when the zombie apocalypse came, I'd be one of the first turned. I can't hunt, I can't build, and I'm marginally afraid of the dark. But maybe I'm selling myself short: while our future zombie warlords won't need advertising copywriters, they might enjoy bards and storytellers and comedians and snarky witticisms, right? Surely they must.

Best not to think about it.

I did spend one college break on the maintenance team of a suburban corporate office park in northern New Jersey. I distinguished myself that humid summer by taking the most coffee breaks and defeating everyone in Rummikub, a tile-based mahjong-rummy game that my bubbe taught me to play when I was eight and which, surprisingly, this team of construction workers played every day during lunch. I also demonstrated my uselessness by riding the lawnmower over a bed of small red rocks (which, apparently, you are not supposed to do). One got sucked up into the blades, and with incredible centrifugal force was flung out the side exhaust of the mower at bullet speed and into the window of a ground-floor office. It left a clean, circular hole in the glass and a rust-colored dent in the sheetrock right behind where someone's head *would* have been had they been sitting at their desk at the time.

Also, I couldn't hammer a nail straight and my power drill was, for some reason, conveniently always out of juice. By the end of August, I was reduced to carrying boxes or whacking weeds (I'm surprised they let me near the weed-whacker) and listening to Howard Stern on the boombox in the warehouse.

That's why this book is about writing and not landscaping.

After college, I applied to several MFA programs in poetry and was soundly rejected by them all. And no, it doesn't still keep me up at night, or make me sad. I swear, it doesn't. Truly. I'm totally fine with it.

Anyway, I moved to Manhattan, bounced around a few different advertising agencies, and worked with some startups. During this time, I completed a Master's in English Literature at NYU.

Why torture myself thusly? Because I've always loved writing, language, and literature. I also secretly hoped that if I wandered around the dusty, forlorn halls of the NYU English Department long enough, Sharon Olds or Zadie Smith might notice my genius—or, at the very least, take pity on me—and allow me into their MFA program. They did not.

Attaining this postgraduate degree was incredibly difficult—and would have been even *without* a full-time job. But I spent my weekends slogging through hundreds of pages of inscrutable theory and criticism—Jacques Derrida, Michel Foucault, and other postmodern continental philosophers (stinky pinkies, if you will)—because there was something about the world I was trying to discover. I knew there was more to life than spreadsheets and media-sponsored happy hours.

Hell, I didn't understand all of it, to be honest. I don't think anyone does. But it did help me learn how to think, really hard, about larger ideas—*the things behind the things*—rather than react instinctually to the banal stimulus of life, like a beast. I enjoyed questioning ("problematizing," as the grad students say) conventional corporate wisdom and looking for the deeper meaning hidden in the morass of sales presentations. Unfortunately, I rarely found any.

Still, even with these "big ideas" floating around in my brain, I was oppressed by the subway commute and the concrete and felt like I was a cog in a terrible instrument, a minute speck of dust on the infinite wheel of money and machinery that processes all New Yorkers—and I got out.

Jump cut to Chicago, where I spent a few years playing in bands and working in digital media. I loved Chicago. But something was always pulling me in a different direction. I never felt satisfied, despite doing well financially. I quit it all and moved to Texas to finally pursue an MFA in fiction writing.

I left a lucrative career to become a poor, full-time graduate student. Why?

Because no amount of money would have made me happy. I was thirty-three when I again applied for an MFA. The same age Jesus went to get that great MFA in the sky. I wasn't sure if any programs would accept me, seeing as I'd gotten shellacked my first go-round ten years earlier. But I knew if I went to my deathbed having never at least *tried* to have a go at being a "real" writer—whatever that means—I would regret it. Plus I had no kids, no mortgage, no relatives in need. Many people in MFA programs are in their twenties, and some go straight from undergrad. This can be risky, as adult life experience outside college offers good writing material. So, actually, I was *lucky* all those poetry programs rejected me. Fuckers.

MFA programs are notoriously difficult to get into—the Iowa Writers' Workshop accepts fewer people by percentage than Harvard—but I was lucky to get into a few. I chose Texas State

University because my literary hero Tim O'Brien taught there, it wasn't as outrageously expensive as some others, and I could live in Austin.

An MFA program, however, isn't "real life." Shocking, I know. And after three years of practicing the craft of writing, my credit cards were maxed out. So I went back to advertising, first in sales, and then launching Mandel Marketing. I founded a literary magazine, *Abandon Journal,* which has afforded me the honor of reading and editing hundreds of terrific stories, poems, and essays from writers around the world.

I enjoyed the MFA experience, and being an editor, a publisher, a marketer, a salesman, and a CEO has allowed me to put into practice the lessons I learned there.

In other words, I had to get back to work.

And now, so do you.

WRITING EXERCISE: EXPECTATIONS AND INTENTIONS

Part I: Think about why you picked up this book. What do you hope to get out of it? What are you struggling with in your career or business right now? What are your short- and long-term goals? What do you wish you could do better?

Now take ten minutes and write these things out. Bullet points are acceptable, and so is paragraph form. A whiteboard with a mind map is fine, too.

Part II: When you're done with your draft of reasons, reread it and start revising. You don't need to change the *content,* necessarily, unless you've been lying to yourself (so be as honest as possible), but do revise the language. Try to make this bullet list or word cloud or paragraph as beautiful and elegant as possible; something you would be proud to hand to your boss or client or partner or kid and say, "I wrote that, and I stand by it."

Now put it aside and keep reading. This isn't some kind of magic "dream it and you'll have it" exercise. It's just some writing practice to get warmed up.

PART I:

ART AND BUSINESS

1: MFA AND MBA

Aesthetics is to artists what ornithology is to birds.

— Barnett Newman (NYC artist)

Similarities Between MFA and MBA Programs

When I refer to MFA programs in this book, I mean in Creative Writing. I specialized in fiction, but writers can also focus on Poetry, Nonfiction, and Playwriting. MFA programs also exist for visual arts such as Painting or Sculpture, as well as Film Direction, Dance, and many other avenues for creative expression.

An MFA is a studio art degree, meaning that significant time is spent on practice, and less energy is devoted to academic and theoretical study than, say, in a PhD program (though there is still plenty of book learning). For writers, this means writing and workshopping stories or poems, while painters and sculptors are in an actual studio, making art standing up.

There are many similarities between MBA and MFA programs, even though the material covered in each is worlds apart. For starters, an MBA—like an MFA—is an expensive piece of paper that can be waved in the face of one's now-lesser peers while shouting, "Listen to me! I'm an expert! I know what I'm talking about! I have an M. F. (or B.) A!!!"

And like an MFA, an MBA is not necessary for success. But it can be helpful. These degree programs allow folks to dig deeper into subject matter than they typically would on their own, and can be excellent for networking. Still, there are tons of successful and talented writers who don't have MFAs, just as many successful, talented business owners and managers don't have MBAs.

Nevertheless, thousands of bright-eyed students enter these programs each year.

The first MFA program began at the University of Iowa in 1936 and by the mid-nineties there were over sixty programs. As of this writing, there are nearly four hundred graduate-level writing programs around the world, according to the Association of Writers and Writing Programs, including PhD and MA programs. This is because these types of programs are known in the education industry as "cash cows."[5] And though that epithet doesn't negate the benefit of an MFA, it does imply that someone is getting rich from this endeavor—and it's not the eager writing student.

So make certain the degree you're aiming for will be beneficial before taking on a mountain of debt, both monetarily and temporally, to obtain it.

Both programs are often expensive, take years to complete, and can be fruitless if not done right. The risk is that you might receive an MBA in name only, while not learning anything useful for your career. Similarly, you might get an MFA and spend three years talking about writing, but not practicing or revising on your own, not reading the assignments (or reading much at all), and not improving. I remember one colleague complaining about "all the shitty stories we have to read for workshop each week," and I thought, *If you don't want to read workshop stories, why are you here?*

So, to all MFA or MBA prospects, or anyone else investing time and money into their educational aspirations: Don't squander it. Neither degree can do the work for you—it must come from within.

The Difference Between MFA and MBA Programs

Besides the content, a glaring *difference* between the programs is that a misspent MBA might still net you a six-figure VP position for which you are not qualified, while a misspent MFA might get you an adjunct professorship position for which you are over-qualified (though at $22K a year with no health insurance, credentials are the least of your problems).

MFA vs. NYC ("School" vs. "Life")

In 2014, an abstruse and self-indulgent book called *MFA vs. NYC* caused a stir amongst the literary crowd. It was a meta and masturbatory collection of navel-gazing essays on a topic for which I doubt many would take up arms: whether 'tis nobler to learn to write by attending an MFA program or by Living (in New York City). That some authors didn't seem to believe "living" could encompass residing anywhere but a gentrified sliver of Brooklyn was not lost on some critics. Regardless, as long as MFA programs have been around, writers and academics have debated their merits. The argument boils down to whether writing can really be taught. And if it can't, then are MFA programs just a scam, selling a dream to unwitting suckers?

Well, I definitely became a better writer through my MFA experience. But I acknowledge MFA programs are not for everyone. In addition, I also spent nine years in NYC *before* my MFA doing a whole lot of "living." Sadly, I didn't get much writing done during that time, and what I did manage to produce wasn't good. I was too goddamn exhausted from all that living to think deeply about anything other than paying rent, nursing hangovers, and fighting FOMO. I had little time to generate new work, and no energy to revise.

Either way, the reality is neither an MFA nor a bohemian lifestyle creates a decent writer. Only time, effort, and patience does. And reading a lot.

After all, how did novelists and poets master the craft before MFA programs? Just as with any skill, they practiced.

And don't worry, it only takes a few million words.

Value

What about an MBA? Is spending oodles of cash on one worth it, or should you go to the University of Life (a.k.a. the "School of Hard Knocks") like dear old granddad did? Can you "teach" business skills, or are MBA programs just extended networking events, precursors to deals made on the golf course?

In the quote at the beginning of this chapter (go back and read the goddamn quote!), the Abstract Expressionist painter Barnett Newman is saying that true artists don't worry about aesthetics (the critical study of beauty and how things look) just as birds don't think about ornithology (the branch of zoology concerned with birds and bird behavior). The latter half of this aphorism is obvious, since birds don't know ornithology exists, as they can't read or talk and have tiny bird brains. But even if they *did* know humans were studying them, would they care? Probably not, as they're more focused on building nests and eating worms and doing that amazing thing they do, *flying*.

What about artists? They are certainly aware of aesthetics and philosophies of art. But do they care? A little, sure. But their main focus is on creating art.

Similarly, writers and businesspeople should only care so much about the study of writing and the study of business. I estimate somewhere between 12 and 23 percent. The rest should be actually writing and working.

Still, I *do* believe writing can be taught—that's why I wrote this book—and I believe business principles can be learned. But just as the paper upon which an MFA degree is printed doesn't make you a better writer, an MBA *itself* won't make you a better manager to your subordinates, a better financial advisor, or a better marketer.

That said, if you need an MBA to move forward in your career, that's as good a reason as any to get one.

But how many people can honestly, *truly* say they "learned how to do business" in an MBA program? Maybe they learned some basic principles of marketing, how to do a regression analysis, and some palaver about ethics (quick business tip: if you

Harvard Business School
CONFIDENTIAL: For Private Distribution Only

1921

L
1

THE GENERAL SHOE COMPANY

In a plant of the General Shoe Company it has come to the attention of the chief executive that many of the piece workers throughout the plant are in the habit of discontinuing their work three-quarters of an hour before closing time, both at noon and at night. This seriously interferes with production since the processes are continuous and the production of each department depends on a steady flow of material from the preceding department. The condition has become acute at the present time, April 1919, because the company has more orders than it can fill. Commodity prices are beginning to advance again and there is general unrest among working men because of the cost of living which has increased 95% since 1914.

Wages have not been correspondingly increased, being only 90% higher than in 1914. The earning of the piece workers are being held up to standard with difficulty. The average earnings of the employees for last month, March 1919, were $18 – $20 per week.

The rule of the shop is that all piece workers are to remain at work until 10 minutes before quitting time. A whistle is blown at this time and the employees are allowed to leave their work to wash up. The foremen report difficulty in enforcing this rule. It is observed by about 30% of the employees who did not wash up before going out. Others take 45 minutes or less from their working time. They argue that unless they are in the washrooms they have to wait their turns and are unable to leave the shop promptly at 12 o'clock or at 5 o'clock. Frequently attempts on the part of the foremen to enforce the rule have caused temporary improvement but eventually there is a relapse to the old way.

There are 700 employees in the shop, of whom 650 are piece workers. 60% of the employees are men and 40% are women. The washrooms are small rooms containing troughs with a few faucets at intervals. This makes it necessary for the employees to wash in running water. The clothing of the employees is not kept in the washrooms but is hung on nails near the machines of the operators. The plant is five stories high and has machines in every available space. Room cannot be made in the building as it stands for a new washroom because it would involve a rearrangement of all the machinery and change in routing, the cost of which would be prohibitive. The cost of building additional floor space, however, is about $4 per square foot.

What factors should be developed in the investigation on the part of the management? What are the general policies in accordance with which these conditions should be remedied?

Figure 4. "The General Shoe Company," perhaps the first case study ever, from Harvard Business School in 1922.

wouldn't tell your mother, don't do it). And maybe case studies such as "The General Shoe Company" in Figure 4 provided "valuable insights" into "best practices." Okay. In other words, the MBA refined their edges and gave their career a nice polish.

An MBA program provides structure, education, time, experience, and expert advice. But people learn how to do well in business by...well, working. By conducting business. You can learn about economics by reading books like *Economics in One Lesson* by Henry Hazlitt and *Capital in the Twenty-First Century* by Thomas Piketty, but you get better at sales by losing pitches. You become a better speaker by speaking and presenting a hundred times.

Likewise, people learn how to write by writing a lot, and the MFA program provides a supportive community, instructions and education, and that most precious resource of all, time.

The point is, "Is it worth it?" is the wrong question to ask.

Uniformity and Conformity

One complaint about MFA programs is that they can, however unintentionally, tend to make new writing sound identical—or at least similar. It follows from people reading the same works of the canon and emulating the same writers. There is even a mini-genre of literature called "*The New Yorker* Short Story," wherein a distinct style and common theme (upper-class white suburbanites stuck in bad marriages) dominated the publishing industry for a time.[6]

Trends are nothing new: think of the prevalence of books with the word "Girl" in the title (see Figure 5). But MFA programs are sometimes accused of forcibly hemming new writers into the same boxes. Not maliciously, but by default: the well-intentioned professors of these programs have themselves been taught what makes "good" writing, and for centuries it's been predominantly straight, cis-gender males of European descent. They therefore perpetuate this style (inasmuch as a single writing style exists) as "good." Also, workshop stories and poems tend to "borrow" from each other over time.

> *Gone Girl, The Girls, The Girl on the Train, The Girl With The Dragon Tattoo (and its siblings The Girl Who Played With Fire and The Girl Who Kicked the Hornet's Nest), Girl With a Pearl Earring, Girl Interrupted, The Girl With All the Gifts, The Good Girl, Kiss the Girls, The Other Boleyn Girl, Pretty Girls, Me and Earl and the Dying Girl, Girl Wash Your Face, Girl in the Dark, Luckiest Girl Alive, Twenties Girl, The Girl of Fire and Thorns, The Girl You Left Behind, The House Girl,* and so on and so on, ad infinitum, until our bodies decompose into worm food.*

Figure 5. Books with the word "Girl" in the title.

This happens in MBA programs, too, where students read the same case studies and business books (see Figure 6), deify and mythologize the same luminaries, such as Phil Jackson, Warren Buffet, and Steve Jobs; and pore over the same archive of Berkshire Hathaway *Letters to Shareholders*.

Over the decades I've worked at huge ad agencies, growing startups, small businesses with a handful of employees, and everything in between. I've encountered the same tripe ("circle back," "think outside the box," "rock star") and the same practices (weekly status updates, boring and pointless time-wasting

Figure 6. It's all the same!

meetings, cold and lifeless emails).

I've heard tell of innovative—though hardly revolutionary—variations on that theme: the "two-pizza team" at Amazon is interesting, though its effectiveness is debatable, and while their "narrative memos" seem like perfect fodder for a book such as this, everyone I asked hated having to write them. And anyway, the best inventions are surely well-kept company secrets that we'll never get to know, such as sacrificing a baby lamb and drawing a pentacle on the boardroom table with its still-warm blood before reporting company earnings. For example.

I always found it sad how business whittles away people's individuality and personality quirks. I was a weird kid (my mother said I was "an old soul") and I like my weird personality, now. But you can't be too weird at work—otherwise you might be seen as a "problem employee," or you might alienate your coworkers. I suppose that's why people talk about sports and celebrities in the break room.

When the COVID quarantine began, those who started working from home saw, perhaps for the first time, perhaps with not a small degree of horror, their partner put on their "professional voice." No more baby talk and cuddly-wuddlies, no more cussing and filthy jokes, no more snarky asides and bizarre non-sequiturs.

Nevertheless there's a certain merit to the conformity. Status calls are necessary because you need to know what your coworkers and clients are up to, and you need to let them know what *you're* up to. And constantly blabbing on about your weekend wicca rituals or fascination with snail slime might, indeed, make some of your coworkers uncomfortable.

Similarly, clichés are easy. They're bad, and they're lazy, but they're easy. After all, sometimes popping off an idle "Let's take it offline" during a long meeting is simply more expeditious than arguing over a detail and wasting everyone's time.

I wonder if the Roman general Sulla had morning stand-ups

with his team when he was consul. Or if Hephaestion ever advised Alexander the Great to "go after the low-hanging fruit," or called him a "rock star." Maybe they had better ways back then, ways now lost to time.

But more likely, they *did* do the same things we do now—surely Sulla met with his staff daily during a war, and they told him to "work smarter, not harder." They just had a cool Latin phrase for it, like "scientia potentia est."

It's not even that "*New Yorker* short stories" are bad; in fact, they're usually pretty good. But those are not the *only* types of short stories that should be written or published. And look back at that image of book titles again in Figure 6. How many were written by women? How many were written by people of color? Not many.

And this reveals another, more pernicious similarity between MFA and MBA programs: diversity, or lack thereof. Diversity is a good thing. More diversity is even better. And though things are changing, they are changing at a glacial pace.

The lesson here is that you should strive to differentiate yourself from the rest of the zombie-drones that surround you. That doesn't mean using Comic Sans font in your emails. It *does* mean having a real conversation with one of your colleagues instead of saluting them with a day-old hunk of biscotti as you rip a pathetic "Have a good one!" and steal out of the break room before they can bore you with the details of their basement renovation or their niece's eighth birthday party.

WRITING EXERCISE: THE RULES OF WORK,
ACCORDING TO YOU

Part I: Think back on your career and recall some of the best lessons you've learned in your time. Maybe they came from a mentor or some other sage, or maybe they were learned inadvertently (by observing someone else's mistake, for example). List these out as you think of them, and take your time.

Part II: Take two or three of these lessons and write short nonfiction anecdotes about how they came to be. Describe the scenes and settings of each, and the characters in it. Use dialogue, if possible. One of the characters should, most likely, be you.

Part III: Take another look at the original list of lessons. Hopefully you have at least a half-dozen or so. Now rewrite each in a more elegant, pithy, creative, and interesting bullet in a new list.

For example, the rule, "Watch where you're going" can be rewritten as "Never drive over a bed of rocks with a lawnmower."

Use all of your creativity and writing skill in making this list sparkle. Make it something worthy of a poster on a cubicle wall. Then give it a snappy name, such as "Rules of Work, According to Me." And come up with a better title than that.

2: FANTASY AND REALITY

Hating your job intensely is not a business plan.
>   — Pamela Slim, *Escape from Cubicle Nation* (2009)

PERMISSION

One of the most important gifts I received during the MFA program was on my first day, when my professor Doug Dorst said, "You have the permission to call yourself a writer."

How did he know?

Probably because he'd been teaching in an MFA program for several years already.

I hadn't realized until then how much I needed to hear this. I'd been writing for fun since I was a kid, but I had zero professional publications, and nobody except my friends and family ever read my work. I liked to think of myself as a writer, but I more honestly thought of myself as a fraud (this phenomenon, which cuts across all disciplines, is known as "imposter syndrome").

You don't need to enroll in an MFA program to call yourself a writer, nor do you need a large advance from Random House or a staff job at *The New York Times*. You need, simply, to write.

And in fact, the converse is also true: some people who do MFA programs *aren't* real writers; not in practice, at least, because they don't do much actual writing. They drink (like Hemingway), they hook up with poets (like Sylvia Plath), and they toss off some pages when their stories are due in workshop (like nobody you've ever heard of, because those kinds of "writers" don't get better, and don't get published).

Just because I was once, technically, hired onto a construction crew, I would never call myself a "construction worker." I never "constructed" shit. If anything, I *deconstructed* stuff, which led me inexorably toward Derrida...but that's another story (and already told in the Introduction).

I'm sure in your career you've met people who inexplicably claim a title or profession but never seem to do any work. Seat-warmers with fancy titles such as "Greatest Salesperson This Company Has Ever Seen," but who've never closed a deal, or "Always-Crazed, Hardest Worker In The Department," but whose kid always catches the ol' coronavirus just as everyone else has to stay late to respond to a last-minute client request. Most frustrating of all, sometimes these people fail up.

Nevertheless, don't be that person. Be the person you want to be.

YOU, Dear Reader, do not need a piece of paper to call yourself a...fill-in-the-blank: computer programmer, mentor, manager, salesperson, accountant. You need to write code, mentor people, manage teams, sell product, and...um, account for stuff.

Now, obviously some fields *do* require specific credentials: practicing law or medicine, for example. But I'm sure, even after passing the bar or the boards, some noob doctors or attorneys need more external validation before they can believe in themselves.

Why do we block ourselves? How many times have you refrained from speaking up in a meeting when you *clearly* see a mistake, or a solution to a problem a client is having, or whatever the case? Or you don't ask for that raise or that promotion—even though you know you deserve it.

Well, I hereby grant you permission.

To call yourself a computer programmer, a teacher, a sales professional, an accountant. I give you permission to raise your hand and speak up. I give you permission to ask for a raise. I give you permission to call yourself an expert.

But please, *please* use this permission wisely. I am not telling you to lie on your résumé. I mean, learn how to teach before you get up in front of a classroom.

But if you've been a junior copywriter for three years, well, guess what: you're a writer. Go after that big ad campaign. Or go write that screenplay. It's yours for the taking.

Successful salespeople acquire a knack for obtaining permission. You need to ask for permission to get a meeting. You need to ask for permission to make a pitch. Seth Godin wrote a whole book called *Permission Marketing* (1999).

But you don't need permission to ask for permission. And as all salespeople know, if you don't ask, you don't receive.

So once again, here it is: I hereby grant you permission to give yourself permission.

WORK

> Diversity is the engine that drives this country. We are an immigrant nation! The first generation works their fingers to the bone making things, the next generation goes to college and innovates new ideas, the third generation ... snowboards and takes improv classes.
>
> — Jack Donaghy, *30 Rock*

I spent the first few years of my working life at ad agencies, feeling miserable. The agencies were fine—my colleagues seemed perfectly happy there—but not me. It was because I wanted to be doing something else with my life.

When I found that "something else," I realized I also needed permission to call what I was doing every day as an MFA student "work."

It didn't feel like "work" because I *enjoyed* reading and writing, and now my "work" was reading and writing. It seemed too good to be true. I would sit on my couch and read some novel or story that was assigned for class. Even if I hated the book, I still loved reading it. Then I would speak to my brother, who was making marketing plans; or my lawyer father, who had a trial the next day; or my accountant mother, crunching numbers; or my sister, editing chapters for a textbook. And I'd feel *guilty*. It didn't seem fair that I got to do what I loved and call it "work." You're not supposed to *like* work, right?

In addition, the reality is that writers often don't get paid (or paid well) for creative work, especially at the beginning of their careers. So not only doesn't it *feel* like "work," it doesn't provide a *living*, either.

The premise of the hilarious quote from *30 Rock* that begins this section is that so-called "privileged" third generations trade on their forbearers' hard work so they can engage in fun and frivolous extraneous activities that are very expensive, such as snowboarding and taking improv classes. The joke doesn't work if it's about "playing basketball," which is fun, but is essentially free to do in a city park, or "reading," since that's not fun (to many people) and can also be free if you take out books out from the library. The (meta) irony is that *30 Rock* was created by Tina Fey and produced by Lorne Michaels, who both started in improv.

In any case, many writers or artists need a day job for another source of income, such as teaching or, in my case, running an advertising agency. But if that source was a trust fund, or your spouse's salary, would writing *then* be "work"?

If so, then it's work, regardless of what constitutes the other source—the rent-paying, grocery-buying source—of income. The point is that you shouldn't feel bad about spending time and energy engaging in and practicing your craft.

I was up until 1 a.m. last night writing this book. And I started writing it at 7:45 a.m. this morning. Now, sure, this "work" is not a constant, steady stream of writing and revising—that's simply impossible, because the mind needs a break—but I'm certainly putting in my hours. And if that's not work, what is it? Fun? A hobby? A waste of time?

So take time to consider what you do every day. What parts of your job do you enjoy? When are you in a state of flow, so absorbed in work that when you look up, two hours have flown by?

If your answer is "Never" (if you hate your job every day, all day, no matter what), then I urge you to find an exit strategy. Regardless of how much money you get paid, toiling away at something you despise is no way to spend your life.

Maybe you don't have that option. I feel for you, I really do. I don't have an answer other than to say that you should aspire. Keep looking. Keep exploring. Try new things.

I'm not advising you to quit your job to sell homemade doilies on Etsy because you like knitting. Any new venture will be difficult, stressful, and anxiety-inducing. But if you enjoy doing it, you'll find it worthwhile. Mandel Marketing didn't spring from the ground fully formed out of nowhere—it took an immense amount of work to get going. But to me, the freedom of running my own company was worth it.

On the other hand, working for someone else provides structure, routine, and often a more reliable paycheck. Many are happy to trade eight hours of labor for this and keep the other sixteen hours of their day. I'm not one of those people, but there's nothing wrong with such a transaction.

IMPOSTER SYNDROME

So back to imposter syndrome. It cuts across class, race, ethnicity, gender, industry, job title, socioeconomic status, eye color, hand dominance, hair length, body type, ability, and any other way of parsing a population. We've all felt it, and if you haven't, then I am now giving you permission to be more ambitious.

What's great about imposter syndrome is that it never fully goes away. Even if you write six best-selling books, you probably still think the book you're working on right now sucks.

In my second year of the MFA program, I began sending out stories for publication—and every one was soundly rejected. To me, therefore, I was not a "real writer." I was a hack. I kept thinking, *If I just get one—ONE—single solitary story published, then I will be able to call myself a Writer, with a capital* W.

Then I got a story published. It was even nominated for an award (though I didn't win).

For a while, I was happy. But soon, one publication wasn't enough. After all, maybe it was just luck. I needed two—*TWO*—publications, then I'd truly be a real Writer.

I got a second publication, which held my imposter syndrome at bay again. But then I started to doubt myself because I hadn't yet published in a quote-unquote "top tier journal."

But after I attained my sought-after "prestigious" publication, I couldn't find an agent for the novel on which I had worked so hard. Imposter syndrome moved back into my mental basement.

Maybe you start out as a junior assistant associate, or whatever is the entry-level equivalent in your industry. You think, okay, once I get promoted, *then* I'll be a real professional. You get promoted. It doesn't help because there are still ten titles above you.

As you reach higher on the ladder, imposter syndrome doesn't necessarily abate. For some, the pressure becomes even greater. You get hired as VP of Marketing and suddenly think, *Once they realize I'm the same damn person I was when I was a lowly junior assistant associate I'll be exposed because I don't know shit about marketing and they'll fire me and they'll escort me out of the building and they won't let me return to my desk to get my stuff and one of my colleagues will sift through my shit and put it in a box and they'll look at my search history on my work computer and they'll find that pint of vodka I had in the desk drawer—for emergencies!—and I'll never find another job and soon I'll be living behind a dumpster....* It gets grim fast.

But who are "they," really? Your colleagues? Upper management? Your direct reports? It's an undefinable fear because, in reality, there *is* no "they." It's just your own doubt, personified.

For some writers, an MFA program acts as a bulwark against imposter syndrome. But a crutch is meant to be temporary. Eventually you need to learn how to stand on your own. Perhaps a better metaphor would be training wheels on a bicycle. Eventually they come off.

Also, I'm not sure imposter syndrome is always *all* bad. It keeps you honest about yourself and it keeps you fighting the good fight. As long as you don't let it destroy you first.

WRITING EXERCISE: IMPOSTER SYNDROME AND PERMISSION

Part I: Was there a time you experienced imposter syndrome? What happened, and why? Write 300 words on it (about two healthy paragraphs). Be specific.

When was another time? Give us another 300 words.

Part II: Now, think about your current career. What is holding you back—or what do you feel you need "permission" to do? Write it out, and then write: "I have permission to..."

Then write whatever it is you want to do next, both in business and in your personal life. This could be asking for a raise, taking on a large project, or volunteering to speak at the next event. Maybe it's doing standup comedy, learning how to speak French, baking a cake, writing a novel, or becoming a photographer.

Read those words again, that you yourself wrote: *I have permission...*

3: ARTWORK AND COMMERCE

Art is important because art is part of that nebulous, unquantifiable dimension of reality we sometimes call "the poetic." Religion, magic, and even love, beauty, and other forms of non-rational understanding also fall into this category. The poetic transcends the practical imperatives of life—and yet it is a building-block of the identities we assign to ourselves. The poetic is also (importantly) a wellspring of joy, hope, pleasure, and wonder ... it is a source of comfort and consolation when our fellow human beings let us down, and when we feel that the universe doesn't care ...

— Leonard Koren, *What Artists Do* (2018)

WHAT MAKES ART "ARTFUL"?

In this chapter, we're going to look at the interplay of art and business.

Not fine art as an investment, nor how art classes might raise your GPA and help you get into the Ivy League, nor how your infant might be smarter if you play Mozart at them while they're in the womb. We'll also put to the side the question of making money selling one's paintings.

And celebrating the "poetic" merits of art—those unquantifiable blobs that make one's life worth living, as Leonard Koren does in the quote above—we'll pause on that as well. Such appreciation is all well and good when you aren't working two jobs to feed your family, or when you actually have time to kick back and tour the museum on a lovely Sunday afternoon after a brunch of croque monsieurs and bottomless mimosas.

That's not why you picked up this book. We're here to learn how the lessons and application of art can make one's labor more enjoyable and worth more in the marketplace.

So what makes art "artful"?

This is a question that already fills libraries and museums, so here's a summary: Good art is about making something new—or making something *appear* new in some way. It's about creation. It's about "the sublime."

Yes, Sublime was a singularly great band from the 1990s that I listened to a lot when I was first learning how to smoke weed, but in an aesthetic sense, the term "sublime" describes something that transcends the everyday, quotidian world.

Good art is surprising; it puts you in an unfamiliar place, or makes the familiar feel unfamiliar. In *A Philosophical Enquiry into the Origin of Our Ideas of the Sublime and Beautiful* (1757), the philosopher Edmund Burke extolls the virtues of the sublime in that it invokes mortal terror, pain, and danger in people (in a good way):

> Another source of the sublime is infinity ... Infinity has the tendency to fill the mind with that sort of delightful horror, which is the most genuine effect and truest test of the sublime ... After a long succession of noises, as the fall of waters, or the beating of forge hammers, the hammers beat and the water roars in the imagination long after the first sounds have ceased to affect it; and they die away at last by gradations which are scarcely perceptible.

Later we'll look at Raymond Queneau's *Exercises in Style* (1947), which tells the story of one mundane event in fifty different ways, from standard narration to an interrogation to a haiku. While the book doesn't strike the same deep "delightful horror" in one's soul as contemplating the size of the universe, it delights and surprises by presenting something familiar in a new way. It's not the event itself that is delightful, but rather its unexpected and novel presentation, and this experience of storytelling. In most books, readers are presented with one, or sometimes several, limited point of view, in one style (realism). This book entirely upends that pattern.

This is the essence of good art, to me: the overwhelming feeling one's understanding of the world is altered irrevocably after seeing, reading, or hearing a work for the first time. It hits like a Will Smith-style open-handed slap to the face.

Just as important, it should be something you can revisit often and experience such magic each time. Great art has layers.

Judging the aesthetic value of art and other cultural objects is complicated. I enjoy Surrealist paintings (Magritte, Ernst, Dali), but have a hard time understanding Modern artists such as Piet Mondrian (see Figure 7). Or Robert Rauschenberg: it's a blank canvas...or it's a white canvas painted with white house paint. The only thing you see on it is your own shadow. Maybe

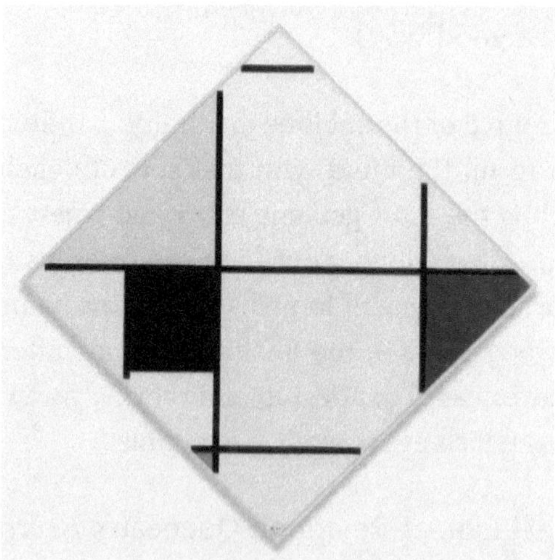

Figure 7. Piet Mondrian. *Lozenge Composition with Yellow, Black, Blue, Red, and Gray* (1921), Art Institute Chicago. This speaks to me. Unfortunately, I'm not entirely sure what it's saying.

dust? (For a great meditation on this, check out the 1994 play *Art* by Yasmina Reza.)

Some art takes your breath away with its beauty, some art makes you want to cry, and some art challenges the definition, usefulness, and meaning of art altogether. However it does it, good art does not let you remain passive.

Instead, it invites the viewer to participate in the art-making through emotion and feeling as well as interpretation. For example, Jackson Pollock's paintings are not representative of things in real life, while many paintings are. You, as viewer, decide what a Pollock painting means to you, but—here's the rub—you *also* decide what the items and people represent in a realist painting, too. The Dutch Modern artist Theo van Doesburg said, "Once the means of expression are liberated from all characteristics they are on their way toward the real goal of art: to create a universal language," and, while I'm not entirely sure I know what he means, I think I agree.

In a novel, a writer can describe a scene, dialogue, and the internal thoughts of a character, but the *reader* imagines them in their own mind.

Theater of the mind is more powerful and effective than sitcoms because the former requires the audience member to become an active participant in its creation. This is why spectacular, big-budget Marvel movies don't feel artistic (though they can be amusing); there is very little nuance, and even less room for interpretation.

So what does all this have to do with business?

Well, I'm not suggesting you create slide presentations full of surreal imagery and leave it up to your client to decide what you mean. But you *should* strive for your audience to actively participate in your work, even if that participation means listening, nodding along, asking questions, understanding. You can feel when you your audience is engaged and present. Business communication isn't a lecture.

Unfortunately, with written communication you don't have

the benefit of immediate feedback. You can't change your tack mid-email if the reader begins showing signs of boredom. They might be reading your email at their desk, or, just as likely, on their phone while sitting on the toilet. This is why business writing needs to be exact, specific, and concise.

THE AUDIENCE

In literary theory circles, much ink has been spilled on the notion of "implied reader" vs. "actual reader," as well as the "ideal reader." Think of it this way: every year, Warren Buffett writes a "Letter to Shareholders of Berkshire Hathaway" to provide a summary of the company's financial performance. The *implied* readers are those who own stock in Berkshire Hathaway, as well as their close associates: attorneys, brokers, financial managers. The *actual* readership of these Letters, however, is much wider, far beyond people who own Berkshire Hathaway shares. Many people in financial markets around the world look to these Letters for guidance and information to use to their advantage in their own portfolios.

Keep this in mind the next time you're writing an email to your subordinates.

An *ideal* reader is different. This is a persona, a made-up fiction—the *kind of* person who would be ideal for whatever you wrote. For a new psychological horror novelist, it might be someone who loves Stephen King and Carl Jung. For a sales director, it might be someone who already has a working knowledge of their product and industry or is dissastified with their current vendor.

Unfortunately for you, and for novelists and poets around the world, the ideal reader doesn't exist. This means your prospect may not know all that industry jargon you're throwing around, or doesn't enjoy reading ten-paragraph emails.

So no matter who is actually reading your material, you

should intend for them to be engaged. Unfortunately, the overwhelming majority of business communication is not engaging at all. The content of most meetings, status calls, pitch decks, emails, online content, and memos is derivative junk, timewasters, clichés, and jargon. Then, in the middle of all this crap, a few original, actionable items are communicated. All the work in the world is built on those few turds of wisdom, and the rest is just noise.

But I'm not trying to make business-speak into modern art. I'm just looking for incremental change. Here's a reasonable goal: if you can manage to take the percentage from 95 percent crap / 5 percent gold to just 70 percent crap / 30 percent gold, then you'll get ten gold stars, a promotion, and a bucket of cash. The best part? You only have to *not* write crap 30 percent of the time, which I think is pretty doable.

Lucky for you, the rest of this book will help you get there.

GENRE FICTION

In Q1 2021, the fastest-growing adult fiction book sales in the US were in the genres of Manga, Contemporary Women's Fiction, Romance, and Fantasy.[7] In the past thirty years, the bestseller lists include Fantasy, Mystery, and Thriller books such as the *Harry Potter* series (1997–2007), *The Da Vinci Code* (2003), *The Girl on the Train* (2015), and *Gone Girl* (2012). But for some reason, I learned in my MFA program that when it came to genre fiction, there was no room in the inn. I'm sure a dozen MFA-types will protest and say they welcome all types of writing, but we all know that isn't the case.

What is "genre fiction" anyway, and why does it matter?

It's probably easier to understand by defining what it's not. Broadly speaking, so-called "literary fiction" focuses on artistic style, realism, character, language, and theme, over more "base" considerations, such as plot, setting, and world-building. (And yes, this is a gross, *gross* simplification.) Genre fiction includes Romance, Fantasy, Science Fiction, Mystery, Spy Thrillers, Westerns, Historical Fiction, Crime novels, and anything you might pick up at an airport or read on the beach. Young Adult and Middle Grade are genres, too.

Historically, MFA programs haven't been interested in this kind of writing because it doesn't seem "artistic" enough.

One reason might be that there are conventions of each genre to which many of the books conform. Romance novels tend to follow this formula (excuse the genders, for the moment): *Boy meets girl, boy loses girl, boy gets girl.* In a Murder Mystery, a dead body almost always appears in the first chapter.

Formulaic writing is less surprising, less "sublime," and therefore less artful.

There are exceptions: sometimes, a "literary" novel *does* focus on setting, such as Marilynne Robinson's *Housekeeping* (1980) or Teju Cole's *Open City* (2011). In these special cases, setting is considered a "character." Lucky them. The pages and pages and pages and pages of descriptive setting in J. R. R. Tolkien's *Lord of the Rings*, well, that's just Fantasy.

And to be fair to the MFA program-slash-literary world, there is room for fantastical work, but it must fall into a predetermined artistic category such as "magical realism," "surrealism," or "fabulism." These are all words for "good" (artful) writing that isn't *quite* straight realism (which, as you'll recall, hearkens back to "*The New Yorker* stories" of Chapter 1). In movies, "magical realism" is *Being John Malkovich* (1999) and *The Shape of Water* (2017), while "realism" is *Marriage Story* (2019) and *Boyhood* (2014).

Jorge Luis Borges, Gabriel García Márquez, Haruki Murakami, and Salman Rushdie are all classic authors whose work has been tagged as both literary and fabulist, though there are tons of others, such as Karen Russell, Kelly Link, Amelia Grey, and Alissa Nutting who are doing some tremendous—and tremendously weird—writing these days.

Oddly, the speculative science fiction of Kurt Vonnegut, Margaret Atwood, or Italo Calvino are considered "literary," but the masterful *Stars in My Pocket Like Grains of Sand* (1984) by Samuel Delany (one of the best titles of a book ever), is just Science Fiction. (Again, I can hear screaming protests, but let's be real.)

And the extra-buttery popcorn, such as *The Wheel of Time* (Robert Jordan, 1990s) or *The Vampire Chronicles* (Anne Rice, 1970s–2020s)? File it under junk food, I guess. And forget about books like Ian Fleming's *James Bond* series, or *Game of Thrones*, or anything by Nora Roberts.

If this sounds stuffy, unfair, snobbish, and somewhat wrong, that's because it is. I, personally, find reading to be great entertainment, and if I'm entertained by *The Wheel of Time*, I don't see how that's any less worthwhile than someone else enjoying Malcolm Lowry's *Under the Volcano* (1947), a very long novel that's been on my nightstand for nigh on eight years now and which, I can safely assume, will go unread in my lifetime.

So why are we talking about genre fiction at all?

It matters because the difference between so-called "entertainment" and "art" can be the difference between getting a job and landing a client, or never getting a call back in the first place.

Maybe George R. R. Martin never set out to change the world when he wrote *Game of Thrones*; he just wanted to tell a fun story that he himself would enjoy reading. Maybe Peter Handke, the 2019 Nobel Prize laureate and author of the "anti-play" *Offending the Audience* (1965) and ennui-inducing novella *The Goalie's Anxiety at the Penalty Kick* (1972), did set out to change the world. One of them became a beloved storyteller, and the other has been relegated to "smart" conversations in graduate programs.

When it comes to business, be realistic about what will make your audience—the implied reader, the ideal reader, and the *actual* reader—sit up in their seat and take notice of your words, ask follow-up questions, and stay engaged until after the last word.

Mastering the Fundamentals

How do you get someone to "sit up in their seat and take notice" of your work? If it were that easy, everyone would be a professional novelist. The reality is that it's difficult work requiring time, practice, patience, and dedication to mastering the fundamentals.

This means you must focus on language (Chapter 5) and style (Chapter 6), and eliminate cliché (Chapter 7). Use figurative language appropriately (Chapter 8), be concise (Chapter 9), write in the active voice (Chapter 10), and offer a believable point of view (Chapter 11). Have empathy for your characters and make them realistic and relatable (Chapter 12). Keep the tension high so your reader can't wait to find out what happens, but ensure you complete a satisfying story arc (Chapter 13). Start with a great first line (Chapter 14) and keep the writing fresh until the end, ensuring thematic resonance provides lasting meaning to the reader after they've finished (Chapter 15). Use humor and irony judiciously (Chapter 16). And perhaps most importantly, never disrupt the reader's "flow" (Chapter 17).

These are the fundamentals for writing anything well, including both genre and literary fiction. We call this mastering one's "craft." I happen to believe the fundamentals also apply to writing emails and sales presentations.

Incidentally, this might explain why many MFA programs don't focus on the publishing part of the business too much, because one need not query agents or learn how to negotiate an advance until one has a manuscript good enough to garner a book deal.

This book is dedicated to helping you master the fundamental techniques of the writing craft and apply them to your business writing.

Writing to Market

Making good art takes time. You can't rush it. If you do, you'll most likely end up with work that is uninspired, unoriginal, boring, and meaningless. Similarly, doing well in business takes time; if you rush it, your product or service won't sell (and if it does sell, by sheer luck, you won't get repeat customers).

There is a difference, however, between *rushing* and doing things *quickly*. Rushing means you are going faster than you should, skipping important steps, cutting corners. Doing things quickly means you're able to do what needs to be done in a short amount of time. For example, I can write an article of one thousand words in about an hour, because I'm so well-practiced at it. But if I *rush* to get it done in thirty minutes, I will no doubt produce a putrid and unusable one thousand words.

And just as you can't rush the process of creation, you can't rush the process of training. Being good at your job, developing your career, becoming a good boss, peer, and colleague—these all take time.

But what about *after*?

Time to cash in, right? Make that bread. Bake that cake. Stack that paper. Bring home a bucket of sizzling, salty bacon.

As the resident spoiler, I'd like to offer a common aphorism that goes around writing craft circles, which is, "Don't write to market." This means don't write what you think will sell.

Like all one-liners, this is not 100 percent true all the time. But generally speaking, it's good advice.

Creating art should, at first, be for the artist. Write the novel *you'd* like to read, not one you think will sell because "cozy mysteries with dinosaurs are hot right now."

It's not because that book will be artless and derivative. You might write the *Finnegans Wake* of dinosaur thrillers (I would read this, by the way). But by the time the book is finished, edited, and ready for publication, "cozy dinosaur mysteries" may no longer be trendy.

So don't write to market...until you have to.

See, whenever you make something, there will eventually come a point when you show it to someone—your spouse, your friends, your peers. Or your agent, your editor, your publisher, gallery viewers, the general internet, people at a bar, fans in a rock club, your boss, your client, your colleagues. Nothing exists in a vacuum forever, unless you never show it to anyone, and unfortunately you won't have that luxury in your professional life.

At some point you have to please the stakeholders in your life—those constituents who will throw your book into the furnace if they don't like it, or turn their back on you while you're on stage and start talking to their friends (loudly) over that sweet love song you wrote about your darling, or walk out of your art show and into the bar next door to the gallery. The moral purity of art is not completely useless, but it can be counterproductive. For every genius who went unrecognized and underappreciated in their lifetime, there are thousands— millions—of unrecognized and underappreciated mediocres. Going unrecognized and underappreciated in your life is not a virtue.

And in business, going unrecognized and underappreciated doesn't pay the rent. So yes, art is great and the sublime is great, but keep it in perspective.

If your job is to hit a quota each month, your boss won't keep you on staff when you tell them your clients simply don't appreciate your unique, artistic sales pitch, which consists of five minutes of Catskills schtick and an interpretive dance to Enya's "Orinoco Flow." Or if you're an accountant, you can't explain to your coworkers that they aren't getting reimbursed for their expenses because "math is just an illusion."

It's true, in a way, that an artist need not please anyone if they don't wish to. If my prospective publisher won't publish my book—my *artwork*—unless I revise the plot to include werewolves, I have the right to shop around for a new publisher. Or I can publish it myself, or leave it in the drawer unread until I die.

However, if my publisher suggests a better title and I *still* resist, then it's just my pride getting in the way. F. Scott Fitzgerald had many different titles for *The Great Gatsby*, including *Under the Red, White, and Blue* and *Trimalchio in West Egg*. One of my favorite books, *1984*, was originally called *The Last Man in Europe*. In Sweden, Stieg Larsson's 2005 thriller is called *Män som hatar kvinnor*, which roughly translates as *Men Who Hate Women*. In English, however, the publishers gave it a new name: *The Girl with the Dragon Tattoo*. Not as risqué, but a wise decision.

Truthfully, most people don't have the luxury to shop around, or to tell their clients to take a hike. If I signed a contract to deliver a piece of material—even an *artistic* one, such as a novel or a screenplay, or even a *less* artistic one, like a script for a television commercial or a corporate white paper—I can't just tell my client to screw off. I'd be in breach of contract.

There's no shame in it. Every copywriter knows that when you give a few options to a client, nine times out of ten they pick the lamest (or safest) option. Work is work. A job is still a job.

The MFA program taught us that you shouldn't write to market. This is sound advice, at the outset. You can use this as permission to think more creatively and broadly when you start a project. But after the contract is signed and money is at stake, you must begin writing (or working) to market, or else your publisher/agent/music booker/boss/gallery owner/sales prospect/client will find someone else who will.

Let's use the rest of this book to make sure the product you make is as awesome as it can be.

WRITING EXERCISE: THINGS I LOVE

Part I: Spend some time making a few lists:

- My favorite books
- My favorite movies
- My favorite songs
- My favorite television shows
- My favorite (you decide)

Now pick one item from each list and think about why you love these things. Write one paragraph on why you love each thing, describing what you love about it and what it makes you feel. You can talk about the artistry of the item, the aesthetics, the idea, whatever you like. Here's my example:

I love the movie *Terminator 2* because of the action and suspense of the main characters being chased by a seemingly impervious creature the entire movie. It seems impossible that John Connor can escape. Every time something seems to go well, it goes wrong. I am also fascinated with the ideas, concepts, and philosophy of the movie. I constantly wonder and daydream about artificial intelligence and what will happen when/if humanity reaches the "singularity," when AI designs intelligences greater than our own. Are we doomed to become slaves to their power? I love thinking about the future, both its prospects and dangers. Also, the aesthetics and special effects of the movie are amazing (for 1991, when I was eleven), perfect for capturing my imagination. Finally, I feel nostalgic when I watch the movie because I saw it for my friend's birthday—and I didn't have many friends back then—and in a movie theater, no less. Going to the movies was a rare and very special experience for me during childhood, and I can remember almost all of the movies I saw in the theater: *Jurassic Park*, *Jumanji*, *Robin Hood*, *He-Man*, and of course, *Terminator 2*.

Part II: Now comes the hard part. Examine a recent project you've worked on—something where you had to spend considerable time and energy on its creation.

- How much care did you put into the work, and how much did you rush to get it done? Does it matter?

- Who was the intended audience, the ideal audience, and the actual audience? Was there a difference? How was the project received?

- Was there anything you could've done differently?

If I were a merciless taskmaster, I'd say you should revise the project and do it again with more intention. But you probably have better things to do. So instead, let's just agree that for the *next* big project, you're going to think of these questions *before* you start, and again take them into consideration while you're working on the project, and then a third time in revision.

4: CREATIVITY AND IMAGINATION

Decades into my career, with many albums and songs under my belt, I still don't know if I am truly creative. Most days I spend more time absorbing the creative work around me than actually creating myself. At times I feel like I'm a way better student than I am a teacher or a maker. The most creative thing I did today, for example, was waking up and texting Jimmy Jam about an obscure B-side from 1987.

— Questlove, Creative Quest (2018)

How to Be Creative

There are hundreds, if not trillions, of books already written on "how to be more creative," or "how to harness your creative energy," or "how to find your creative north star/pole/horse" (including the excellent book by Questlove quoted above). This is because our world fetishizes creative artists, and many people fantasize about being one. Perhaps they think it'll make them famous, rich, or get them laid.

It won't.

But there is a certain something, a *je ne sais quoi* (a faux-pretentious cliché in French meaning "I don't know what") to real creativity. A true artist is often regarded as some kind of genius, a special person to which so-called "normal" people could never even aspire. Oddly, and ironically, they are also sometimes—in a quiet, insidious way—derided and marginalized for being weird or useless, or for not contributing anything to the economy. Being an artist myself, I don't buy into that nonsense—though I imagine the forming of such opinions is less about principle and more about jealousy, insecurity, and bitterness.

Truth is, artists are normal people. They simply have dedicated a practice to a different craft. While everyone else was out playing and having fun, they were inside, sculpting, singing, drawing, painting. Maybe crying.

Many writers in my MFA program were not athletes. Sure, some were athletic, but I'd say, on average, we were at most one-sport athletes in high school. Maybe track, or baseball. I personally was a zero-sport athlete, though I play basketball now and again for fun. *But Phil,* you're already saying, *David Foster Wallace was famous for tennis—he almost went pro,* and I will respond by saying, *Yes, and he's the exception that proves the rule.* How many celebrities have written amazing novels, or any novels for that matter, without the help of a professional ghostwriter?

Most of us in my MFA program didn't really follow sports, either. Sure, we were in Texas so everyone by default kind of cheered for the UT Longhorns or the Aggies or whatever, but nobody went to Texas State Bobcats Football games, and when the Mets were playing the Royals in the World Series, only I (from NY) and the dude from Kansas City (who wasn't *in* the program, but whose girlfriend was) watched it. Rather than spending our time with sports, we writers spent our time with books.

But Phil, you're already saying, *Fred Exley wrote an entire novel about being a fan of the New York Giants!* True, he did, and it's a great one (*A Fan's Notes,* 1968). But that, again, is the exception that proves the rule, and that book came out, like, a hundred years ago.

The pro wrestler Mick Foley (a.k.a. Cactus Jack, a.k.a. Mankind, a.k.a. Dude Love) wrote a novel I haven't read called *Tietem Brown* (2003), so there's that.

This is a gross generalization, but my point is that writers and artists become Writers and Artists by spending a lot of time practicing and thinking about writing and art—just as great athletes become professionals by playing their sport *all day, every day*. And, with no exaggeration, I write every day. Every single day.

Creativity, too, can be learned only through practice (even though it's true that, like sports, it comes more easily and naturally to some gifted people).

That's why I'm a bit skeptical when I see how many of these books purport to change your life and show you how to be creative, if you only follow some magical formula. This formula inevitably involves a liberal use of exclamation points and some permutation of the buzzwords found in Figure 8. These words could, presumably, be combined in any order to create a bestseller (or, at least, a career as a "life coach," whatever that is):

These aren't *bad* words, in and of themselves, (except for "zig," "zag," "ninja," and "rock star"). Many of them, in fact—maybe all of them, I haven't checked—are used in this book. But they are repeated so much that, in a vacuum, they become meaningless.

Don't believe me? Here are some random book titles generated from this list:

- *Ninjas & Rock Stars: How to Harness Your Power to Identify Your True Vocation!*

- *The Zig-Zag Journey from Reflection to Achievement*

- *Imagination & Daring: Your Maverick Calling*

- *Just Breathe: The Guide to Magical Ideation and Accomplishment*

Accomplishment	Encourage	Maker	Resist
Achievement	Energy	Master	Restless
Actionable	Epiphany	Maverick	Right
Agile	Escape	Meditate	Roadmap
Apply	Evolve	Milestone	Rock Star
Artificial	Executive	Mindfulness	Routine
Aspirational	Experience	Miracle	Rules
Attitude	Experiment	Model	Safe
Authenticity	Extreme	Motivation	Self-Care
Awareness	Failure	Multidimensional	Science
Awesome	Fear	Mystery	Shape
Barefoot	Force	Myth	Sharpen
Belief	Flow	Naked	Shortcut
Blind spot	Flux	Navigate	Small
Boss	Focus	Negative	Smart
Brain	Formula	Ninja	Special
Build	Freedom	Occupy	Solution
Calling	Govern	Occupation	Soul
Challenge	Growth	Optimize	Stand Out
Champion	Guide	Organize	Step Up
Changemaker	Guru	Overwhelm	Strategize
Channel	Habit	Passion	Stuck
Command	Happen	Path	Success
Community	Happiness	Pattern	Surprise
Complex	Harness	Perform	System
Confidence	Help	Personal	Test
Conquer	Hierarchy	Permission	The Way
Connection	Holistic	Pivot	Think
Consciousness	Honesty	Positive	Thrive
Constraint	Ideation	Possible	Tools
Conventional	Identify	Potential	Triangulate
Courage	Identity	Power	True / Truth
Crave	Illuminate	Practice	Ultimate
Curate	Imagination	Practical	Unconscious
Curve	Innovate	Problem	Unconventional
Daring	Insightful	Production	Underlying
Defiance	Inspire	Profession	Understand
Design	Intention	Profit	Unleash
Desire	Invent	Prosperity	Unmistakable
Destiny	Journey	Psychological	Unstuck
Detox	Jumpstart	Purpose	Validate
Develop	Just Breathe	Quality / Quantity	Virtual
Different	Kickass	Radical	Vision
Differentiated	Knowledge	Reflection	Vocation
Difficult	Learn	Rebel	War
Discover	Lesson	Reframe	Wiring
Disrupt	Lifestyle	Reimagine	Wish
Dream	Love	Reinvent	Whole
Embrace	Magical	Reshape	Zig-Zag

Figure 8. Self-improvement buzzwords.

- *Reinvent Your Milestones to Test Your Soul*

- *The Kickass Power of Practical Myth*

- *Psychological Prosperity, the Confidence-Based System of Unconventional Habit*

- *Unleash the Roadmap of Strategizing Complex Self-Care*

- *The Differentiated Detox Model: Curate Multidimensional Energy*

- *Insightful & Aspirational Mindfulness: Overwhelm & Conquer*

The last one sounds more like a mash-up of a yoga video and a WWII video game, but you see what I mean. Countless book titles are vapid arrangements of the words above, and more are published every day.

There are over a million words in the English language and about 170,000 in common usage today. Each person has a vocabulary of twenty to thirty thousand words—yet this list has only about 200 phrases on it. Why aren't we using any of these other 169,800 words? What's wrong with the other words?

If it sounds like I'm denigrating these books (or, at least, the titles of these books), it's because I am. That's not to say I don't find such insipid poppycock to, occasionally, be quite inspiring. And if it works for you, then have at it

Unfortunately, a catch-all solution to "be more creative" doesn't exist. Some people have a natural propensity to daydream, think unconventional thoughts, and come up with wacky premises, while others are more analytical, seeing things in black and white and putting objects into categories. These people like to make lists.

Most people, however, are a bit of both.

If you're already a super-creative person—you doodle

fantastical creatures in your notebook during status calls, you come up with hundreds of taglines for nonexistent products all day, you write poetry in the office toilet (see Chapter 17)—then the exercises and tools in this book will help you harness that into more professional work. If you're more the analytical type, then the exercises and tools in this book will help you think and express yourself more creatively at work.

POSSIBILITIES

> Imagination is more important than knowledge. For knowledge is limited, whereas imagination embraces the entire world, stimulating progress, giving birth to evolution.
>
> — Albert Einstein[8]

Imagination fuels creativity. For many writers, dreaming up a plot and inventing a main character is what makes writing enjoyable. Anything can happen in a story, just like anyone can appear in a story. A planet of hyper-evolved, super-smart spiders battle against a psychotic computer-person and the last dregs of humanity? Cool. A doctor is framed for the murder of his wife (who was actually bludgeoned to death by a one-armed man)? Sure. A woman kills her children and her unfaithful husband's new woman to get revenge? Sounds great.

These are, by the way, the plots of *Children of Time* by Adrian Tchaikovsky (2015), *The Fugitive* (1993), and *Medea* by Euripides (430 BC).

Imagination is crucial in business as well because unforeseen scenarios and problems arise without warning all the time. You need to be flexible and imaginative to come up with solutions. You need to be able to work through the various options in your head: *What if we try this, or what if we do it this way?* An exemplar of the unexpected event happened when COVID-19 appeared and upended the world.

Sometimes you don't know what will work unless you try it out. Many a time have I written a story and thought, well... what if Jack *doesn't* get married now, but instead takes a trip around the world? This can lead to pages of revisions that lead nowhere (though I wouldn't dare think of them as wasted), or it can lead to a necessary breakthrough. Unfortunately, you usually have to write it all out to see if it's the right way to go.

Similarly, many hours are spent brainstorming products, services, and solutions for businesses that sometimes work and sometimes don't. The entire concept of a business pivot is based on imagining new possibilities. This is why a core rule of brainstorming is to not immediately say no to any new idea.

When it comes to writing at work, stop yourself before pressing "send" and consider alternate ways of communicating your message. Perhaps the sales numbers would be easier to read as a chart, instead of a list. Or the blueprints could use a paragraph of background so your audience can understand your larger vision. Maybe add a few sincere words of encouragement to the team on Friday afternoon before asking them to come in on Saturday.

This doesn't mean you won't proceed with what you already have, but it will mean that you can be sure you've given it your best effort.

WRITING EXERCISE: AUTOMATIC WRITING

Part I: There's no trick to being creative, but it takes time and practice. One strategy is to remove your own snap judgment of what you produce, so you don't prematurely revise your thoughts or shut down ideas before they've had a chance to blossom (or, in many cases, wither). This technique is called "automatic writing."

Set a timer for six minutes. Then put pen to paper (or fingers to keyboard) and start writing. **Do not stop until the timer goes off.**

You'll quickly see that six minutes is a *long* fucking time to write continuously.

Nevertheless, keep going. Even if you write the words "I am writing I am writing I am doing automatic writing blah blah blah" and so on, just keep writing until the timer goes off. Often your mind will eventually wander elsewhere and you'll start writing something more substantial again.

And if it doesn't, that's okay. Do this exercise once or twice a week, and I promise you'll start writing some more interesting material over time. Don't expect Shakespeare or Faulkner just yet, because "great" writing happens in revision (see Chapter 21). But your ideas will come ever more quickly, and they'll grow more imaginative over time.

If you have any experience with meditation, you might find this exercise analogous, and six minutes may be easy. If so, just set the timer for longer, or do two to three automatic writing sprints in a row.

Part II: Automatic writing only works if you allow yourself the freedom to throw away what you've written.

You don't need it. You aren't submitting for publication or sending it out as an email.

Unless there's some gold in what you generated that you might want to mine for some other project, don't worry too much about what you write in these automatic pages. Think of it as swimming laps, shooting free throws, or hitting the driving range. It's just practice, and you're not keeping score.

PART II:

CRAFT AND TECHNIQUE

5: LANGUAGE

"The day waves yellow with all its crops." That is [Virginia] Woolf, from *The Waves*. I am consumed by this sentence, partly because I cannot quite explain why it moves me so much. I can see, hear, its beauty, its strangeness. Its music is very simple. Its words are simple. And its meaning is simple, too. Woolf is describing the sun rising and finally filling the day with its yellow fire. The sentence means something like: this is what the field of corn on a summer's day will look like when everything is blazing with sunlight—a yellow semaphore, a sea of moving color. We *know* exactly and instantly what Woolf means, and we think: That could not be put any better. The secret lies in the decision to avoid the usual image of crops waving, and instead, to write "the day waves": the effect is suddenly that the day itself, the very fabric and temporality of the day, seems saturated in yellow. And then that peculiar, apparently nonsensical "waves yellow" (how can anything wave yellow?), conveys a sense that yellowness has so intensely taken over the day itself that it has taken over our verbs, too—yellowness has conquered our agency. How do we wave? We wave yellow. That is all we can do. The sunlight is so absolute that it stuns us, makes us sluggish, robs us of will. Eight simple words evoke color, high summer, warm lethargy, ripeness.

— James Wood, *How Fiction Works* (2008)

SEVEN PERCENT

Why is writing so hard? Perhaps a better question: Why is writing *well* so hard? It's because writing is a skill, and just like with any other skill, humans have to learn it, then practice a lot to get better. Unlike eating and pooping, we aren't born with the ability to read and write. Writing clearly and thoughtfully also takes a lot of concentration and work, which is anathema to those of us who prefer doomscrolling or playing video games all day.

But there's more to it. In the 1960s, a college professor named Albert Mehrabian came up with a formulation of face-to-face communication called the "7-38-55" model. This posited that only seven percent of feelings and attitudes are communicated through the actual words we speak, while thirty-eight percent comes through tone and voice. The other fifty-five percent is in body language.

It makes sense to me, then, that if most of the time people are able to get across what they mean largely—ninety-three percent, in fact—through means *other* than words, then they won't think about word choice because it isn't necessary. People who don't make their living from writing don't need to focus on it, as long as they can convey what they need through the other ninety-three percent.

But writing isolates word choice. There is no voice, tone, or body language to communicate what you *really* mean. You have to say it right the first time. So we're going to start at the beginning.

The *way* beginning.

Vocabulary

Writing is, for the most part, made up of language, which is, for the most part, made up of words. In addition to tone, voice, and body language, some business communication will also have charts, figures, data points, illustrations, numbers, and (hopefully) a lot of dollar signs. But this book isn't about graphic design. We're here to talk about words. And sentences. And paragraphs.

The human use of language is a wondrous piece of evolution, and it provides me my daily bread. We communicate using thousands of words, most of which we repeat constantly—such as (in English) the participles "the," "a," "at," simple verbs and their conjugations like "to be" or "to go," and pronouns.

Reading is a wonderful way of improving your vocabulary and is essential to becoming a good writer. I used to read the dictionary and the encyclopedia when I was a kid (because I'm a fucking nerd, you see), though I'm not suggesting that for everyone. But if you're not already working on your vocabulary, at least a little, then now is a great time to start.

When it comes to both business and creative writing, one or two recherché words go a long way. See what I did there? "Recherché" means exotic or rare, and that I am now defining it for you means that I've stopped your forward progress in consuming the material (the "flow" of reading, discussed in Chapter 17).

In any type of communication, you almost never want to confuse or disrupt your reader's experience, unless part of the pleasure is "figuring it out." An example of this might be a purposefully quixotic or modernist text such as *Ulysses* (1920) by James Joyce, *Infinite Jest* (1996) by David Foster Wallace, or *House of Leaves* (2000) by Mark Danielewski. Leave that for the Modernists. Business communication should be clear and concise.

The minor feud between two twentieth-century giants of literature, William Faulkner and Ernest Hemingway, demonstrates this idea, as the former once quipped that the latter had "never been known to use a word that might send a reader to the dictionary."

As if that was a bad thing. Hemingway, in his typical style, responded, "Poor Faulkner. Does he really think big emotions come from big words? He thinks I don't know the ten-dollar words. I know them all right. But there are older and simpler and better words, and those are the ones I use."

Hemingway is correct, for the most part, though finding the *precise word* to convey meaning is more important than worrying whether the word is too complex or too simple.

One more quick writing tip on language: vary your word usage within a text. Repeating words, especially those that are a bit recherché, is noticeable and distracting.

Observing the World

More important than building a huge and abstruse vocabulary is the practice of observation. Many professional writers carry with them a notebook (I use the Notes app on my phone) to write details, anecdotes, ideas, bits of conversation, and anything they notice and want to reserve in their minds but know they'll forget. Sometimes one of these tidbits will make it into a story, sometimes they won't—but the practice of scribbling it down is what matters.

Every time you stop to write something—*and I promise you, for real, professional writers do this*—you get more practice noticing the world. You may not know what certain things are called at first, or how to describe them in florid detail, but you will start observing bits of your world you had previously ignored, and this skill will work its way into your career and business writing.

Here are some examples from the Notes app on my iPhone, without context:

- at a doctor appointment: a muzak version of the cure's "boys don't cry" with classical nylon string guitar

- one of those independent coffee shops that burn their coffee

- the difference between a cross and a crucifix

- hate speech vs. mind control, or occasional casualties (the "purge" principal) and liberty vs. tyranny and oppression

- bringer shows, myspace bands, doggy daycare worker, breaking pencil during lsat exam

What does it all mean? Well, let's just agree that for this book, it doesn't matter.

THE NAMES OF THINGS

> I want you to touch that lil' dangly thing that swing in the back
> of my throat.
>
> — Cardi B, "WAP"

Have you ever seen a pile of rocks stacked one on top of each other, balancing precariously? Of course you have. Did you know this object has a name? It's called a *cairn*. Maybe you already knew that, and good for you.

An *aglet* is the plastic nub at the end of a shoelace that keeps the fibers from fraying. *Dysthymia* is a long-term, but mild, state of depression.

Writers need to know the names of rarefied objects so we can describe the world to our readers. It's part of the job, just as graphic designers and interior decorators must know the difference between shades of red, which colors complement each other, and which colors evoke different emotions (apparently red makes people angry and green is soothing). Writers sharpen their vocabularies like carpenters sharpen their saws.

The divot above your lip and under your nostrils is called a *philtrum*, which beautifully comes from the Ancient Greek, via Latin: φίλτρον or phíltron, meaning "love charm."

And that "little dangly thing" in the back of one's throat? It's called a *uvula*, a word that sounds much dirtier than it is.

As a true word nerd, I love archaic phrases nobody uses anymore, such as "donnybrook" (a fistfight) and "Good Thunderation!" (the "Holy fuck!" of the 1800s). I also love wordplay, such as puns, spoonerisms, and palindromes ("Able was I ere I saw Elba"). Untranslatable words are also a delight: the Spanish *sobremesa* is translated as "dessert" but really means that hour or so you spend warmly chatting at the table after a long meal, while the Japanese *tsundoku* is an act of which I am guilty: the acquisition of reading materials such as books and magazines and letting them pile up in your house, unread. (It's a lifestyle.)

In business, it is also important to know the names of things. You need to know the difference between a lead and a prospect, or revenue and profit, or a balloon mortgage and an ARM. This isn't only because you don't want to look inept in a meeting (by, for example, confusing EBITDA and Ebola), but because much of the modern economy is conceptual and idea-driven.

Consider the phrase "consumer path to purchase." This concept describes a reality upon which marketers depend, even if most shoppers don't know they're a part of it. One doesn't simply acquire products or services. There is a process in which a potential consumer becomes aware of and learns about a product, considers it, compares it to competitive products, perhaps reads reviews and testimonials, goes to a store (online or in person), considers it again, then purchases it. If the product is consumable, or is a service, they may use it and purchase it many times. Marketers—and all business owners, really—need to know their own customers' path to purchase, and, more importantly, that there is one.

If I told you that a conditional trade over a specific timeframe that combines the features of a stop-on-quote order and a limit order in order to mitigate the risk of transacting on a security is called a "stop-limit order," you would also have to know what "transacting on a security" means, as well as what a "stop order" is, and a "limit order." Those in finance should know such terms. If you want your website to be at the top of the organic search listings, you need to know what "organic search listings" are, and that there is a strategy to achieve this called "search engine optimization," or "SEO." Someone who runs a residential home construction company should know the difference between veneer and cladding.

I've always loved to learn, and one of the joys of being a writer is that I have to (get to) delve into literally myriad topics I'd never otherwise research. Wait. Go look at Figure 9.

I have a book called *The Writer's Guide to Weapons* that goes into detail about guns and other weaponry, and it's useful when describing battle or fight scenes. When I moved to Texas, I met people who'd been around guns their entire lives and knew the difference between a bullet, shell, cartridge, and round. When I was growing up in New York City suburbs,

Let's look more closely at this sentence:

> I've always loved to learn, and one of the joys of being a writer is that I have to (get to) delve into literally myriad topics I'd never otherwise research.

My intentional use of "myriad" is an example of precision with vocabulary because it is often used improperly. Technically, the word "myriad" means "ten thousand" and therefore doesn't need the word "of" after it. "Myriad topics" is grammatically correct, meaning "ten thousand topics," while the phrase "myriad of topics" is incorrect.

Also, the use of "myriad" and "literally" in this sentence could be considered examples of hyperbole (see Chapter 7), in that I haven't literally researched ten thousand topics—probably more like a hundred. The exaggeration communicates that I've done a lot of research.

But the rules of grammar, as well as definitions of words, evolve over time. Just like how the word "literally" now means both "literally" and "figuratively," the word "myriad" now means "a lot," and most people use the word "of" after it. So it's generally no longer incorrect to say "a myriad of topics." In fact, not using "of" might sound overly formal or awkward to some ears.

Figure 9. On "myriad," "literally," and "figuratively."

however, these terms could be used interchangeably. Through research, though, I now know important details such as a Winchester Model 70 is a bolt-action rifle, while a Winchester Model 94 is a lever-action rifle.

The trouble is, as a writer, you cannot fake this knowledge. Some readers may have intimate knowledge of the subject and will spot even the most minute errors. This undermines your credibility as an author, just as faking it in business can undermine your job.

Every field of human endeavor has deep-level intricacies and terminology that you pick up over time: painters learn the names and uses of each different brush, sound engineers know how to identify and correct audio phase issues, quants know the difference between alpha and beta performance, real estate agents know about closing costs, eminent domain, and titles.

Take time to educate yourself on the more arcane terminology of your business. It may come in handy one day.

Le Mot Juste

Once you've learned the terminology of your field, you must implement it correctly. The name of this section, *le mot juste*, is an example of itself. I'd like to think every word I've chosen in this book is an example of *le mot juste*, in fact.

Le mot juste is a French phrase meaning "the exact right word." I could have used the word "specificity," but that wasn't *exactly* the right word I needed, or "particularity," which features prominently in Sol Stein's *Stein on Writing* (1995). But "le mot juste" *is* the right phrase. And I'm not being particular for the sake of perfectionism or being persnickety for fun. Picking the exact right word is crucial to communicating the *exact* message you want your audience to understand. This especially goes for written communication, because you won't have a chance to clarify your words or provide additional context in the moment of reading.

It's about *meaning*. Unless you are speaking (or writing) just to hear yourself talk (in which case, stop), then you are likely communicating with someone to get a message across, whether it's "The report is due at 2 p.m.," or "The fridge is being cleaned out this weekend," or "If you don't hit your numbers this quarter, you'll be fired."

When Sol Stein discusses "particularity," he advocates for the use of fresh and precise detail. This doesn't mean adding words for the sake of itself, but rather adding the *right* details to bring the world alive, as Stein says: "It is not just detail that distinguishes good writing, it is *detail that individualizes*." Consider:

The used AirPods she tried to sell me were kind of dirty.

Versus

The AirPods she tried to sell me were crusted over with an oily, sour-smelling, yellow-brownish earwax.

More specific, and more gross. You can envision these AirPods, you know exactly what they look like. You know what they smell like, you can *feel* their oleaginous slime on your hands. You know she's been wearing them all day, every day, and you can smell the yellow-brownish earwax. Even the phrase "yellow-brownish" is specific—not quite yellow, not quite brown.

It makes for better writing, but only if the extra details are crucial to communicating what you mean. By being specific and accurate with your word choice, you will be more articulate and more successful in conveying what you mean. Sacrificing brevity, however, is only recommended if you can't find fewer and better words.

Consider a salesperson reporting to their manager why a sale was lost:

They said the product is too expensive.

Versus

They said the product is overpriced.

Technically, the second sentence has one fewer word, so that's a win, but more importantly, the second sentence is more specific. While both "too expensive" and "overpriced" mean that someone is not willing to pay a certain amount of money for a product, the former may result from more than one reason, such as the customer thinks the price is too high for the value, *or* the customer thinks the product is priced correctly but doesn't have the budget for the product at the time. Choosing the right word can help with negotiation—if the price is too high for the value, you might be able to lower it, but if the customer doesn't have the money, then the time isn't right no matter what it costs.

Let's look at one more example from the book *Traction* (2011) by Gino Wickman:

> My typical client is an entrepreneurial small to mid- size organization ($2 million to $50 million in revenue with 10 to 250 employees), growth oriented, willing to change, and willing to be vulnerable (as in being open- minded, willing to admit weaknesses, and willing to face reality).

What if he'd written:

My typical client is an entrepreneur.

Both sentences have their time and place, which is what *le mot juste* (the perfect word) is all about. In an introductory email or in an elevator, you may want to summarize, so the second sentence would be appropriate. In a long-form explanation, however, you can provide specific details to communicate who and how your service can help.

No matter what, though, vagueness often leads to ignorance and confusion. It breaks down trust. It leads to pointless meetings. It's one more reason to avoid clichés (see Chapter 7): they are not specific, and they have no meaning.

Unfortunately, it takes a lot of effort to come up with the right word; to sit and envision what *exactly* you're trying to communicate. This is why people use clichés and jargon—because they're easier. Nevertheless, *le mot juste* is worth it.

Et Cetera

The opposite of *le mot juste* is the dreaded "stuff like that." There are many variations of this phrase: "things of that nature," "and the like," "and so on," "and so forth," or "you know what I'm saying." These are all loosey-goosey forms of the Latin phrase *Et Cetera*, which means "bad writing." (No, no, of course it doesn't. *Et* means "and," and *cetera* means "the rest." It literally means "and the rest.")

"Etc." is easy, it's convenient, and it's a cop-out. When you use a phrase like this, you are abdicating your job of communicating information and instead making your listener or reader do the work of figuring out what you actually mean, or what "the rest" actually is.

Furthermore, it leaves a lot of room for interpretation, misinterpretation, and confusion. If I ask my intern Blake to put together a marketing report "with all of the data, such as impressions, clicks, etc.," then Blake only knows I want a marketing report, and that it should include impressions, clicks, and at least one more field. But do I want engagements, cost, views, cost per click, cost per engagement, or something else? Blake can never be sure. Either Blake pulls a report with every possible metric, which is unwieldy and useless, or Blake tries to read my mind and ends up omitting a handful of metrics I actually do need. Now Blake needs to redo it, and I've wasted everyone's time.

People use shorthand because it's easy, and I understand the impulse. When you must specify "stuff," you have to think of a list, and thinking is hard.

Unfortunately for you, that's the theme of this book: *Think harder.*

NEOLOGISMS

A "neologism" is a new word—a term that didn't exist before someone coined it. We encounter neologisms all the time, especially as technology expands, though they eventually become commonplace words in the zeitgesit (think of "internet," "meme," or "lol").

Authors, too, invent many words:

- **Robot** comes from Karel Čapek's novel *Rossum's Universal Robots* (1922), which derives from the Czech word *robotnik*, meaning serf or slave.

- **Utopia** literally means "nowhere," and Sir Thomas More coined it, from Ancient Greek, in *Utopia* (1516) for the name of a perfect, ideal nation (because such a place does not, and could not, exist).

- **Lilliputian** means small, and comes from Lilliput, a small island nation in Jonathan Swift's *Gulliver's Travels* (1726) full of diminutive people called Lilliputians.

William Shakespeare coined hundreds of words and phrases, including "a rose by any other name," "green-eyed monster," and "disgraceful."

A neologism can help elucidate or crystalize an idea, and if you actually coin one, you're a freaking genius. "Stuplime" is a great neologism, a portmanteau (see Figure 10) of "stupid"

> A **portmanteau** is a new word made from the combination of two other words, such as "brunch" (breakfast + lunch), "smog" (smoke + fog), or "spork" (spoon + fork). Or for you frat boys, a "kegerator" (keg + refrigerator).
>
> We encounter portmanteaus all the time, such as with new dog breeds (I personally have an "Aussiedoodle," named Marty, who is a mix of an Australian Shepherd and a Poodle). They are especially common with journalists trying to sound more clever than they actually are, which is why you should approach your own invention of a portmanteau with caution.

Figure 10. Portmanteau.

and "sublime."[9] The *Jackass* movies are stuplime.

I'm not instructing you to come up with hundreds of new words like Shakespeare did. If you're a professional writer or poet, it's an impressive achievement, but hardly worth the effort. As a normal everyday knowledge worker, your goal is to get your meaning across easily and memorably so you don't confuse your team or client, and don't have to repeat yourself endlessly. That's it: be clear, get your point across.

But you can *think* like a neologist.

As in much of life, tips and tricks that purport to be easy ("life hacks," if you will) do not work. Anything worthwhile usually takes time and effort, and anything that seems too good to be true usually is. If getting six-pack abs were easy, everyone would have them. So while it isn't *easy* to think like a neologist, it will help your writing.

If this seems monumental, remember that thinking like a neologist doesn't have to take place on the first draft. Ideally you want to spend your first go-round getting down your thoughts and ideas—*then* go back and polish that turd. It's not an issue if your first draft contains clichés or imprecise wording. That's what rewrites are for.

Let's look at an example from the inimitable Terrance Hayes. In his poem "Barberism," he describes cutting his father-in-law's hair:

It was light and lusterless and somehow luckless,
The hair I cut from the head of my father-in-law,

It was pepper-blanched and wind-scuffed, thin
As a blown bulb's filament, it stuck to the teeth

Of my clippers like a dark language, the static
Covering his mind stuck to my fingers, it mingled

In halfhearted tufts with the dust.

The title of this poem is an example of neologism: "barberism" mashes up "barber" and "barbarism" (barbaric), and he describes his father-in-law's hair using original metaphors: "pepper-blanched" and "thin as a blown bulb's filament."

But Terrance Hayes is a genius poet, and you're just writing an email. If you try to be too clever coming up with new words, you'll just sound like a pompous jerk, or worse, you'll come off like Michael Scott from *The Office*.

All you need to do is look at what you're writing and dissect it into each sentence, one by one: is there a fresher way of saying what you're saying? The most common phrases at work are typically horrible clichés, and this is where you can try to remove some from your life.

WORDPLAY

Wordplay such as "barberism" is exciting, fresh, and pleasing. In creative writing, these kinds of language games can be fun, though en masse they can also become tiresome and self-indulgent, especially if used for no other reason than for their own existence.

In business, a smidge of wordplay goes a long way in keeping your communications fresh and interesting. But be careful. Puns, as much as I love them, will induce an eye roll rather

Figure 11. "Fly the coop?" Are they fucking kidding?

than a smile. See Figure 11 for a pun so revolting it led me to not only unsubscribe from Peacock's promotional emails, but cancel the service altogether.

Another type of wordplay is chiasmus, a rhetorical device that switches two words around to create an often memorable, poignant, and repeatable phrase:

Ask not what your country can do for you; ask what you can do for your country. (John F. Kennedy, 1961)

Do I love you because you're beautiful or are you beautiful because I love you? (Rodgers & Hammerstein, "Cinderella")

If you are a speechwriter or songwriter, a chiasmus is a nice turn of phrase that, once in a while, can be great. But use wordplay with *discretion*. This horrible, awful, and detestable phrase is *also* an example of chiasmus:

You working hard, or hardly working?

The Sound of Language

> Of course I stole the title for this talk, from George Orwell. One rea-
> son I stole it was that I like the sound of the words: Why I Write.
> There you have three short unambiguous words that share a sound,
> and the sound they share is this:
>
> I
>
> I
>
> I
>
> — Joan Didion, "Why I Write" (1976)

I always read my work out loud. If someone were in the room with me, they might think I'm a loon, but hearing the sound of the language of my words is helpful for revision. Not only do I pick up on typos and errors, clunky syntax, and/or ambiguous phrasing I would have otherwise missed, but I also get a sense of the variety of how my writing might be interpreted.

See, everyone reads in a way suited to their own mind and brings their own interpretation to your work. It can be surprising when someone reads something you wrote and thinks it means something totally different than what you intended. This is because *their* emphasis fell on *certain* words instead of *others*, whereas my *intended* emphasis *was* on different *phrases*.

An example of this occurred in a workshop during my MFA: I submitted a story in which the narrator thought about his mother, who'd died after a long battle with cancer. In his internal monologue, the character thinks, "The doctor had given her three months, but she stayed in the goddamn ring for two years." Maybe it's because I'm from New York, but I heard "goddamn" as signaling pride and admiration at his mother's grit. But some people read "goddamn" as anger. It made no sense in the context of the story—as if he were inexplicably pissed off his mother wouldn't just die—and was the opposite of what I intended (my readers, too, were confused).

That's the risk of writing: once your idea is transmitted from mind to pen to page, you're out of the equation, and you can't explain, modify, or interpret your words for your audience. So you have to be precise.

Much can (and has) also been said about the *actual* sound and rhythm of language. It applies a bit more to poetry than it does to prose, and even less so to emails or sales decks—but we shouldn't ignore it entirely.

One more time, let's look to Terrance Hayes, in "As Traffic." Read this one aloud:

> Sounds like the hook in a chart topper
> A rapper mouths squatting like a gilded animal
> In the middle of a bustling boulevard
> Of bumpers and bumping bikini rumps,
> Chains, chains, chains, but it meant to conjure
> My half brother, and the girls the news says
> He'd kidnapped or persuaded with knuckles
> Before the police rushed in knocking him
> Like a lover no longer loved to the motel floor

The sound of the language here—"a bustling boulevard of bumpers and bumping bikini rumps, chains, chains, chains"—is as gorgeous as the content is graphic.

This attribute is called *euphony*, by the way, and it is subjective. For example, one of the most beautiful phrases in the English language is said to be "cellar door." I don't know about all that. I believe the perceived beauty of language is in part determined by the meaning of the words, not just the phonemes. "Sick, twisted, sad son of a bitch" is also full of internal near rhymes and alliteration, but I wouldn't call this group of words "beautiful."

In any case, I recommend that whenever possible, find somewhere private and read your work out loud, be it a slide presentation, a white paper, or just an email. Listen and be astonished by the sound of your own language.

Connotation and Denotation

Put simply, "denotation" is the literal definition of a word, while "connotation" is the underlying or implied meaning. In creative writing, a word with ambiguous or double connotation can be used slyly for effect, but in business communication it will just be confusing. Just like how a wicked *double entendre* can be clever and flirty over a dirty martini at the hotel bar, while embarrassing or offensive in the conference room.

The section "The Names of Things" deals with knowing the denotation or definition of words and phrases, as well as knowing how they are used colloquially. The word "peruse," for example, *technically* means to read carefully and thoroughly, but everyone uses it to mean "skim." I'm not sure why, it's just the way it is.

Unfortunately, you can sometimes only learn connotation through usage and experience—especially because words have different connotations in different communities and at different times. In American English, for example, the word "pants" refers to what the Brits would call "trousers," while in British English, the word "pants" refers to what we Americans call "underwear" (or underpants, if you're being super weird).

For a business example, the words "economical," "reasonable," and "inexpensive" all denote a product or service has a relatively low cost. However, the word "cheap"—which also denotes a low cost—might also imply (or connote) to your client or prospect that it is cheaply-made, and thus inferior or of lower quality.

Another example: any time you would say "if you get my drift" with a raise of one eyebrow, that would be connotation—and as you can imagine, it doesn't work well in a corporate setting:

Let's meet in my office this afternoon to go over your latest sales figures.

Versus

Let's meet in my office this afternoon to go over your latest sales figures, if you catch my drift.

Synonyms

Some writing books caution new writers to avoid using a thesaurus because a common and plain word is often a better choice than an obscure "ten-dollar" word. Well, I like using the thesaurus because my old and tired brain only has ready access to a small portion of the words I've learned, and so it's handy to have a list when I need it. For what it's worth, I use *The Synonym Finder* by J. I. Rodale, thesaurus.com, and sometimes WordHippo.

But don't fall under the illusion that using a thesaurus will save you time. If I don't have the exact word I need—*le mot juste*—readily available to call to mind, it might still take me a good ten minutes trying to find it. And I'll go back two or three times on revision, still debating which word is the right one.

My other note of caution with using a thesaurus is that you ought not choose a word that you don't already know. The English language has incorporated many thousands of words that have precise meanings and have become obscure over time, and using the same boring or simple word twice is much better than using one word incorrectly. Consider the following:

This is a story about love and death in the golden land, and begins with the country. (Joan Didion, "Slouching Towards Bethlehem," 1968)

Versus

This is a peroration about concupiscence and necrosis in the aureate terra firma, and precipitates with the palatinate.

There is no need to explicate why this is terrible. Large and uncommon words can make you seem pompous, and words with the wrong connotation can make you seem stupid.

WRITING EXERCISE: LANGUAGE

Part I: For the next day or so, try to notice new details of life and write them in a notebook or phone app. Don't judge what you write or even reread it—just write and move on. In a week, reread your observations. You'll be surprised by what you find.

Part II: Learn the names of things. Whatever your industry, do some research into different terminology and see what you do or don't know. Especially for anything new you noticed in the notes you took from Part I.

Part III: Grab a couple of recent documents you've produced and read them over carefully. See if you used any "et cetera" language to avoid doing the hard work of enumerating specifics. Do you think your audience truly knew what exactly you meant, or do you think you may have inadvertently been vague and caused confusion?

Part IV: Read these same documents aloud and listen for the language. Did you use any stale or clunky phrasing? Take a few minutes and see if you can rewrite a part of one of these documents with more specific points and fresher language.

6: STYLE

When I was in an MFA program—one of the most respected, highly touted, expensive, and therefore, one of the most flawed—"structure" was a dirty word and "craft" was something for carpenters, or the rubes upstairs in the film school. The education I received for over $30,000 can be condensed to eight easy-to-forget points...

1. Write what you know; don't write what you don't know.
2. Flashy style or language without a story to tell is "all dressed up with nowhere to go."
3. Writing can't be taught.
4. Cut out adverbs.
5. Never use the word "always."
6. "You will never be fictionists."
7. Don't write screenplays; they will destroy your ability to write prose fiction.
8. There are kinds of stories.

Aside from the vapid number three and the asinine number six, none of these is wrong, but they're all useless.

> — Tim Tomlinson, *The Portable MFA in Creative Writing* (2006)

DEFINING STYLE

In this book, "style" is less about what you're saying (content), and more about how you say it. Or as the English writer Jonathan

Swift defined it, "proper words in proper places."

Ernest Hemingway and James Joyce both had famously notable writing styles: the former was sparse and direct, while the latter was maximalist and dense. Style is easy to see in movies, particularly with certain directors such as Quentin Tarantino or Wes Anderson. Their work is so stylized you can almost immediately guess the director by watching one scene.

Style is important when writing creatively, and it develops and changes over the course of one's career. I tend to write in long sentences with multiple clauses and punctuated by asides and parentheticals. The style of E. E. Cummings' poems often features a lack of punctuation, while the detective novels of Dashiell Hammett, Elmore Leonard, and Raymond Chandler have a style called "hard-boiled."

Many authors, however, prefer to write in an unobtrusive style that doesn't call attention to itself, thus allowing the story, characters, and plot to shine. They follow standard structural rules, such as each paragraph having a topic sentence supported by all other sentences, and they keep sentences short and readable.

In business writing especially, there tends to be less room for overly stylized writing, as the content of what you're saying is ephemeral, timely, and of utmost importance. Business communication is not meant for perpetuity, to be read casually, or for its artistic merit, so the style tends to be dry. Consider the following:

Dear Client,

Can we meet at 11am on Friday for our status call?

Thanks,

Phillip Mandel

Versus

Dea
    r (c)
            lie
    nt
,——   can
    WE
m(e)a)t
    eleven 11 XI
morning sunshine/rise and shine/coffee
F
    ri
                    dayismyfavoriteday
4 hour status   call
            ?   ?   ?

Or consider this:

Dear Client,

Item 4 on the creative brief is unclear. Can you please provide additional demographic information about the target audience?

Thanks,

Phillip

Versus

Hey hot stuff,

Your creative brief reads like yesterday's newspaper after it's been chewed by a dog and left in the rain. I looked at item four and thought, "Whaddaya mean, Jelly Bean? This sonofabitch isn't making any sense!"

So give me a break, will ya? I'm all over this like stink on

shit, but I need to know which side of the highway you're driving on.

P

Personally, I would love to write all my emails like either of the second versions—but I might lose all my clients if I did.

Nevertheless, your personal writing style *is* important, and it *will* have an effect on how you are understood and how your audience reacts. For example, using (or not using) clichés is a choice of style, as is using humor, ornate or sparse language, or the passive voice. Puns, wordplay, and the sound of your language all make up your style.

In a famous writing book, *The Elements of Style*, William Strunk, Jr. and E. B. White lay out a series of proscriptive and rigid tenets about how to write properly. This book should be required reading for anyone whose living depends on writing. But read with a degree of skepticism—or at least one upturned eyebrow—as Strunk and White can be stodgy and old-fashioned. For example, their rant about orthodox spelling was perhaps relevant in 1979, but has since been rendered passé by the internet and social media. Indeed, the book has found strong critics over the years. But I've found it useful.

FORM

Style is more than just grammar and split infinitives and being concise. It's also about tone and voice. It affects what your audience takes away from your communication. For example, in the first sentence of this paragraph, I broke the rules of grammar by using "and" twice. Technically it's a run-on sentence, but I like the way it sounds. It goes well with my conversational tone and the cadence of my persuasive voice.

Another important aspect of style is form. In *Exercises in Style* (1947), the French author Raymond Queneau presents ninety-nine versions of one trite anecdote, ranging from a haiku to an official letter to cockney to operatic languages. In one version he tells it backwards, in another he uses only metaphors, in another he writes it as a sonnet. Some are straightforward and easy to understand, some are nonsensical or whimsically funny. As a lover of language, I am into this kind of book. But for learning to be a better writer at work, this book is an object lesson on style and presentation.

The "Narrative" chapter, which is the most straightforward, presents the incident like this:

> One day at about midday in the Parc Monceau district, on the back platform of a more or less full S bus (now No. 84), I observed a person with a very long neck who was wearing a felt hat which had a plaited cord round it instead of a ribbon. This individual suddenly addressed the man standing next to him, accusing him of purposely treading on his toes every time any passengers got on or got off.
>
> However, he quickly abandoned the dispute and threw himself on to a seat which had become vacant. Two hours later I saw him in front of the Gare Saint-Lazare engaged in earnest conversation with a friend who was advising him to reduce the space between the lapels of his overcoat by getting a competent tailor to raise the top button.

The same story is told backwards in the "Retrograde" chapter:

> You ought to put another button on your overcoat, his friend told him. I met him in the middle of the Cour de Rome, after having left him rushing avidly towards a seat. He had just protested against being pushed by another passenger who, he said, was jostling him every time anyone got off. This scraggy young man was the wearer of a ridiculous hat. This took place on the platform of an S bus which was full that particular midday.

The content of the anecdote doesn't change, but the style of its presentation does.

Poetry, as an art form, has all manner of structure, though free verse—which doesn't focus on rhyme or meter—has been the dominant form for decades. The sonnet, a fourteen-line poem with a specific rhyme scheme, is probably the most famous of formal poems for English speakers, as Shakespeare wrote many that are commonly taught in high school. Haiku is also a well-known short form of poetry from Japan, and limericks are famous as dirty jokes. But what about the aubade? It's a morning poem, while an elegy is a mourning poem. Poets can also work with the nineteen-line villanelle, or a thirty-nine-line sestina that repeats specific words.

There are specific parts of poems to know as well, such as a couplet, a trochee, and a caesura (none of which need defining here). The point is that just as poetry is more than line breaks, writing in general is more than just putting words down on a page one after the other.

Business communication is fairly limited in the types and styles you can use. You're not going to present a sales presentation as a skit or a play, for example, and you're not going to email your board the quarterly report as a haiku.

Obviously.

But although much business communication is strict, formal, and precise, there are still many considerations to enhance your style so your communication flows better. Your writing will be more polished, and your words will be remembered and understood.

VOICE

In art, the subject of "voice" can get metaphysical pretty quickly. It's a mix of both technique and ideology. A writer's voice is derived from mastery of their craft, their style, and what they are saying in their work.

It takes a long time to find. As noted elsewhere in the book, one of the benefits of an MFA program is gaining the time to experiment and find one's voice. It stems from your *weltanschauung*, which is a terrific German word meaning "worldview," or overall philosophy about life and one's place in the universe.

And it's not only for artists.

Voice applies to your career, your company, and your everyday business communication. Consider the different "voices" of Facebook founder Mark Zuckerberg, industrialist Elon Musk, and veteran investor Warren Buffett. They are all billionaires, all business leaders, and all very famous—but they each speak to the world differently. Zuckerberg is somewhat reserved and conservative, using redundant words like "really" and "clearly" to hedge; Musk is more chaotic and direct, using internet slang "imo" in a tweet; Buffett is folksy and straightforward. In the following, pay attention less to what they're saying and more to *how* they're saying it:

- **Zuckerberg**, in response to a question about competition from Apple: "One of the things I think is interesting is that it's not really clear upfront whether an open or closed ecosystem is going to be better. If you look back to PCs, Windows was clearly the one that had a lot more scale and became the default and norm that people used. And Mac did fine, but I think PC and Windows were, I think, the premier ecosystem in that environment."[10]

- **Musk**: "Tesla stock price is too high imo," in a tweet on May 1, 2020, that led to shares plunging more than 10 percent.

- **Buffett**, providing some folk wisdom: "Someone's sitting in the shade today because someone planted a tree a long time ago."

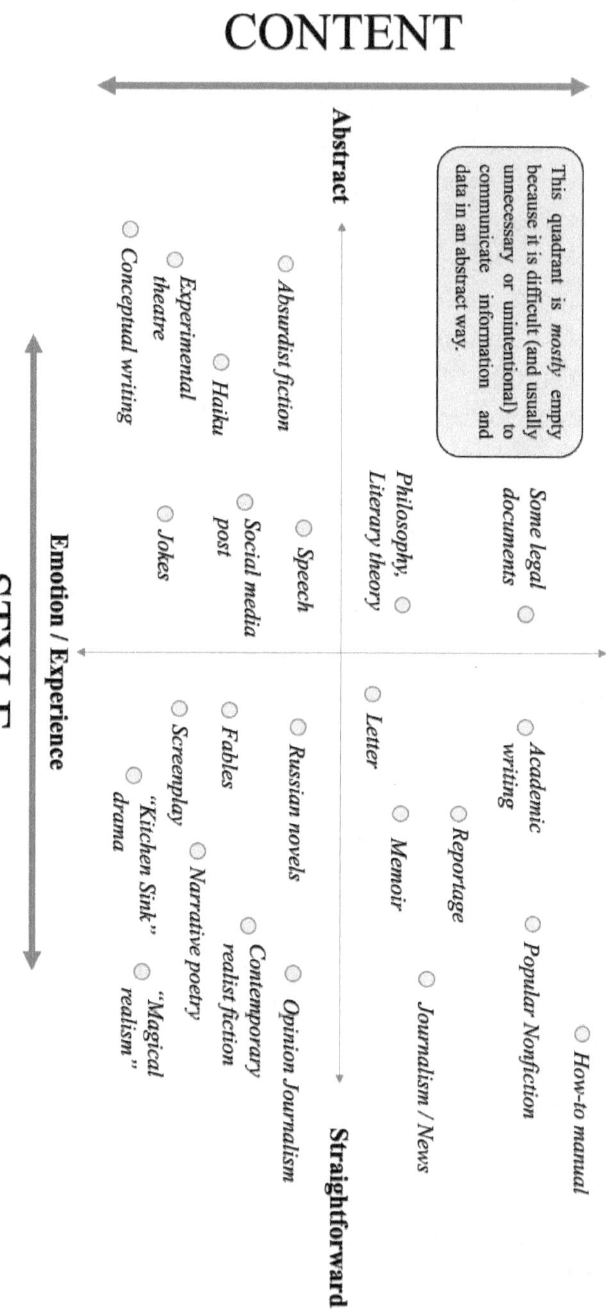

Figure 12. Style vs. Content in creative writing and nonfiction.

Yes, you may be a CPA, but that is not your voice. Maybe there are a limited number of writing styles when filing taxes, but there's surely a lot more to your career than that. You can and must have your own Voice—your unique way of seeing things and acting in the world—not only to differentiate yourself from every other Joe and Jane Calculator out there and get more business, but to retain clients, work better, and get more enjoyment out of your life.

CONTENT VS. STYLE

For those who find experimental art exciting, I recommend *Against Expression: An Anthology of Conceptual Writing* (2011), edited by Craig Dworkin and Kenneth Goldsmith. This challenging yet rewarding book showcases work that doesn't feel like "traditional" writing, though they are, technically, words on a page (and in some cases, not).

Here is a snippet from a work called "I Was Told to Write Fifty Words," by Vladimir Zykov, in which he paid five cents to dozens of random people on Amazon's Mechanical Turk to write fifty words:

> I was told to write fifty words, so that is what I am doing.
> I was not told what to write, how to write, or why to write
> fifty words. I was told to write fifty words, nothing more. I
> hope the fifty words that I have chosen are fine.

Another example of conceptual and experimental writing is *Day*, by Kenneth Goldsmith himself, which is a line-by-line reproduction of *The New York Times* issue of September 1, 2000, set in nine-point font, including advertisements, stock quotes—everything.

The ideas and concepts this kind of work communicates are not as easily definable or understandable as, say, an illustrated manual of a specific task. So in Figure 12, let's imagine a scale of ideas and communication, with CONTENT as one axis: "information / data" on one side, and "emotion / experience" on the other. The other axis is STYLE, where "straightforward" is one way of communicating, and "abstract" is the other.

Naturally, this is just demonstrative and there are thousands of examples that don't fit where I've plotted them, but it works for these purposes.

Let's look at a few examples on this chart:

- **Illustrated how-to manual**: Conveys information and data only, intended to describe specifically and exactly how to do or make something, with no room for interpretation.

- **Nonfiction**: Conveys factual information objectively (supposedly) but allows the reader to interpret that information.

- **Memoir**: Conveys factual (supposedly) information and emotion, but filtered through the lens of the author, and allows the reader to interpret that information and emotion.

- **Realist fiction**: Conveys universal truths and emotion through a fake yet realistic story.

- **Poetry**: Conveys universal truths and emotion through language, sometimes with realism, sometimes with story, sometimes without either.

- **Conceptual writing**: Open to interpretation.

In *Against Expression*, Goldsmith argues that much contemporary conceptual writing is a response to the rise of technology. He thinks the internet, computer technology, and "copy / paste" has done to writing what photography did to painting; that is, when painting was no longer needed to reproduce images (because a new technology—photography—accomplished this more easily, and with better quality), painters were given freedom to play with their craft. This gave rise to impressionism, minimalism, surrealism, modernism, and other schools of representative visual art that value emotion and experience over a factual replication of what can be seen in the world with one's eyeballs.

Similarly, he argues, formal writing is no longer needed to communicate information, as the glut of content on the internet can do that. Now, artistic writers are free to play with form. One example he highlights is how some writers appropriate text from other sources and refashion them as new works, thereby exploding and challenging conventional notions of "literature," "communication," "meaning," and "expression."[11]

If this sounds like horseshit, that's okay. I don't agree with him, completely—but I do find it a kind of maddening, inspirational fun to "read" a book that is just the letter "t" hundreds of times (see *Soldatmarkedet*, by Monica Aasprong).

There is, however, an analog for the workplace: phone technology reduced the time it took to communicate with people, email reduced it more, and instant message, Slack, and Zoom have brought it down to almost zero. And yet, is the exchange of ideas any *easier*?

In his book *The Bias of Communication* (1951), Canadian political economist Harold Innis states that "Improvements in communication ... make for increased difficulties of understanding." He wrote that way before television exploded the reality of mass media and the advent of the twenty-four-hour news cycle distorted what information was deemed "important," before the internet "democratized" information (said sarcastically, FYI), and before Facebook, Twitter, and "fake news" completely muddled any semblance of understanding in the first place. Dude was ahead of his time, really.

Nevertheless, due to these improvements in technology, productivity has increased. Far more business gets done every day because of it. Now, instead of spending the afternoon shooting baskets into your garbage can with crumpled pieces of paper while you wait for your letter to get to Acme Industries in Cleveland, let alone receive a reply, you can conduct that business in real-time and go home early to spend time with your kids, or write that novel, or play real basketball.

But has meaningful communication and understanding increased as well?

If we map business writing on the same scatter chart of *content* and *style* (see Figure 13), we can see where most communication *should* land—in the upper right quadrant.

When it comes to more creative documents, such as a pitch deck, or advertising copy, there is room for stylization, as well as emotion (especially in, say, a television commercial). A poorly constructed presentation, however, may land in the upper left quadrant, where the author *intends* to convey information but is unsuccessful.

Let's return to the Zykov quote above. The work was created by Vladimir Zykov, but he didn't write the words himself. Instead, he used Amazon's Mechanical Turk to commission random, anonymous people from around the world to write fifty words in return for one cent. Ultimately, he collected five hundred sets (for a total of five dollars) and left them unedited. Though its literary merit is debatable, *I Was Told to Write Fifty Words* asks some serious and important questions:

- What kind of world do we live in, where people sell their labor on Mechanical Turk in this way?

- What is the *value* of this labor?

- What is the value of writing and words in general?

This last question is ever more important as AI gets more powerful and takes a larger role in creating words and images in business settings, and in the culture at large. It is also somewhat reminiscent, to me, of the endless repetition of trash that gets thrown about the office on a daily basis: pointless meetings, pointless emails, pointless tasks. Sometimes it feels like

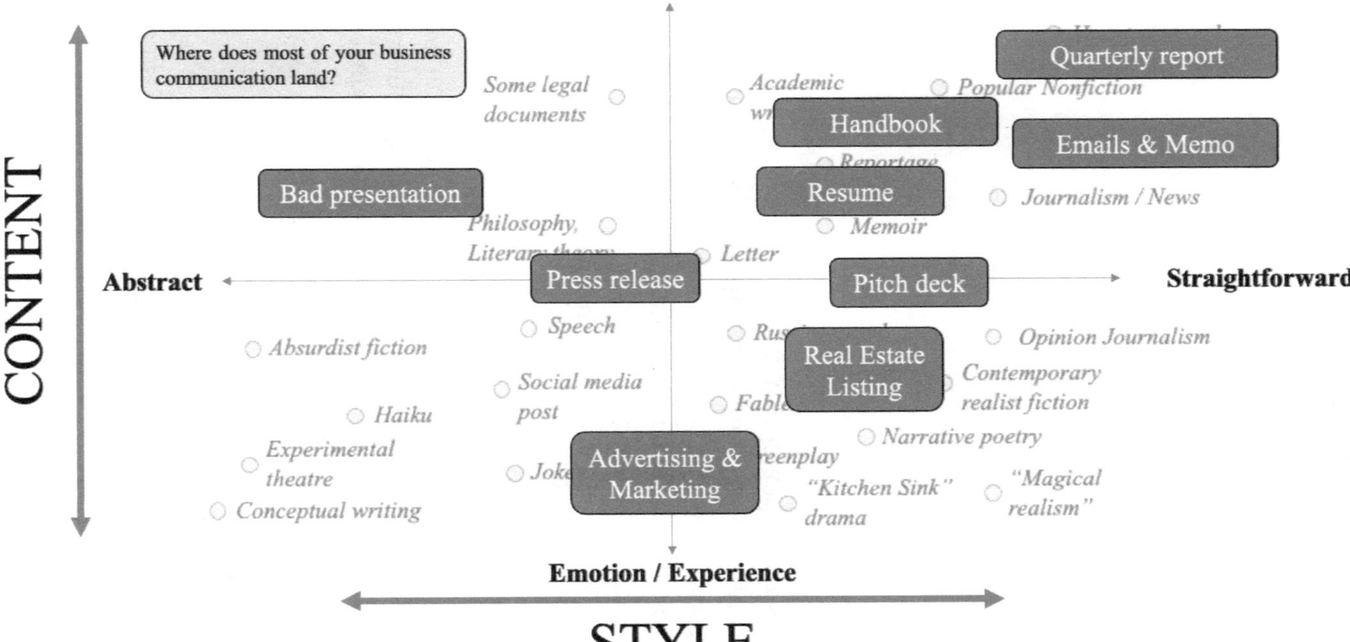

Figure 13. Style vs. Content in Business Writing.

you're being told to dig a hole and fill it back in just because they're paying you a salary and there are still three hours left in the day. You can't very well go home and enjoy yourself, right?

In any case, use the charts in Figures 12 and 13 to examine where most of your writing should be, and – be honest – where most of it currently is.

DON'T USE COMIC SANS

What is it about using the Comic Sans font in email that annoys people so much? It's distracting, sure, but it's *legible*—so it really *shouldn't* bother the reader, right? What should matter is the content of an email, not the font used. Right?

It puts me in a shit mood to see that stupid font. It makes me assume the sender is a moron. I want to mark it as spam. I already don't like this person.

Maybe people choose Comic Sans because it seems "playful" and disarming. They want to come across as nice, non-threatening, and fun. Instead, it comes across as unsophisticated and doltish. It's also disingenuous. The content of your character will be evident in your words and actions, not in your font (see Figure 14):

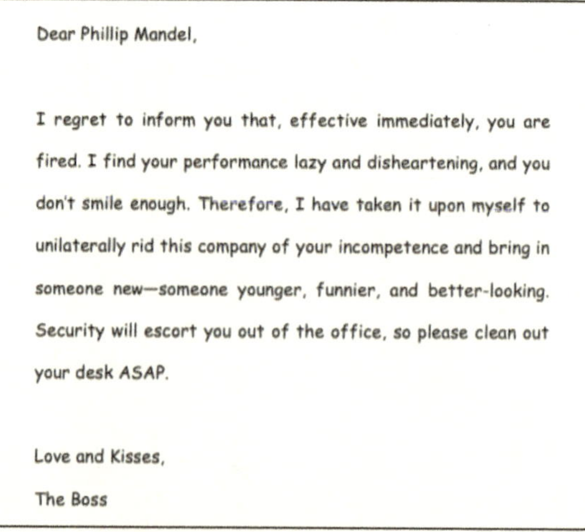

Figure 14. Comic Sans is vile.

I don't care what kind of font it's in, that email is terrible, and that boss is a jerk.

The same goes for using different colors, formats, cases, sizes, and fonts (see Figure 15):

> Dear VALUED CUSTOMER,
>
> It has come to our attention that some or all of your *account information* appEars to BE MISSING or incorrect. We need to **verify your account information** IN ORDER FOR YOU to *continue using your product.* Please verify your account information by clicking on the link below to verify your license.
>
> Click here to **verify** your identification and ACCOUNT information.

Figure 15. This is obscene.

The overuse of bold, italics, and underlining is not only bothersome and distracting, but it also becomes meaningless. One italic, one bold, or one underline per email—that's all you get.

The issue is style. Your words must speak for themselves, regardless of the format. Check this by copying your text and pasting it into a new document without any formatting. If the meaning changes, then you have work to do. Choosing the right words to convey what you mean is superior to qualifying the wrong words with underlines, bolding, or "wacky" fonts.

Writing Exercise: Style

Part I: Review the "Style vs. Content" matrices in Figures 12 and 13 against recent communications you've written. Look at big, important stuff, such as a speech, pitch deck, or report, as well as minor, everyday stuff, such as email or Slack messages.

Where does the bulk of your work lie? Are you being informative and clear, or vague? Does your work often involve conveying data and fact, or emotion and experience—or perhaps a combination? Are you short and to the point, or flowery and descriptive? Do you make jokes and asides in your writing, or are you cold and formal? Is it cluttered or brief? Do you use a lot of adverbs or the word *very* a lot? Are you resorting to gimmicks, such as non-standard fonts or different colors?

And why does your work tend to read this way? Were you taught to write in this style, or is it standard for the industry? Is it correct, for that matter? Would your business or career be better served if you deviated more toward clear, factual information, or do you need to bring some human emotion into your writing?

Write 250 words describing your style, as you see it, and why you write that way.

Part II: Now take 250 words to answer each of these questions:

- Describe your "voice" at work, and in your career. Not your *style*, but your voice—what are you trying to say?

- What are your values at work, and in your career? What do you believe in?

- Describe your personal brand.

Part III: Take a recent communication and rewrite it using a different style. If you're excessively descriptive ("purple prose," as it's sometimes called), use fewer words and go straight to the point. If you're sober and humorless, add a joke. Try locating it in an entirely different quadrant of the chart.

For example, what would an ad campaign look like if it were only straightforward and data-driven? Old print ads used to be full of copy—would they be successful today? How about a quarterly report that focuses more on the emotions and experience of your business, and is presented in an abstract style?

Figure 16 shows a simplistic example from my favorite resource, the Berkshire Hathaway "Letters to Shareholders" from 2021, and my revision:

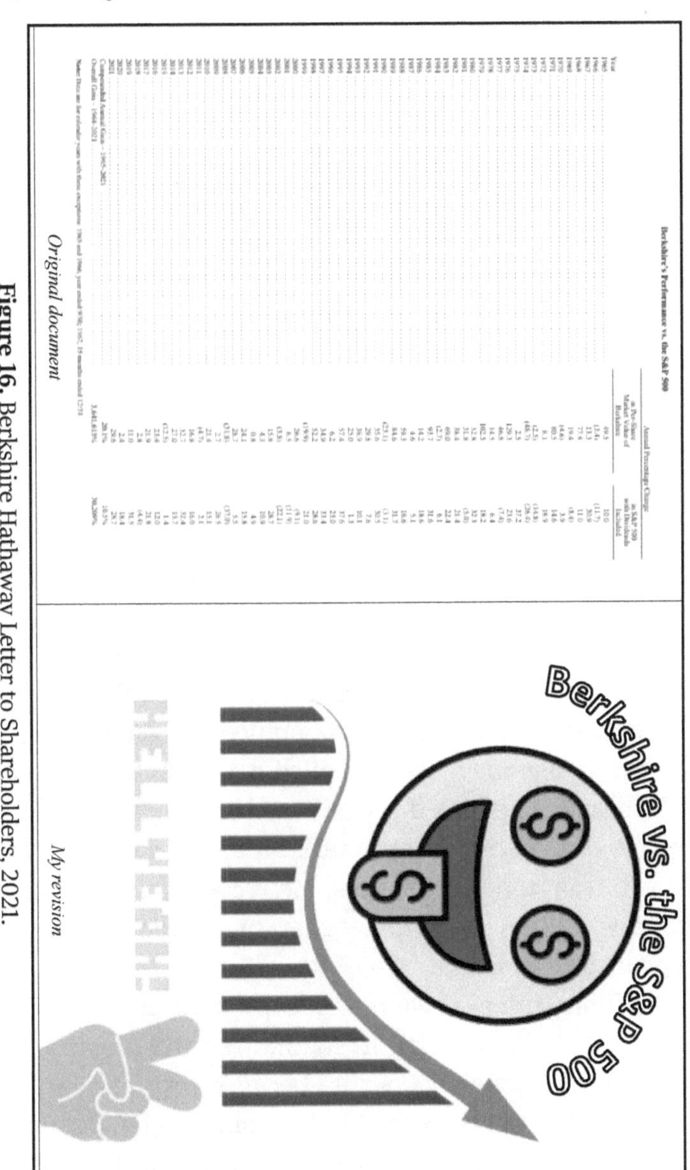

Figure 16. Berkshire Hathaway Letter to Shareholders, 2021.

7: CLICHÉ AND JARGON

All writing is a campaign against cliché. Not just clichés of the pen but clichés of the mind and clichés of the heart. When I dispraise, I am usually quoting clichés. When I praise, I am usually quoting the opposed qualities of freshness, energy, and reverberation of voice.

— Martin Amis, The War Against Cliché: Essays and Reviews 1971–2000 (2001)

AVOID CLICHÉ

If there was only one piece of advice I could give to anyone, whether it be about making any kind of art or conducting any kind of business, it would be to avoid cliché. The rest of this book is commentary (see Hillel and the Golden Rule).

Cliché and jargon seem to spontaneously generate in business writing like maggots in spoiled meat. (In the olden days, people did actually think this was what happened. Idiots.) Cliché is so prevalent in our work life that it appears constantly and we don't even notice. Go read some recent email or whatever website you're on right now—guaranteed you'll spot clichés once you start looking.

The funny thing is, we humans are naturally more drawn to things that are original, fresh, and *not* full of cliché—even if we've never thought about it—because they are surprising and pleasing. Great comedy doesn't utilize cliché, because if it did, you'd be able to predict the punchline and it wouldn't be funny. Live sports are exciting because anything can happen and, by definition, it's never happened before. Online memes, too—when they first arrive—are not cliché (though they may use cliché to satirize something else in popular culture).

However, clichés are hard to escape when you're writing. These bad, bad, bad bad bad bad words appear in the shitty first drafts of many works-in-progress—but what distinguishes great writing is that great writers edit these phrases out in subsequent drafts.

As discussed in Chapter 3, compelling and "artful" material is surprising and makes the familiar feel unfamiliar (the "sublime," if you recall). Clichés are anathema to this because they are overused, played out, and meaningless. When encountered in email or other business writing, clichés invoke the movement of a reader's eye across the words without really reading them.

Here are some examples:

- A mile in someone else's moccasins

- A peek under the kimono, inside the tent, or behind the curtain

- Low-hanging fruit

- Think outside the box

- Rock star / ninja / killer / Jedi master

- Run it up the flagpole and see which way the wind is blowing

- Avoid something like the plague (this includes the unfunny, self-referential writing advice "Avoid cliché like the plague," which is also a cliché)

If I'm not making myself clear enough, clichés are the Adolf Hitlers and Stalins and Pol Pots of the written word.

So why are they so prevalent? Probably because they *seem* useful and easy, and they play to our inner laziness. They seem to be a shorthand way of communicating more complex ideas. But they don't.

Clichés are ineffective. They do not do what you want them to do. They make your writing weak, and they weaken your argument.

Yes, it is easier to write a cliché than to think of a better, more original way of phrasing something. It takes less energy and less time. But if you intend your work to convey anything of importance, using a cliché is not worth it.

"Low-hanging fruit" is both a cliché and a euphemism. As a cliché it is over-used, and as a euphemism it stands for the concept of "doing the easiest task first" (thus, as a cliché it is autological, or an example of itself—like the word "sesquipedalian," or "pentasyballic"). But in most professional settings, you can't actually admit to your boss or client you'll be doing the easiest thing first for fear of seeming like the kind of person who is lazy and prefers doing the easiest thing possible first. You can't justify your salary (or fee) that way, right? So instead of coming up with a clever and interesting way of communicating this idea, you can just use the easy and lazy pablum, "low-hanging fruit."

Sometimes this is okay. If it's midnight and you need to go home and you can wrap up a meeting by using the term "low-hanging fruit," I say go for it.

But if you're writing anything significant, know this phrase is almost meaningless. The audience will see the words, but they won't read them. You'll be more effective and memorable by being original and interesting—perhaps even coining a new phrase, if possible (think like a neologist!)—and by being specific and explicit with what you mean. Though not exactly deathless prose, it is still more effective to say:

We can generate $4 million in new sales by targeting

**consumers that have already demonstrated a preference
to our product.**

Versus

Let's just go after the low-hanging fruit.

The cliché "think outside the box" is even more disturbing because it is anti-autological, or an autoantonym. It is a demonstration of the opposite of itself, similar to the new meaning of the word "literally," which can, sometimes, *literally* mean "figuratively."

At least "low-hanging fruit" is a low-hanging fruit way of communicating. Using the phrase "think outside of the box" is *literally not thinking outside of the box* when trying to communicate the idea of thinking original and creative thoughts that challenge status quo ideas and practices. It is a regurgitated, semi-degraded, half-digested bolus. It is word-puke. Cud.

While we're at it, I also hate "ninja," "rock star," and "killer." These are insulting to both the complimented and the represented. A competent realtor is in no way a "ninja," in that a "ninja" (or "shinobi") was a trained mercenary assassin in feudal Japan.

Maybe I'm nitpicking.

But when you call your new assistant junior intern Blake a "rock star" because they brought the right coffee this time, *they know this does not make them a rock star*. Mick Jagger is a rock star. David Bowie was a rock star. Hell, even Chad Kroeger from Nickelback is, in a way, a rock star (and by the way, making fun of Nickelback is *also* a cliché). But Blake is just a lowly intern. A worm. And they know it. That's why Blake is *in* your stupid internship program in the first place, to gain experience and move up in their career (so that, eventually, they'll have their *own* dirtbag intern fetching coffee). If you think calling Blake a "rock star" makes them feel good, you're being both lazy and ignorant. You're deluding yourself. All you are doing is reminding Blake that they are definitely *not* a rock star, but instead a peon not even worth the effort it would take to say "thank you" and come up with something original, like "The Blakester," or "Sir Blakes-A-Lot," or "Blake-Me-A-Cake."

Don't call Blake a "rock star," because you don't mean it. Just say "Thank you," "nice job," and pay them a living fucking wage.

And while we're at it, if being good at creating sales presentations makes me a "killer," then lock me up and throw away the key. Also, "lock me up and throw away the key" is a cliché.

They're everywhere!

Jargon

> Simplification is useful and can be a great aid to those business persons and academicians who tend to inflate their sentences with excess verbiage and pompous jargon.
>
> —Sol Stein, *Stein on Writing* (1995)

Jargon is a cousin to cliché, and not the cool cousin from the Bronx who introduces you to rap music and SimCity and drives an IROC-Z (shout out to my cousin Noah). Like cliché, jargon is antithetical to good writing. It is the enemy of truth, using the familiar to obfuscate the unfamiliar. It does the *opposite* of what we want. Jargon is poison.

Nevertheless, it will no doubt appear in first drafts as you think through your topic because jargon represents or alludes to valid ideas. In later drafts, you must revise your jargon into plain English that is more original and precise.

Outside of work, we don't use all that much jargon, and when we do, it's grotesque. Imagine a parent tucking in their child at night and saying, "I'd like your buy-in to circle back with you tomorrow about that tantrum you had during dinner." Or two lovers in bed, trying to "align their goals," if you get my drift, and at the moment of climax, one says, "This is really moving the needle for me." Or someone sitting at their beloved grandmother's deathbed, weeping but willful and resigned, determined and courageous, as they ask the doctor, "What's the ROI on pulling the plug?"

So why *do* people use jargon in the first place if it's so horrible?

Well, from a practical standpoint, some jargon is useful and, frankly, accurate. The much-lambasted word "synergy" does have a specific meaning: it's when the process of mixing two things creates something better than the sum of their parts alone. For example, a clownfish and a sea anemone create a shield when they're together that protects them both from harm, but not when they're apart. This is synergy.

When a great salesperson teams up with a great account manager, their partnership will bring in new deals and upsell current clients. This is a fine use of the word "synergy."

But when you fire half of Accounts Payable because a new AI made their jobs redundant, that's not synergy.

Jargon often appears when someone is unsure of what they are talking about, they want to appear more knowledgeable than they are, or they want to create a power dynamic in which they are the expert in some subject and the other person is not. That last one is also known as trying to talk over someone's head—and nobody likes it.

I've seen this often from poor sales professionals, or even great salespeople laden with a bad product. It's a defense mechanism. A good seller with a good product is confident and wants to sincerely and generously educate their prospective customer. They will answer questions in a forthcoming and clear manner and not obfuscate the details with vagueness or jargon.

I experienced a lot of jargon-talk and obfuscation when I was buying internet advertising in the mid-2000s. I'd ask a sales rep how exactly their ad tech worked or what was *in* their supposedly "premium" online network, and they'd go on and on about "scaling efficiencies" and "CTR optimization." I happened to know what CTR optimization was because I was a digital media planner, but there were a lot of senior-level media directors whose careers had been built on cable TV GRPs ("Gross Rating Points," another media jargon word, and a way of measuring the audience of a given show) and "spots and dots" (more jargon, meaning commercials). They were unfamiliar with new digital media terminology, and many millions of client dollars were wasted because of it.

Jargon abounds in job listings. Perhaps they think it's a way of weeding out bad candidates; that is, those who don't already know industry terms won't apply.

To be fair, jargon is an effective way of communicating much information in a small space. "KPI" uses fewer characters than "email newsletter signups," after all. But a job listing full of jargon also communicates to the potential employee a level of bureaucratic ennui that already exists in your organization such that the hiring manager can't be bothered to write anything interesting or original in the post. It doesn't distinguish the company or the position, and many highly-qualified and interesting people won't bother.

So don't use jargon. Think harder. Slow down. Choose your words carefully.

As with mansplaining, the hardest part is to recognize when you're doing it. You must slowly reread your work—aloud, if possible—and isolate the jargon.

There isn't really a trick to it—simply follow George Orwell's advice from his essay, *Politics and English Language* (1946): "Never use a ... scientific word, or a jargon word if you can think of an everyday English equivalent."

For Orwell, the use of jargon was not simply a matter of business. He insisted there were political ramifications to such "pretentious diction." Dire ones. He warned that people would use words such as "epic" and "historic" to "dignify the sordid process of international politics" and "glorify war," which could lead to terrible people getting into positions of power. From there, disaster would be inevitable: fascism, torture, mass death, starvation.

He was correct.

But our concerns are not so grand. I don't think over-using the term "KPI" is going to cause thermonuclear war. But I'll still argue for militating against its usage, just in case.

So what's wrong with "KPI?" Well, nothing, if it's used in the proper context.

But I have, in many business conversations, heard the term "KPI" bandied about worse than a lithe young meth-addicted lot lizard in a West Texas truck stop. And, like life for that poor tweaker, the term "KPI" loses its meaning after enough turns 'round the circle.

What people *mean* with "KPI" is "what we need to measure because it impacts our business the most." But until that metric has been defined, it is only a placeholder. Better to spend a minute defining your KPI than confusing everyone by talking around it.

Slang

By now, I'm sure you can guess that I'm going to advise against using slang in professional communication. Slang is the jargon of any specific community, and while it is certainly appropriate to use in casual conversation, it is informal and doesn't translate well onto the page (or in email). Self-evident examples are words such as "ain't," "brb," or "lol."

Slang really only works in certain creative writing styles, too, such as in dialogue, interior monologue, and voice-driven poetry. Work that evokes a community or era—be it street slang of a neighborhood in the 1990s, hippie slang of the 1960s, or internet slang on Reddit in the 2010s—can use nonstandard words (judiciously) to tell a story, but otherwise such language will detract from the piece and interrupt the reader's flow.

Slang also changes rapidly and, therefore, doesn't age well. If you're over the age of, say, twenty-seven, you may come across as ridiculous, desperate, or tragically hip trying to use words at work that you hear younger colleagues (or your kids) use.

More importantly, your audience may not know what the hell you're talking about—especially if they're not familiar with the community from which the slang words arise. And if the purpose of business communication is to actually communicate information, then slang might stop this from happening.

This makes me sound stodgy and conservative, but oh well. Don't use slang.

DECONSTRUCTING THE PROCTOLOGY EXAM (*AN MFA FOR YOUR MBA* IN PRACTICE)

Someone had to be the first person to ever say "Working hard or hardly working," and I assume it had the cubicle farm in stitches. Then every manager started saying it (because it was so funny and clever, you see), and it became an odious cliché. Memes, viral videos, and social media are accelerating the pace of cliché-making. *Tiger King* (2020) was passé in a matter of weeks—just as soon as I downloaded a virtual background of it for Zoom.

Everyone hears a cliché for the first time, of course. In elementary school I remember answering a question with apprehension, unsure if I was right. It went something like this:

Teacher: Who was the thirteenth president of the United States?

Me: Um, Millard Fillmore?

Teacher: Are you asking me or telling me?

Despite my humiliation, it was the most cunning retort I'd ever heard. *Did she just come up with that?* I wondered. *She might be funnier than "Weird Al" Yankovic!*

As time passed, I lived my life and went through puberty and lost my virginity and learned to drive and graduated college and bought my first house and started a business, and at some point I realized this dumb phrase is used by wiseacres all the time, and my fourth-grade teacher had not invented it. Was I let down? Yes, you could say I was let down.

In any case, you, too, may also be fooled into thinking some phrase is funny and/or interesting, or original and/or fresh, only to find out (upon using such a phrase yourself) that it's a worn-out cliché everyone has been using for years. For example, the other day my CEO friend was telling me his company was being acquired and he had to provide a "proctology exam" of the "company books" to the buyer.

I chuckled outwardly, because he was trying to be funny, but grimaced inwardly, for the idea of applying this metaphor to his company seemed wrong and slightly nauseating.

So let's deconstruct this: I believe my friend meant he was going to provide a thorough, in-depth analysis (no pun intended) of his company's liabilities and assets (no pun intended) for the constituents of the acquiring company, so they could see what they were buying. He would *administer* a proctology exam to his company and provide the *results* of said exam to the buyer.

That imprecision notwithstanding, does the metaphor stand? *Is* a "proctology exam" a thorough, in-depth analysis? A proctologist specializes in diseases and abnormalities of the colon, rectum, and anus. Besides the well-known colonoscopy, some of the bodily investigations they perform include:

- Defecating proctogram

- Pudendal nerve test

- "Transit time" test (guess what that means)

- Fecal Occult Blood Test, which I pray is the name of a death metal band in Florida

I'll assume my friend meant the well-known probe known as a Digital Rectal Exam (the word "digital" in this usage does not refer to computers, but rather to someone's finger, or "digit"). Contrary to my friend's metaphor, the DRE is a *specific* test that provides minimal information about a person's general health outside of one's colon, anus, and rectum.

It won't show your cholesterol, blood pressure, or resting heart rate. It won't identify plantar fasciitis, tennis elbow, or a crick in your neck. It's really only specific to the colon, anus, and rectum.

My friend, however, needed to show the "books" in *many* areas of his company, not a specific one. One measly P&L statement from last quarter from one division wouldn't suffice. The acquiring company wanted a *comprehensive*—rather than specific—look at the finances of the company—obviously. The word "books" is also a figure of speech. In this context, "books" is a metonymy for the company's finances (as well as a cliché) because my friend does not *actually* use a large book, or ledger, to keep track of his company's finances. He uses software and spreadsheets.

Well, okay...so maybe that wasn't why he called it a proctology exam. Maybe it has to do with the shame and embarrassment of having another person stick their digit somewhere uncomfortable?

But does my friend's *company* feel shame when he "exposes the books," so to speak, for all to see? Do they feel embarrassed for being "opened up" like this? No, of course not. It doesn't have a colon, anus, or rectum. A company is not a person; it is a concept, a fake thing, in name only, that represents a collective. It is a willing delusion. It is many things, but it does not feel shame or embarrassment.

A company comprises individuals, though. So maybe it's the *workers* who feel ashamed for being looked at, poked, and prodded in such an unusual and uncomfortable way.

Perhaps. But I'd venture that only people with something

to hide would feel uneasy about a financial inspection. Other people may actually be *proud* of what this so-called "proctologist" will see, and they will bend over and spread with aplomb.

So why did he call it a proctology exam?

Because it's a cliché. Because it's easy. Because it's shorthand.

The lesson? Don't use cliché because it makes you sound like an asshole (pun intended).

JUST FOR FUN: ART JARGON

Artists and writers are just as prone to their own set of clichés and jargon as anyone else. If you're not living in this world, these words may not seem like clichés because you're not hearing them every day, but trust me, they are—and they're just as awful and overused and eye-roll-inducing as "think outside the box."

See Figure 17 for a charcuterie board of art jargon. These terms might "sound smart" at first blush, but once you've heard them enough times, they lose meaning and become sort of groan-worthy. Here are some examples of randomized sentences from this list, all guaranteed to make you throw up in your mouth (an image that is, itself, a cliché):

- I'm interested in challenging the ontological functionality of hybridity.

- This postmodern work interrogates the vocabulary of performative myth.

- Where is the heat in this piece?

- Can you tease out or contextualize the epistemological and teleological—ugh, I can't even continue...

A Priori	Heat	Performance
Abstract	Hedonic	Performative
Academia	Hegemonic	Perspective
Alienation	Heretofore	Phenomenology
Anticipatory	Hermeneutics	Piece
Arbitrariness	Heteronormative	Post- anything
Baroque	Homologous	Postcolonial
Bifurcate	Hybridity	Postmodern
Canon	Iconography	Post-postmodern
Capitalist	Immersive	Praxis
Challenge	Implementation	Predicated
Co-opt	Incorporate	Presuppose
Conceptual	Independent	Problematic
Concern	Informed by	Problematize
Constellation	Inspiration	Profound
Contemporary	Installation	Provisional
Contextualize	Interconnected	Questions
Controversy	Interdisciplinary	Rationale
Convergence	Interested	Readymade
Correlative	Interrogates	Realism
Cultural	Intersectional	Reductive
Curate	Kafkaesque	Reification
Dada	Legendary	Repurpose
Deconstruct	Legitimate	Robust
Dialectic	Liminal (space)	Rococo
Dialogic	Logos	Semantics
Dichotomy	Manifest	Semiotics
Discipline	Marginal	Sign / signified
Discourse	Marginalize	Simulacrum
Disenfranchise	Marxism	Structural
Disjunctive	Maximalist	Structuralist
Electricity	Meaning	Subjugate
Elements	Metaphysics	Sublimation
Elucidate	Minimalism	Subsume
Epistemological	Modality	Symbolism
Ergo	Multi-faceted	Syntax
Exegesis	Mythic	Tease out
Existential	Narrative	Teleological
Exploration	Necessitate	Temporal
Fabrication	Niche	The other
Fetishize	Object	Theory
Folklore	Objective correlative	Therefore
Foucault	Objectivism	Transcendental
Form	Ontological	Transgressive
Found	Orientalism	Triangulate
Framework	Palimpsest	Unmediated
Functionalality	Panopticon	Unpack
Gaze	Paradigm	Vocabulary
Gestalt	Pedagogy	Zeitgeist

Figure 17. Art jargon.

Figure 18. This slide makes me sick!

A Case Study in Meaning(less)

Figure 18 is a real slide I came across while researching online. It is an object lesson in visual form of how jargon and cliché can ruin communication. If you refer to the matrix of Style vs. Content in the previous chapter (Figure 13), you'll agree the slide belongs in the dreaded upper left quadrant.

View this slide and drink in how worthless and horrible it is. None of these words mean anything.

"Train?" Train what?

"Engage?" Engage whom?

"Perform?" How?

"Enhance productivity." This is at least a sentence, with an object and a predicate. (For all you grammar nerds, the subject in this imperative statement is "you," that lamentable soul who is receiving this godawful presentation, and it is implied.) But it lacks some important detail.

If I worked at the company for which this was produced, I would cut all the words from this slide, then drag the designer of this presentation into the break room and fire them twice.

How to Avoid Cliché

I've made my case *that* one should avoid cliché, jargon, and slang, but *how* does one go about doing it? Here are some strategies:

Delete. Expunge. Cut. Excise. Remove. Eliminate. Reject. Erase.

The simplest solution is to cut a cliché when you see it. That's right, just highlight the offending phrase and delete it. If your sentence still makes sense, then all the better, because it's now shorter.

For example, a cliché such as "in this day and age" can be cut, rather than re-worded, because it's implied. If you are referring to something other than the present—such as the Ancient Greeks, or the 1970s—you would no doubt specify that first.

And if the goal is to surprise your audience with your language because it will get them to engage with you, you can't simply re-word a cliché with another cliché. You must avoid them altogether:

- The intern brought the right coffee this morning. You're a rock star, Blake! ←NO

- The intern brought the right coffee this morning. You're a ninja, Blake! ←NO

- The intern brought the right coffee this morning. Thank you, Blake! ←YES

Envision and Describe

Unfortunately, the more difficult and more common solution for avoiding clichés is...well, *thinking harder.*

Are you sensing a theme? Writing well is difficult. I'm not going to pretend that there are simple tricks and easy shortcuts. No four-hour work week or seven-minute abs here.

You have to just sit and think about what you're working on, and continue to think about it until you can envision it clearly in your mind's eye. Then describe it.

Often our first few thoughts about something are familiar, conventional, lazy, and boring, and thus we can throw them away.

It means not rushing through your work, but sitting with it, concentrating, and putting in the effort. At first it's uncomfortable and rather difficult, but I promise it does get easier with time. It's the reason I can whip up a long article in about forty-five minutes, while it might take someone else three hours.

For example, instead of saying "Our software solutions really take the cake," you might list out the different awards your company has won. Or you can specify that "Dr. Schmendrick has forty-five years of experience as a board-certified surgeon" instead of "Dr. Schmendrick is older than dirt." Note: "older

<hr>

This aside will take you no time to read. **Hyperbole** is a figure of speech in which you exaggerate wildly to make a point, but should not be taken literally. People use hyperbole constantly, which is a hyperbolic way of saying people use hyperbole frequently in everyday speech, not literally "constantly." Also, while this section is short and won't take long to read, even thirty seconds is longer than "no time." Hyperbole can be effective, but be aware that many common hyperbolic metaphors are clichés:

- Sleeping like a rock
- It's a jungle out there
- Drowning in paperwork
- Slow as molasses
- So hungry I could eat a horse
- I could hear you from a mile away
- This costs an arm and a leg
- Cry me a river
- When pigs fly

You shouldn't need overblown and overused phrases like these to make your point. But like all clichés, they are readily at hand and easier than being original and creative. But originality will make your point better, and creativity will make your work memorable.

<hr>

Figure 19. Hyperbole.

than dirt" is an example of hyperbole, which is exaggeration for effect (see Figure 19).

Free Association

A great brainstorming technique, free association is when you enunciate or write the first thoughts, words, and images that come to mind without censoring yourself.

Practicing free association will help you become more creative with language and generate more ideas overall. Improv comedy works off free association. And while you may hate improv or think it's not funny, you have to admit it's original and creative.

In this example, a master improv comedian, Matt Besser, explains how he free associated on the word "pumpernickel," which was suggested by his audience:

Pumpernickel. So, have I eaten pumpernickel bread? Maybe. Do I have a story on it? Definitely not. But if I need to start talking, I can't just sit there and say "Pumpernickel … pumpernickel." I can't force myself to have a memory about pumpernickel if it doesn't occur to me right away. So I have to free associate.

The most simple way to go here is bread, but I should probably try to be more specific, like "What kind of bread?" How about fancy bread? Oh, that makes me think of the deli that my dad would take me to when I was a kid over in Little Rock, Arkansas. So now I'm starting to launch into the story. I could just say my dad took me to a deli, but it's more interesting to say that my dad took me to a deli in Little Rock, Arkansas, as opposed to New York. That's another thing to look out for—details. Details make the story better.

So, my dad used to take us to the only deli in town, which also makes me think that we were basically the only Jews in town. We used to go to this deli, and we would get lox. Lox, that's a very Jewish thing. I don't think many other people in Little Rock had lox, or if they did, they called it smoked salmon ...[12]

Don't Steal

Do the opposite of what Picasso (or Steve Jobs, depending on who you ask) said: *don't* borrow (or steal) someone else's work.

If you catch yourself using a figure of speech, expression, phrase, idiom (see Figure 20), or other word you've heard elsewhere, you're probably wandering into cliché territory.

> An **idiom** is an expression or phrase common to a dialect, such as "under the weather," which means feeling sick or ill. "Once in a blue moon" is an idiom referring to something that happens infrequently, and "hit the sack" or "hit the hay" mean going to bed. In normal speech, idioms are easy and useful, but in writing they tend to stick out like any other cliché and should be avoided.

Figure 20. Defining "idiom."

I've called out many of the clichés that made it into the final draft of this book (avoiding 100 percent of all clichés is an impossible task), but trust me, the first draft had many more. They were all phrases that popped into my mind and were fine as placeholders until I could go back in revision and spend the time to think of something better.

Be Aware of Stereotypes

The word "cliché" comes from the French word *clichér*, which means "to stereotype." Since a cliché is an overused word or phrase, a stereotype is a type of cliché in that it is an overused descriptor of something or someone. It also often becomes somewhat denigrating or offensive, but even if it isn't, it is still weak writing.

For example, avoid using "Red-headed stepchild," as well as the phrase (and the idea) "damsel in distress."

Understand What You Want to Say

Clichéd *thinking* is also a trap, and one which we all fall into sometimes.

Consider this classic thought-cliché: "I learned more from them than they learned from me." What are you really trying to say? Did you really learn more from "them," whoever they are? How and why? What were the circumstances? *What*, precisely, did everyone learn in that experience? What did *they* learn? *Why* did you learn more?

Whatever your answers are to those questions—write and say that, instead. My hunch is that what you really mean is that the experience in question was unexpectedly rewarding, or rewarding in an unexpected way.

Similarly, if you want people to "think outside the box," then *you* should think harder about what you want. What hackneyed ideas have already been tried in your circumstance? What are some examples of this thinking? What kind of brain leaps, interesting options, or novel ideas are you looking for? Do you want something new but still reasonable, or do you want to throw out all the rules and hear anything rational or irrational, however outlandish?

And why? Is your business problem so intractable that nobody has encountered it before? Or is your company, brand, or product being buried in competition and you simply want to stand out a bit more?

In other words, do you want **2 + 2 = 5**, or **2 + 2 = Potato**?

Be Direct

Perhaps the most effective technique is to simply be authentic and direct. Don't try to write around what you're trying to say or obfuscate the meaning with a metaphor, idiom, hyperbole, or cliché. Be straightforward, honest, and simple.

Strangely, it sometimes takes longer to write simply and directly than to write with indirect, metaphorical language. This is because you are forced to concentrate and distill exactly what you mean, rather than to describe with "sort of this" and "kind of like that."

Clear and direct writing can spring only from clear and direct thinking—but this is a good thing. It leads to more effective communication and better overall productivity. It will translate into more sales, better products, shorter meetings, happier coworkers, and more effective employees.

Writing Exercise: Cliché

Part I: Look at some recent projects you've worked on and emails you've written. Identify all of the clichés. This may take a couple of passes, as you may not recognize clichés at first glance. But do not be generous to yourself. Mark *each* one, even the seemingly innocuous ones, like "in this day and age," and clichés of thought, like "that day I learned more from my intern Blake than Blake learned from me."

Be brutal with yourself. Anything you think *might* be a cliché, mark it. It's a word or phrase you've seen elsewhere. It's a shorthand, bullshit way of saying something. Circle them in bright red marker or highlight them on the computer.

Think about why you wrote each of them. Was it for expediency (that is, it was easier and took less time), or were you really unable to think of a better way to say what you meant?

And does it *matter*? If it's a toss-off, inconsequential email, then maybe it doesn't matter, and you can let yourself have that cliché. But if it's an important project that has gravity, then it probably does.

Part II: Find a better, more original turn of phrase or description for each place you marked. It doesn't have to be Shakespeare or James Joyce, but you should write something original, direct, and authentic that communicates your message both in tone and meaning. And for the love of God, don't call it a proctology exam. Also, "for the love of God" is both an idiom and a cliché.

8: METAPHOR

Shall I compare thee to a summer's day?

> — Shakespeare, "Sonnet 18" (1609)

COMPARISONS AND ANALOGIES

Cold as ice. You ain't nothin' but a hound dog. Don't go chasing waterfalls. Watermelon sugar. Life is a highway. A spectre is haunting Europe.

Our culture is infused with figurative language because analogies and comparisons can communicate ideas, emotion, and meaning better, more quickly, or in a more memorable way than literal descriptions.

Analogy and metaphor abound in business as well, but to my dismay they're often related to sports. This new project management tool is a slam dunk. Her presentation to the board really knocked it out of the park. This sales pitch is a "Hail Mary" (which is, itself, a prayer metaphor in football).

Interestingly, in a 2017 essay from *Harvard Business Review*,[13] Bill Taylor gives several reasons why sports metaphors are *not* accurate analogies for business, including "the logic of competition and success is completely different," "the dynamics of talent and teamwork are completely different," and "the creation of economic value is completely different." Maybe he's right, but sports are so universal in our culture that almost everyone understands what sports metaphors mean—*that's* why they're so easy to use.

In any case, our interest right now is in the *language* of sports metaphors, not their accuracy.

I never much liked hearing my sales managers talk about "blocking and tackling" when it came to making cold calls, but the comparison made sense: "blocking and tackling" are fundamental football skills, and making cold calls is fundamental to making sales. In other words, you've got to learn how to dribble before you hit a grand salami and you've got to learn how to skate on the ice backwards before you can kick a touchdown. Or something like that.

You see, metaphor, in writing, is like getting free cocaine from a stranger: it can be so good, but it can also be ruinously bad—and regardless of how you cut it, any more than a bump is too much. That sentence, by the way, contains both an analogy—comparing the literary device of metaphor to cocaine—as well as a pun ("regardless of how you cut it"). And while a great metaphor is original, memorable, and presents the familiar in an unfamiliar way, a bad metaphor—or a glut of metaphors— will arrest the reader's flow (see Chapter 17).

Strong, original metaphors are a hallmark of fine writing and communicate ideas and emotion effectively. Let's read some in the poem "The Rose Has Teeth," by Terrance Hayes:

> I was trying to play "Autumn Leaves"
> because that's what my lady's falling dress
> sounds like to me. Before you, Piano, I was just a rap
> of knuckles on a windowsill. I am filled with the sound
> of my lover's breathing and only you can bring it out of me.

The narrator of this poem is a human being who plays the piano and is not *literally* a rap of knuckles on a windowsill, but the metaphor is so strong that it provides the reader with an entire life's worth of emotion and memory. The narrator is not also literally filled with the sound of their lover's breathing (he is filled with air, muscle, bones, cells, and water), but the reader understands from the metaphor that the narrator thinks constantly about their lover, and it inspires them to play the piano.

This is the power of metaphor.

But metaphor for the sake of metaphor is not good enough! A bad metaphor will also stick out in your reader's mind, as well as call attention to itself, thus interrupting the flow.

Bad metaphor can destroy your work, no matter how many books you sell. Take this **simile** (see Figure 21) from *Fifty Shades of Grey* (2011) by E. L. James:

His voice is warm and husky like dark melted chocolate fudge caramel ... or something.

Now, James isn't known for artful prose, but this line is so bad it reads like parody.

> A **simile** is a type of metaphor that uses "like" or "as" to make the comparison. "Sly like a fox" and "sharp as a tack" are similes.

Figure 21. Simile.

The lesson is that if you're going to use metaphor and simile, *be precise*. To communicate my company's services cost less than a competitor, I could say, "Mandel Marketing is cheaper than a dime-store whore!" Unfortunately, that also connotes my firm doesn't do high quality work, and might give you the clap.

Let's look at an example of a metaphor I found in a business book that is not overplayed, so it's not a cliché. Nor is it vague and simplistic, so it's not meaningless. In the chapter "Overcome the Permission Paradox" in the book *The 5 Patterns of Extraordinary Careers* (2003), authors James Citrin and Richard Smith discuss a universal conundrum people face: you can't get the experience you need without getting a certain job, but you can't get that job without having the experience first. They call it the "Career Catch-22," and, by now I'm sure you're already anticipating that I'm going to call out "catch-22" as a cliché.

Indeed, the phrase "catch-22" is a cliché—now. But when first coined by Joseph Heller in his novel *Catch-22* (1961), it was not. "Catch-22" describes a logical paradox: To get out of fighting in combat, you have to prove you're insane. However, wanting to get out of combat duty is proof of sanity, and thus you have to keep fighting.

In any case, "Career Catch-22" is not the metaphor I'm talking about. No—it's when Citrin and Smith discuss a phenomenon they call "career lahars." I had to read that phrase again because I'd never seen the word "lahar."

Earlier in this book (Chapter 5), I encourage the use of specific and precise words because they are both interesting and meaningful. Turns out "lahar" is a word of Javanese origin (from Indonesia) describing a huge, violent mud flow down the side of a volcano. It was, according to this book, one of the main powers that created the Grand Canyon, rather than simply eons of steady erosion. They offered this definition in the first paragraph of the section, because they rightly predicted that few readers would know this word. If you use an unfamiliar word and don't define it, you better give your reader a good reason to look it up.

The authors use "lahar" as a metaphor for similarly impactful one-time events in people's careers that give them access to opportunities to get the experience they need to get the job they want. It isn't relevant to me whether this is true, or if Citrin and Smith know what the hell they're talking about. I just like the use of "lahar" as a metaphor, which I've never seen elsewhere.

The authors could've just as easily used a cliché like "paradigm shift" or "disruptor," but chose to be creative instead. So, nice job to those guys.

You could say that using a word nobody knows is pretentious rather than creative, but I don't think that's the case here. They define the word immediately, and it's a good metaphor for what they're talking about. Now, employing a recondite shibboleth in one's oeuvre for no other reason than to show off one's lexicon, *that* is pretentious. And trust me, I have an MFA. I know all about being pretentious.

But.

But, but, but.

Just because you've been creative and original and particular doesn't mean you've been precise or accurate. In the same section, Citrin and Smith write, "like a river flowing continually over time, steady access to new experiences met with strong performance is required to keep your career on an upward trajectory." Wooden prose aside, I'm on board with this notion. But then they predict that there will be "a limited number of lahar opportunities ... that, if taken full advantage of, will positively and dramatically change your career's direction."

Is this true? Lahars are certainly dramatic events. But they are also, in fact, extremely *destructive*. Everything I could find on the internet told me how horrible lahars are, and if you see one, you should run way the hell in the other direction as fast as you can. Maybe back during the era of the formation of the Grand Canyon, a lahar simply broke a bunch of earth into a beautiful landscape, but nowadays there are cities and farms and towns and highways in the path of lahars, and people can die. Isn't it akin to saying that there are limited opportunities for meteors, or zombie-apocalypse-like events? COVID-19 was an event like this (hopefully, in that it was a one-time thing). Certainly much changes, but it isn't all good.

Truthfully, I don't think any readers of this nice career-help book will really look into the meaning of "lahar" as much as I have, and their point about big earth-quaking events in people's lives is effective enough to get meaning across. Indeed, you can use Derrida-style Deconstructionism to ruin anything. But, like the "proctology exam" we discussed a few pages ago, it is important to be precise and deliberate.

MAKING METAPHORS

Some people are slow writers, controlling for every word perfectly before committing it to paper and thereby needing fewer subsequent revisions. I'm a quick writer, though, meaning I get my first draft down and revise extensively in later drafts. Sometimes I'll use a temporary, clichéd metaphor or the placeholder XXXX HERE for something I will tackle later. Then, on my second draft, I'll sit and stare off into space as I rack my brain trying to invent something interesting, clever, fresh, and precise. Like men, good metaphors are hard to find.

But either way you do it, you must sit there and do the thinking.

There is one technique—the "mash-up"—that can help. This is when you take seemingly disparate objects and combine them. It can spawn an evocative and original metaphor, such as Groucho Marx's "A hospital bed is a parked taxi with the meter running."

It doesn't always work, though, and you may have to go through a few rounds before hitting upon a good one. For example: a book is made of paper and is therefore flammable, so I can mash up those two ideas into the metaphor of a "burning book."

It's a suggestive image, but what it's suggesting isn't clear. Do I mean the book is literally burning, and I should dunk it in water? Or are the *ideas* in the book incendiary, inciting me to violence? Perhaps the book is full of fiery prose—but what even *is* "fiery prose"? Maybe what I mean is the words were burned into my mind and, after reading the book, I was never the same person.

Also, an inventive metaphor can go from whimsical to cringeworthy pretty quickly, so be careful:

He felt his cashew become a banana, and then a rippled yam, bursting with weight.
— John Updike, *Brazil* (1994)

Even the immortal, prize-winning John Updike of *Rabbit* fame can bungle it by trying too hard, no pun intended (because it's about his penis, you see).

Sometimes you might be lightning-struck by a great turn of phrase, and, lucky you. But, as with everything else in this book, most often you have to just spend the time thinking deeply to get there. So if anyone tries to sell you an easy trick for difficult metaphors, well, it's probably just snake oil. That metaphor is a cliché, by the way.

Euphemism

> The more syllables a euphemism has, the further divorced from reality it is.
>
> — George Carlin

Unlike a high-quality and original metaphor, a euphemism is often a clichéd phrase that masks something unpleasant with innocuous words that don't sound so bad—sometimes employed to be polite, sometimes to elide responsibility or truth.

For example, "passing away" is a euphemism for dying and "passing gas" is a euphemism for flatus. "Between jobs" is a euphemism for being unemployed, while the phrase "downsizing" or "right-sizing" is a nicer way of saying "laying people off" or "letting them go," which is a nicer way of saying "taking away someone's livelihood."

Political language is rife with euphemism: the phrase "enhanced-interrogation techniques" is often seen as a euphemism for torture, while "collateral damage" means killing civilians, noncombatants, and/or destroying nonmilitary targets.

So that's euphemism.

And by now you're probably already anticipating what I'm about to say, but here goes: unless a euphemism is *original* or *necessary*, don't use it. Most likely it's a cliché, it's vague, or it obfuscates meaning and makes your writing weaker.

WRITING EXERCISE: FIGURATIVE LANGUAGE

Part I: Reread some communications and projects you've written and received over the past week. Identify the metaphors, similes, analogies, euphemisms, and hyperbole. What are you communicating through figurative language? Are your comparisons doing their best work? Why or why not? Are certain types of documents you use regularly, or certain colleagues prone to more metaphor usage than others?

Let's examine the first few paragraphs from the Berkshire Hathaway "Letter to Shareholders" from 1980 (Figure 22), since

To the Shareholders of Berkshire Hathaway Inc.:

Operating earnings improved to $41.9 million in 1980 from $36.0 million in 1979, but return on beginning equity capital (with securities valued at cost) fell to 17.8% from 18.6%. We believe the latter yardstick to be the most appropriate measure of single-year managerial economic performance. Informed use of that yardstick, however, requires an understanding of many factors, including accounting policies, historical carrying values of assets, financial leverage, and industry conditions.

In your evaluation of our economic performance, we suggest that two factors should receive your special attention - one of a positive nature peculiar, to a large extent, to our own operation, and one of a negative nature applicable to corporate performance generally. Let's look at the bright side first.

Non-Controlled Ownership Earnings

When one company owns part of another company, appropriate accounting procedures pertaining to that ownership interest must be selected from one of three major categories. The percentage of voting stock that is owned, in large part, determines which category of accounting principles should be utilized.

Generally accepted accounting principles require (subject to exceptions, naturally, as with our former bank subsidiary) full consolidation of sales, expenses, taxes, and earnings of business holdings more than 50% owned. Blue Chip Stamps, 60% owned by Berkshire Hathaway Inc., falls into this category. Therefore, all Blue Chip income and expense items are included in full in Berkshire's Consolidated Statement of Earnings, with the 40% ownership interest of others in Blue Chip's net earnings reflected in the Statement as a deduction for "minority interest".

Figure 22. Berkshire Hathaway Letter to Shareholders, 1980.

that was the year I was born.

In this exceedingly dry financial report, two analogies are used: "yardstick" and "bright side." That's it. All other language is literal and clear. Don't be fooled by the phrase "Blue Chip," which is also highlighted, because in this usage it is *not* metaphorical. The phrase "blue chip stocks" dates to the 1930s and refers, *metaphorically*, to strong, healthy companies with

Figure 23. Yes, this is an ad for cocaine mirrors.

expensive share prices that can weather financial downturns and always perform well. It refers to the color of the highest-value poker chip (blue). Here, however, it refers to an *actual* company called Blue Chip Stamps.

Contrast this with a magazine ad from the same time period (Figure 23) and note how much figurative language is used (though, admittedly, all centered on one specific metaphor).

Part II: Have fun and come up with some outlandish figurative language for your more dry material. You won't be sending these emails or projects out, but it's good practice to exercise the metaphor-making center in your brain and stretch your vocabulary to corners rarely used.

9: BREVITY

Vigorous writing is concise. A sentence should contain no unnecessary words, a paragraph no unnecessary sentences, for the same reason that a drawing should have no unnecessary lines and a machine no unnecessary parts. This requires not that the writer make all [their] sentences short, or that [they] avoid all detail and treat [their] subjects only in outline, but that every word tell.

> — William Strunk, Jr. And E. B. White, *The Elements of Style*, Third Edition (1979)

Clutter is the disease of American writing. We are a society strangling in unnecessary words, circular constructions, pompous frills and meaningless jargon.

> — William Zinsser, *On Writing Well*, Third Edition (1985)

CLUTTER

Why is being concise so important? How do you know *which* words are necessary, and which can be cut? When are *two* quotes one too many?

Let's answer the last question first: don't worry about it.

As for the second question, any words that don't add meaning to your writing are unnecessary and can be cut.

Phrases such as "at this time" or "it's important to note that" do not add meaning:

At this time, we are having a fire drill. Please exit the building.

We are having a drill. Please exit the building.

Or

It's important to note that shirt and shoes are required to dine at Olive Garden.

Shirt and shoes are required to dine at Olive Garden.

Similarly, the most elementary public speaking advice starts with removing "uh," "um," and "like" from one's speech.

Later we'll look more in depth at the adverb, which is a part of speech that modifies or describes another word, usually a verb or an adjective. They often end in "-ly," but not always. "Fast" and "quickly" are both adverbs ("she runs fast" and "she runs quickly").

Adverbs *typically* don't add much meaning to a sentence and can *usually* be cut. But not always. The first sentence of this paragraph contains two qualifying adverbs: "typically" and "usually." I feel the need to qualify the sentence because the common and pithy writing advice to cut all adverbs is wrong.

But back to the first question: why bother doing the work? What's an extra word or two going to hurt anybody?

Shame on you!

Consider the acronym TL;DR, which stands for "too long; didn't read." It often applies to articles posted online that are longer than a few hundred words, or emails longer than two paragraphs. People simply won't read them. And it's not because of the internet or social media, though they've surely made the problem worse. It's because people don't have long attention spans, and unless your writing is super compelling, they won't make the effort.

It doesn't really matter why people won't read long blocks

of text—they just won't. When was the last time you read a full contract, or the T's & C's before signing them?

Never, that's when.

Advertising copywriters abide by this dictum as part of their job:

- Just do it. (Nike)

- Impossible is nothing. (Adidas)

- A diamond is forever. (De Beers)

- The happiest place on earth. (Disneyland)

- You're in good hands. (Allstate)

- What's in your wallet? (Capital One)

- Snap! Crackle! Pop! (Rice Krispies)

- Finger lickin' good. (KFC)

- America runs on Dunkin'. (Dunkin' Donuts)

- Breakfast of champions. (Wheaties)

- Think outside the bun. (Taco Bell)

- Betcha can't eat just one. (Lay's Potato Chips)

So while the motto "less is more" is, by now, a cliché, it's nevertheless true. This is why taglines, at best, are only a few words long, and headlines should be kept to fewer than five. Old print ads have a shocking amount of text on the page, but those days are long gone (Figure 24).

This leaves two options:

1. Make your writing more compelling and less boring.

2. Make your writing shorter.

You can try enticing your reader with something hokey like an email subject line that says "You *must* read this entire email,

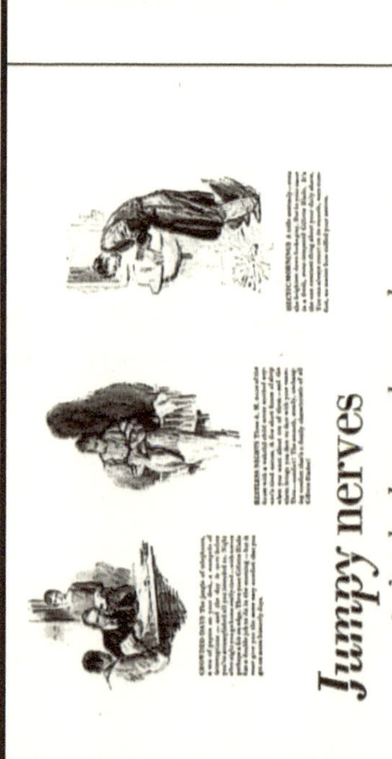

Figure 24. Two magazine ads from 1928.

or you're going to prison," but most people will skip it anyway if they can't see it all on one screen on their phone. This is why your writing needs to be both concise *and* engaging.

Slide presentations are another arena where brevity is preferable to verbosity. Fewer words on a slide are almost always better than more. People won't read text-heavy slides, which is why full sentences are rarely used, and why presentations are meant to be *presented*. Not read. See Figure 25 for proof, which is a slide based on this chapter.

Cutting Clutter

Unfortunately, clutter is sometimes easier to spot than it is to remove. This is because cutting words requires courage and confidence. You must trust your audience to understand you. This is why people so often reiterate their point, though repetition can usually be cut. Have confidence in your audience or reader to not think less of you for using a simple word instead of a sesquipedalian one.

Emails abound with unnecessary words and phrases, such as:

- My schedule is currently open Tuesday afternoon, and I've also got availability on both Thursday and Friday. (17 words)

  - **I'm available Tuesday afternoon and all-day Thursday or Friday.** (10 words)

- I'd like to start by sharing a few more details about the roles I have identified. (16 words)

  - **Here are details about the roles.** (6 words)

- Feel free to give me a ring at your convenience. (10 words)

  - **Call me back.** (3 words)

Chapter 9: Brevity

- **Clutter:** Why is being concise so important? How do you know *which* words are necessary, and which can be cut? When are *two* quotes one too many?
  - Let's answer the last question first: don't worry about it.
  - As for the second question, any words that don't add meaning to your writing are unnecessary and can be cut.
- Phrases such as "at this time" or "it's important to note that" do not add meaning:
  - **At this time, we are having a fire drill. Please exit the building.**
  - **We are having a drill. Please exit the building.**
    - Or
  - **It's important to note that shirt and shoes are required to dine at Olive Garden.**
  - **Shirt and shoes are required to dine at Olive Garden.**
- Similarly, for public speaking you might want to practice removing "uh," "um," and "like" from your speech.
- Later we'll look at the adverb, which is a part of speech that modifies or describes another word, usually a verb or an adjective. They often end in "-ly," but not always. "Fast" and "quickly" are both adverbs ("she runs fast" and "she runs quickly").
  - Adverbs *typically* don't add much meaning to a sentence and can *usually* be cut. But not always. That sentence itself contains two qualifying adverbs: "typically" and "usually." I feel the need to qualify the sentence because the common and pithy writing advice to cut all adverbs is wrong.
- But back to the first question: why bother doing the work? What's an extra word or two going to hurt anybody?
  - Shame on you!
  - Consider the acronym TL;DR, which stands for "too long; didn't read." It often applies to articles posted online that are longer than a few hundred words, or emails longer than two paragraphs. People simply won't read them. And it's not because of the internet or social media, though they've surely made the problem worse. It's because people don't have long attention spans, and unless your writing is super compelling, they won't make the effort.
- It doesn't really matter why people won't read long blocks of text—they just won't. When was the last time you read a full contract, or the T's & C's before signing them?
  - Never, that's when.
- So while the motto "less is more" is, by now, a cliché, it's nevertheless true. This is why taglines, at best, are only a few words long, and headlines should be kept to fewer than five. Old print ads have a shocking amount of text on the page, but those days are long gone (Figure 24).
- This leaves two options:
  1. Make your writing more compelling and less boring.
  2. Make your writing shorter.
- You can try enticing your reader with something hokey like an email subject line that says "You *must* read this entire email, or you're going to prison," but most people will skip it anyway if they can't see it all on one screen on their phone. This is why your writing needs to be both concise *and* engaging.

Figure 24. Two magazine ads from 1928

Advertising copywriters abide by this dictum as part of their job:
- Just do it. (Nike)
- Impossible is nothing. (Adidas)
- A diamond is forever. (De Beers)
- The happiest place on earth. (Disneyland)
- You're in good hands. (Allstate)
- What's in your wallet? (Capital One)
- Snap! Crackle! Pop! (Rice Krispies)
- Finger lickin' good. (KFC)
- America runs on Dunkin'. (Dunkin' Donuts)
- Breakfast of champions. (Wheaties)
- Think outside the bun. (Taco Bell)
- Betcha can't eat just one. (Lay's Potato Chips)

Figure 25. Proof.

- As I mentioned, I just wanted to confirm your details below so that we can update your profile accordingly. (19 words)
  - **Confirm your details to update your profile.** (7 words)

Some of these polite, generic words are used to soften the tone, which is fine in small doses. But every extra word puffs up the length of your communication and reduces the chance it'll be read and understood.

Other unnecessary clauses that weaken your writing are qualifiers, such as "I think," or "try to." This may feel illogical, at first, but it's true. Consider:

- I think you should try to cut all unnecessary qualifying language from your writing, if you can. (17 words)
  - **Cut unnecessary qualifying language from your writing.** (7 words)

Saved ten words (59 percent) *and* the sentence is stronger—not a bad ROI on that one!

THEMATIC RESONANCE

Cut anything—sentences, paragraphs, entire slides—that don't have thematic resonance to your presentation, email, or story at large. We'll discuss Theme at length in Chapter 15, but for now think of it as the core of what your communication is "about."

For example, it is typically unnecessary for a real estate listing to include biographical information about the realtor, such as where they went to college or if they're married. Likewise, an email debriefing a presentation doesn't need to include what everyone was wearing, or if the air conditioning in the conference room was too strong.

Take this book, which is about business communication. While it may be true that I used to play in a punk band in New York City—and I love talking about my glory days—it is irrelevant to the subject matter (the Theme) and was removed from the final version of the Introduction.

CLARITY AND BREVITY

Avoid using two (or more) words when one will do. People often use larger, more complex, unwieldy, inelegant, clunky, and less meaningful phrases because they think it makes them sound smarter. It doesn't.

It also isn't necessary. "Keep in mind" is no better than "remember," just as "make use of" is no better than "use."

- We can make use of this empty bathroom to serve the purpose of being our secret hideout during lunch breaks. (20 words)

    - **Let's hide in this empty bathroom during lunch.** (9 words)

However, do not sacrifice clarity for brevity. Using the word "nudiustertian" instead of "the day before yesterday" simply because there are fewer words does not help convey meaning. Rather, it interrupts the reader as they wonder what the hell "nudiustertian" means. Generally speaking, stopping the reader is the worst thing you can do, as it disrupts the flow of your narrative.

THROAT-CLEARING

The term "throat-clearing" is something of a cliché, and it's difficult to define, but like obscenity, you know it when you see it.

It's when the presenter isn't saying anything useful, such as giving background on the project that everybody already knows or reading numbers on a chart that people can see for themselves. It's the extra pages of a book where an author "introduces" a subject with a bunch of clever twaddle instead of getting right into it.

This delaying tactic can ruin a presentation, meeting, story, book, your life.

A tiny amount of throat-clearing goes a long way, and I'm sure you can already guess my advice: locate these phrases and delete them. To help you, here is a list of phrases you can eliminate without sacrificing meaning:

- It is important to note that
- It should be noted that
- It's clear that
- Keep in mind that
- Please note that
- It is important to remember that
- It should not be overlooked
- I contend that
- The fact that
- Go ahead and
- Feel free to

There are ~~far~~ too many phrases like this to list ~~them all~~, but when you ~~start to~~ become aware of them, you'll see them everywhere. ~~Feel free to go ahead and~~ Delete them ~~when you see them.~~

Adverbs

Okay, let's talk about adverbs. There is an oft-repeated basic piece of advice for writers: Cut all adverbs.

True, strong writing usually contains few adverbs, as they are often redundant. But they do have a place.

Adverbs qualify the verbs in your sentence, like adjectives do for nouns. You may describe your desk as "blue" and "sturdy," and these are adjectives. But an adverb describes how you're doing something:

I'm running quickly.

In this sentence, "running" is the verb—the action—and "quickly" is the adverb. But is it necessary? One hallmark of strong writing is using specific words that don't require extra descriptions. It is possibly more accurate to say:

I'm sprinting.

This is shorter sentence, and therefore possibly stronger—but either one will do, especially because there is a difference between sprinting, which usually means running as fast as possible, and running quickly, which might mean any variety of running speeds.

Thus, you run into the problem of vagueness again. Do you need to specify *how* quickly? Will it not suffice to simply say, "I'm running"? The listener or reader already knows, in this word alone, that you are trying to move faster than a walk. Does it matter if you're running at 75 percent max capacity, or running as quickly as a deer? Or perhaps "quickly" does suffice— you're merely trying to say you're running faster than usual.

The point is, to make this decision, you need to think deeply about what you're trying to communicate. Sadly, you have to spend *extra* time *eliminating* words from your writing to make it concise and strong versus something wordy and weak.

"Screaming loudly" and "ruminating thoughtfully" are examples of unnecessary adverbs. Screaming is, by definition, loud, and rumination is, by definition, thought. If, for some reason, a writer wanted to say someone was screaming *quietly*, or ruminating *unwittingly*, then those would be opportunities for necessary adverbs.

Nevertheless, from a style perspective, you want to avoid this:

I'm sprinting quickly.

The word "sprinting" implies "quickly," so is an unnecessary adverb. Let's look at another example:

He's talking quietly.

You could also write, if it is true:

He's whispering.

This eliminates the adverb and gets more specific. However, there can indeed be a difference between "talking quietly" and "whispering," so you need to make sure what you're saying is accurate, rather than merely short. Either way, you should rarely ever need to write:

He's whispering quietly.

Again, "whisper" implies "quiet." However, *you* may, at some point, want to say,

He's whispering *loudly*.

This is also sometimes called a "stage whisper," which is when someone is using their "whisper voice" loud enough that people in another room can hear.

All of these rules can be broken whenever necessary, but

generally speaking, most adverbs can go, because you should try to come up with a better word.

Some very nerdalicious research (Ben Blatt's 2017 book, *Nabokov's Favorite Word Is Mauve: What the Numbers Reveal About the Classics, Bestsellers, and Our Own Writing*) showed that literary giant Toni Morrison was one of the most adverb-averse writers in recent history (along with another you might expect, Ernest Hemingway):

> Morrison has said in multiple interviews that she doesn't use adverbs. Why? Because when she's writing at her best, she can do without: "I never say 'She says softly,'" Morrison tells us. "If it's not already soft, you know, I have to leave a lot of space around it so a reader can hear that it's soft."[14]

In the first chapter of Blatt's book, he uses statistics and hard data to demonstrate how many of the most successful writers—and in their most successful books—use fewer adverbs.

It would be easy, then, to conclude one should simply cut all words that end in "-ly." But that's not the lesson. The real lesson is that you need to go back through your writing thoroughly to find the best way of saying what you mean, and not *relying* on adverbs to do the work for you. Like clichés, adverbs are shortcuts that ruin your work.

VERY, SORT OF, REALLY, SOMEWHAT, AND OTHER QUALIFIERS

The word "very" is another one that can be cut almost all the time. You may think it emphasizes the word you're trying to qualify, but it doesn't. Seriously. Truly. It doesn't make your work stronger, it makes it weaker:

I'm mad at you.
I'm very mad at you.

This may seem counterintuitive, but the first one is stronger writing because it gets the same meaning across with 20 percent fewer words.

But what if "mad" isn't strong enough? Exchange it for a more precise word: "furious," "angry," or "enraged."

What I usually do, in a later draft of my work, is find all instances of the word "very" and start deleting.

Phrases such as "really," "kind of," "sort of," "pretty," and "somewhat" can also usually be deleted, unless they are being used to soften your tone.

Consider the phrases "kind of unique" and "really unique." The word "unique" means "singular," so by definition, something is either unique or it is not unique. Without getting philosophical, there are not different shades, or degrees, of "unique."

Same goes for being pregnant: you either are or you aren't, but you can't be "somewhat pregnant."

Colloquially, people typically use the term "very pregnant" to describe someone who is in their third trimester, but in this usage the term is not indicating *whether* someone is pregnant, but instead how far along they are, or how much the baby is showing, or how much has changed in relation to one's life before being pregnant (as in, "Diane is very pregnant and can't tie her own shoes or go skiing this weekend").

In a business setting, the problem with these phrases is that they aren't specific enough. "These sales figures are somewhat good" is not actionable feedback. Consider instead: "These sales figures are not at goal, but they are high enough to earn your bonus," or "These sales figures are not at goal, and therefore you are fired."

The phrase "We're pretty close to budget" doesn't fly, either. Does that mean you're 20 percent to budget, or 5 percent to budget, or 10 percent over budget?

THAT

Another word to cut is "that." Many instances of "that" are unnecessary and cutting them will reduce clutter and word count:

I think that you're a great person.
I believe that I love you.
The next time that I see you will be the last.

These work better as:

I think you're a great person.
I believe I love you.
The next time I see you will be the last.

In the first trio of sentences, the word "that" is superfluous and can be deleted.

However, there are cases where the word "that" refers to something, so you can't simply do a "find all" in your document and delete. For example:

Will you pick that up for me?
I would do anything for love, but I won't do that.

~~Nevertheless, you'll note that~~ Many examples ~~that are~~ in the section on "throat-clearing" contain the word "that," which ~~is a good indication that~~ indicates something is awry.

WRITING EXERCISE: CONCISION

Part I: Take a recent communication or other written work and find extra phrases and clutter. Locate and highlight all the adverbs, throat-clearing, clutter, uses of the words "very," "that," and the others we've agreed to hate.

You don't need to rewrite anything right now, just cut what

you highlighted. Look at what you have. It's better, isn't it?

Well, it's *shorter*, I hope. Let's look more carefully. Have you lost meaning anywhere? If so, identify what was cut and see if there could've been a better way of phrasing your sentence in the first place. Remember, sometimes "that" *does* have meaning (though "very," "sort of," and "kinda" do not).

Part II: Find some other written work or communication from your job that others have written—emails, blog posts, articles, memos, presentations, anything—and see if you can identify where there are extra words and clutter. Reflect on the work that *doesn't* contain much clutter—is it easier to read and understand? Is that author similarly concise in their other written work?

Part III: Now, the hard part. Take something you're working on right now and bring out the scalpel. Don't send it out until you've done some major surgery.

10: GRAMMAR

Grammar is a piano I play by ear, since I seem to have been out of school the year the rules were mentioned. All I know about grammar is its infinite power. To shift the structure of a sentence alters the meaning of that sentence, as definitely and inflexibly as the position of a camera alters the meaning of the object photographed.

— Joan Didion, "Why I Write" (1976)

GRAMMAR

This book is not a guide to grammar, as there are thousands of resources already available for that, and there are many automated programs that will fix bad grammar for you. The rules of grammar are also different in different languages. For this book, what I want you to know about grammar is that bad grammar will confuse your reader, interrupt the flow of reading, and make them question your authority as a writer. Thus, if the function of business writing is to convey information, then improper grammar stands in the way.

When writing creatively, you don't always have to follow all the rules of grammar. James Joyce famously started a book in the middle of a sentence:

riverrun, past Eve and Adam's from swerve of shore to bend of bay, brings us by a commodius vicus of recirculation back to Howth Castle and Environs.

That's the beginning of *Finnegans Wake* (1939), a novel that few people have ever read and even fewer understand.

Also, Joyce wrote millions of words *with* standard grammar.

The point is, you must know the rules, and have a solid reason for intentionally breaking them—otherwise, it looks like a mistake. So put a period where it belongs, capitalize sentences, and know the difference between their/they're/there, fewer/less than, and lay/lie/laid (a tricky one, even for a professional like me).

It may seem unfair that mistakes in grammar can convey to your reader a lack of education, leading to distrust of your expertise—just as typos on a résumé can prevent someone from getting an interview—but it's reality. Confusing it's/its and your/you're are red flags. Run-on sentences and sentence fragments cause warning signals to go off for your audience, as they make your writing difficult to read and understand. Misusing a semi-colon is also a no-no (see Figure 26).

Similar to the infield fly rule, the use of a **semicolon** is an oft-debated yet esoteric topic that nobody but the most ardent of writing folks will care about. A semicolon bridges two discrete independent clauses into one sentence. A comma does this as well, but needs a conjunction:

- I wrote a book about writing, but I had to revise it extensively.
- I wrote a book about writing; I had to revise it extensively.

There are other reasons to use a semicolon, such as in making lists, but you'll have to look those up on your own time.

E. L. Doctorow said he detested semicolons, though I'm not sure why. Kurt Vonnegut also had a something to say about semicolons in *A Man Without A Country* (2005):

"Here is a lesson in creative writing. First rule: Do not use semicolons. They are transvestite hermaphrodites representing absolutely nothing. All they do is show you've been to college."

I'll leave it to you to decide if he was kidding.

Figure 26. Semicolons.

Creatively, messing with grammar can (if done well) conjure new emotion, feeling, and ideas. For example, in the masterful poetry collection *How to Be Drawn*, Terrance Hayes uses proper grammar, and messes with grammar, to great effect:

> I was trying to play the twelve-bar blues
> with two bars. I was trying to fill the room
> with a shocked and awkward color, I was trying
> to limber your shuffle, the muscle wired
> to muscle. I wanted to be a lucid hammer.
>
> — "The Rose Has Teeth"

> *The Spikes* \Incisor/
> Of twanging that talk that sounds like money, that ricochet
> encasement that's twelve degrees wide. Oooed & Eeeeked
> with possibility. & that able-joyed.
>
> — "Who Are The Tribes"

And lest you think playing with grammar is just for the poets, many novelists do it too. The "stream of consciousness" style in prose is meant to elicit a feeling of being inside a character's mind, experiencing a continuous stream of thoughts in real time, just as the character does. In *The Handmaid's Tale* (1985), Margaret Atwood achieves this effect using incomplete sentences to mimic Offred's eye jumping from point to point in her room:

> A chair, a table, a lamp. Above, on the white ceiling, a relief
> ornament in the shape of a wreath, and in the centre of it
> a blank space, plastered over, like the place in a face where
> the eye has been taken out. (Chapter 2)

In *Mrs. Dalloway* (1925), Virginia Woolf shows how thoughts interrupt each other using nonstandard punctuation and run-on sentences:

The aeroplane turned and raced and swooped exactly where
it liked, swiftly, freely, like a skater—
"That's an E," said Mrs. Bletchley—
or a dancer—
"It's toffee," murmured Mr. Bowley—
(and the car went in at the gates and nobody looked at
it), and shutting off the smoke, away and away it rushed,
and the smoke faded and assembled itself round the broad
white shapes of the clouds.

When done poorly, stream of consciousness can become
tedious—but in a business setting it would be unreadable. The
point is, creative writing can take liberties with grammar that
business writing cannot. If you reach out to a cold lead with
an email full of grammar mistakes, you are (unfairly or not)
unlikely to get a response.

> **Deer client, I'm reaching out to try hard to get a meeting
> with ur procurment ppl can you give me there email
> please; thanx? – philm andel**

Grammar is generally learned along with language, and largely
becomes known inherently or as you learn to read. (You can
read more about universal grammar and linguistics, especially
as developed by Noam Chomsky, if you like this kind of thing...
but I wouldn't necessarily recommend it.) There are a handful
of byzantine grammar rules that I see no harm in breaking so
long as the meaning of your ideas comes across. For example,
split infinitives ("to sing proudly" versus "to proudly sing" or
"to type quietly" versus "to quietly type") are supposedly a no-
no, but I disagree. You're also not supposed to end a sentence
with a preposition. Or start a sentence with a conjunction (such
as "and," "but," "or," and "if"). But I do it all the time.
Grammar changes over time, as do the meanings of some
words (such as "literally"). For example, until recently, the word

"they" was a pronoun that only represented a plural group. Now, "they" can be a singular pronoun representing a person who doesn't identify as "he" or "she." Other grammar rules are evolving, too, such as how and where to use hyphens, or the archaic and draconian distinctions between "who" and "whom."

Outside of these exceptions, however, proper grammar is essential to business communication. This is because grammar helps people understand what you are saying. If grammar mistakes prevent you from being understood, you have to fix them. It's not because the great Grammar Teacher in the sky is grading you and you'll get grounded or go to jail if you make mistakes. It's because poor grammar obscures the meaning of your words.

As an example, let's look at a minor—but specific—error that should always be fixed, as it can cause needless confusion in your reader: pronouns and antecedents.

Pronouns and Antecedents

This teeny boo-boo is an easy fix once you learn to notice it. A *pronoun*—"he," "she," "it," "they," and so on—is a word that refers to a noun, without having to use the noun again:

> **I brought a sandwich with me to work, and someone else ate it.**

The word "it" in that sentence refers to my sandwich. We use pronouns in exchange for repeating the same noun over and over:

> **I brought a sandwich with me to work, and someone else ate my sandwich.**

This is obvious. But for a pronoun to work, the reader must

know what it represents. This is the "antecedent." Consider this sentence:

Someone else ate it.

What is "it" in this sentence? It could be my sandwich, it could be an apple, or it could mean someone fell off their skateboard, or down the stairs. If the previous sentence was "I cooked my chicken pot pie in the break room microwave," then the reader will know the "it" refers to a chicken pot pie. But in a vacuum, the word "it" has no meaning.

The pronoun "it," in this example, has no *antecedent*. The *antecedent* is the word that specifies what the pronoun refers to.

In everyday speech, this happens less often because there are other context clues and body language to help convey meaning—such as nodding toward the microwave in the break room, or grabbing an empty paper bag with your name on it out of the trash and waving it around furiously.

But in writing, this pitfall happens to the best of us. The technical term is "pronoun-antecedent agreement," and if there isn't any, the result is confusion:

I synced my laptop and my phone and now it's not working.

Which device is not working, the laptop or the phone?

So even though it may seem clunky, you should specify, for accuracy in writing—especially when it comes to important business matters:

I synced my laptop and my phone and now the phone is not working.

Stylistically, it might feel awkward to repeat the same word twice in a sentence, and usually it is. But you don't want to sacrifice meaning for style, so in this case you have to. Also, you must resist the temptation to "solve" this problem by using a synonym:

I synced my laptop and my phone and now my Samsung Galaxy is not working.

Substituting the brand name Samsung Galaxy for "phone" to avoid using the word "phone" twice is no solution. It may seem obvious to the writer, but the reader can't be entirely sure you're referring to the same object. You've introduced a new noun, so it *might* mean there is another phone, this one being a Samsung Galaxy, that is now not working. That's also why I had to use the word "phone" twice in the first sentence of this paragraph.

There are real-world political ramifications to the obfuscation of pronouns and antecedents. Consider the remarks made by President Trump on September 7, 2020, during the height of the COVID pandemic and the election:

So, contrary to all of the lies, the vaccine that they're— they politicalize. They'll say anything. And it's so danger- ous for our country, what they say.[15]

There are many uses of "they" in this passage, none of which have a specific antecedent. Trump was masterful at using "they" ambiguously, which allowed his audience to fill in the anteced- ent however they wanted—whoever *you* think is at fault, that's who it is. I'm calling out Trump here, but all politicians do it. Deliberately.

In business communication, however, you are trying to do the opposite. You want to be clear and convey meaning, so your employees know what is expected of them, so you can influence decision-makers to buy your product, so you can persuade investors to take a risk on your company.

Be aware of pronouns and be careful and specific. We use pronouns so regularly that they're hard to spot and easy to miss.

The Passive Voice

Ah, the Passive Voice. A hallmark of bad writing, and an easy bugaboo for the creative writing workshop schoolmarm.

Like all pithy, universal statements, the advice "never use the passive voice" is *largely*, but not *always*, true. On rare occasions, the passive voice is indeed called for.

To understand the *passive* voice, we'll contrast it with the *active* voice:

- The grouchiest book about business communication ever published, *An MFA for Your MBA*, **was written by** Phillip Scott Mandel. (Passive)

    - Phillip Scott Mandel **wrote** the grouchiest book about business communication ever published, *An MFA for Your MBA*. (Active)

- The largest deal in company history **was closed by** Phillip Scott Mandel. (Passive)

    - Phillip Scott Mandel **closed** the largest deal in company history. (Active)

In these two instances, the active voice is stronger than the passive voice. Mandel is taking action, rather than things having action taken upon them *by* Mandel.

In strong business writing, the passive voice is rare, but it's not 100 percent absent. For example, I just received a newsletter that reads at the bottom:

This email **was sent** to you because you are a user of our website or submitted an inquiry to our company. To update your email subscription...

This is a perfectly fine use of the passive voice. If it were written in the *active* voice, it would read "We sent you this email because…" and the tone might almost sound prematurely defensive. With the passive voice, the subject of the sentence is the email, not the company sending it. With the active voice, it's the other way around.

Use of the passive voice can be more insidious, however, when it comes to business and politics. This is because the passive voice can hide blame and responsibility. Consider this passive sentence:

Our biggest account was lost.

Well, who lost it? It didn't get lost on its own, did it? Now consider the active sentence:

Phillip Scott Mandel lost our biggest account.

Ah, now we know. It's that bastard Mandel's fault.

Sometimes a lost account isn't the fault of someone at the company, but because of other market forces, and "our biggest account was lost" is fair. But I would argue that a better way of framing this is to be active, because it provides more context:

Company X closed their account with us and moved their business to another vendor because our prices are too high and our customer service isn't any good.

Now, the clients at Company X are active—they chose to close the account—and the reasons are clear. We can take action so we don't lose more accounts.

Real-world political ramifications of language abound. Just as with removing antecedents from pronouns, the passive voice allows politicians to elide responsibility for death, destruction, and misery. Here's an easy and all-too-common example:

Mistakes were made.

— Every politician ever

The questions are: *Who* made the mistakes? What were the consequences of the mistakes? Were the people who made the mistakes held accountable? Was anything done to redress the mistakes? Was there justice? And so on.

Automation + AI

These days, software such as Grammarly, ProWritingAid, and even good ol' spellcheck can help you with grammar mistakes, spelling errors, clutter, passive voice, and clarity. I like these programs and have used them with much success to find offending words and phrases that I've missed on manual revision.

However, automation is only one tool that solves only one problem, and you don't want it to become a crutch.

These programs work for me because I'm already a professional writer, and I know why they're fixing certain errors. The program won't, unfortunately, fix most of the problems we discuss in this book. It also won't make you creative.

Using AI to write for you only exacerbates the problem, as it will write badly for you. In fact, tools such as Grammarly and ProWritingAid or AI writing bots might make your writing less original and creative because they operate on a formula. Formulaic writing is boring, trite, weak, and eliminates your unique voice by making everything sound the same.

Writing Exercise: Grammar

Part I: Carefully review some recent items you've written: emails, presentations, reports, anything. Run a spell-check and grammar check.

How's your grammar, friend? Did you use the passive voice? Did you miss any antecedents for your pronouns? Are there any other glaring mistakes?

If so, what happened? Sheer carelessness? Or are there some grammar rules you need to relearn?

Part II: Take a few minutes to fix your grammar errors and brush up on some of the rules you may have forgotten.

11: POINT OF VIEW

As she came nearer and nearer to the familiar breeding places there was more and more earnestness in Laska's exploration. A little marsh bird did not divert her attention for more than an instant. She made one circuit round the clump of reeds, was beginning a second, and suddenly quivered with excitement and became motionless.

— Leo Tolstoy, *Anna Karenina* (1878)

FIRST AND THIRD

One of the primary mistakes new writers make in their fiction is with Point of View (POV). This is the lens through which we view the world and story of your writing. For nearly all writing, there are only a few options:

- First person limited: "I emailed my team to ask for a status on my project."

- Second person: "You emailed your team to ask for a status on your project."

- Third person limited: "Phillip emailed his team to ask for a status on his project."

- Third person omniscient: "Phillip emailed his team to ask for a status on his project, which they had not started yet."

Generally, any story with "I" as narrator is in first person. Most stories with a first-person narrator are told by and about one person, such as the angsty teenager Holden Caulfield in J. D. Salinger's *Catcher in the Rye* (1951):

> If you really want to hear about it, the first thing you'll probably want to know is where I was born, and what my lousy childhood was like, and how my parents were occupied and all before they had me, and all that David Copperfield kind of crap, but I don't feel like going into it, if you want to know the truth.

A first-person shooter video game is so named because you see the world from the eyes of the main character. There aren't many movies made in first person, though *Lady in the Lake* (1947) and *Hardcore Henry* (2016) are examples.

There is also a small subset of books written in first-person plural, which is where the main narrator is "we." *The Virgin Suicides* (1993) by Jeffrey Eugenides and the workplace novel *Then We Came to the End* (2007) by Joshua Ferris are examples of these, and while disorienting at first, this POV can be used to great effect.

In professional writing, you almost certainly use first-person for your resume, as well as most email that has any kind of personal element, such as "I'll be there at 3 for the meeting" or "Attached are the documents I put together."

The first-person *plural* POV often comes into play when writing to represent one's company, rather than oneself:

> **We've been around since 2008, and we provide best-in-class service at unbeatable prices.**

Early in my career I was taught to use "we" rather than "I" whenever possible, especially when communicating with clients or stakeholders. It sounds more collaborative and puts one's team or company into focus, rather than the individual.

THIRD PERSON

A third-person point of view is when there is no "I" telling a story, but the story is being told by an unseen narrator about the characters in it. Many novels and stories are told this way, as well as when you relate an anecdote about someone else:

Jennifer presented to the client alone and wondered why her partner Mike was late to work.

And

Mike stopped for gas on his way to work. It was outrageously expensive and made him late. He wondered if Jennifer was going to present to the client without him, or if she was going to reschedule.

Individually, these are both *limited* points of view, in that in each one, we don't know what's going on outside of Jennifer and Mike's perspectives. A first-person POV is also limited to that narrative "I," but very often a first-person POV will feel more subjective to the reader, while a third-person POV feels more objective.

In professional writing, third-person limited POV might come into play when describing a consumer persona, for example.

Jake is a 26-year-old college graduate who lives in a city and loves pizza and video games. He'll drink a national lite beer every so often, but he craves "authenticity" and wants to show off his bona fides by drinking a local craft brew.

The facts of legal brief are also presented in third person, as is most journalism, meeting notes, press releases, written records, business documents, medical summaries, corporate bylaws, NDAs, contracts, and almost all other objectively-presented written material.

Omniscience ("God Mode")

Omniscient POV is when the narrator knows everything, and is usually told in third person. Omniscient narrators can describe anything and everything they want, because they see and know all and (generally) show no bias preference.

Old-school authors like Dickens and Tolstoy used omniscient POV to zoom in and out in their narrative—from providing a single person's thoughts to describing the political situation in a country in a fashion no individual character *within* the story would be able to do. In the quote from *Anna Karenina* that begins this chapter, Tolstoy even jumps into the perspective of the dog, Laska. This type of narration conveys a heavy authoritative authorial viewpoint and has largely fallen out of favor, though tastes change.

Is there a first-person omniscient? Technically, if a story were told by God, or some all-knowing machine, then you *could* argue that could be first-person omniscient, but outside of those two examples, almost all other "I" fiction is "limited" by the narrator's consciousness and knowledge.

Multiple POV

Omniscient POV shouldn't be confused with *multiple* third-person POV, which can still be limited. In the novels of *A Song of Ice and Fire* (normies may call it *Game of Thrones*), each chapter is titled and told from a different protagonist's viewpoint. The tension surges as readers learn about plotting and politicking in one part of Westeros while characters elsewhere in the world are unaware. Technically, the overall narration of *ASOIF* is "omniscient" in that it jumps to different POVs, but each individual chapter is narrated from a limited third-person POV. In Tyrion's chapters, we only see the world from his sardonic and clever perspective.

The Poisonwood Bible (1998) by Barbara Kingsolver also features multiple POVs, but unlike *ASOIF*, which is in third person ("Bran rode," "Jon saw"), Kingsolver's novel is in first-person limited ("I saw"). Each chapter has its own narrator, and as the plot unfolds, the reader gets a different perspective from each "I" telling their side of the story. This is not first-person *plural*, because the book isn't told from the perspective of "we."

You may have heard of a "Rashomon-style" story, which depicts multiple perspectives of the same event. Named after the movie *Rashomon* (1950) by Akira Kurosawa, this is a fun storytelling technique because each POV is subjective and naturally self-serving to the protagonist. The audience is left to interpret the event however they choose. The book *Gone Girl* by Gillian Flynn (2012) is an example of this, as is the movie *The Last Duel* (2021).

Second Person

Finally, there is second person. This is a direct address to the reader, told in the imperative, or "You." Every so often you'll see a dreaded "You" short story (I wrote one!), and they stand out because they're uncommon, and can sometimes feel gimmicky. They can be tedious to read after a while, so there aren't as many full-length novels written in second person as there are short stories.

Also, the "You" of the story is sometimes really an implied "I," in that the person is really talking to themselves, but aren't able to take responsibility for their feelings or actions. They distance themselves by depersonalizing the situation by pretending that such-and-such is about "you," rather than "me."

This almost automatically evokes a kind of trauma reading in the character, and can be very powerful.

So despite the gimmick warning if done poorly, these kinds of stories can be moving and memorable, if done well, such as the following:

- "Girl" by Jamaica Kincaid

- The short stories in "Self Help" by Lorrie Moore

- "Travel Tips" by Manuel Martinez[16]

- The novel *How to Get Filthy Rich in Rising Asia* by Mohsin Hamid

Unlike in fiction, much business communication has an element of the second person, as it is written with the intention of influencing another person's behavior. You aren't simply telling a story to entertain, but you are providing information so your reader can do something with it.

This is the "action item" (or "call to action") of a presentation, email, advertisement, company handbook, user manual, real estate listing, or other business copy. The first few pages or paragraphs might be a report on some information in either first person or third person: this is who we are, this is what's going on, this is how the printer works, this is the company policy on paid time off.

Then you get to the parts about why it's relevant to "you" (the listener), and what "you" need to do: **buy** our product, **input your sales** calls into the CRM, **contact your supervisor** with questions, **place the printer** on a flat surface, **provide a report** on our quarterly financials, **stop coming in late** to work, or **imagine yourself** in this lovely three-bedroom home.

Consider *this* book, for example, which is written in both the first person *and* second person. *I*, Phillip Scott Mandel, am narrating what I know to help *you*, the reader, take action in your life and career.

Limited POV

As mentioned earlier, a "limited" POV allows a reader to only see and know what a specific narrator or character sees and knows. This is true even if the overarching narrator of the story is omniscient, such as in *A Song of Ice and Fire*, because each chapter presents a certain character's viewpoint of the world.

Limited POV is popular because it feels real for most readers, as it mirrors the way we actually live. In the example under the "Third Person" section, Jennifer doesn't know why Mike was late, and Mike isn't sure if Jennifer is going to present to the client without him. Consider how little we know about the world, or even what's going on in other people's minds, every day at work. Billions of dollars are spent each year on market research to figure it out.

Not only is limited POV more realistic, it naturally builds suspense. Think of a crime narrative that cuts away from the cops to show the criminal doing something terrible to their victim. The thrill for the audience is in knowing the cops don't know what the criminal is up to—especially if he's setting a trap.

Limited POV also allows a reader to see "around" a character. This can happen when a reader figures something out or knows from experience something the characters don't. In the story "Where Are You Going, Where Have You Been?" by Joyce Carol Oates (1966), a fifteen-year-old girl named Connie meets a menacing stranger named Arnold Friend (ignore the Dickensian name). By the end of the story, you want to jump into the page and scream at Connie not to talk to Arnold, but *she*, being a naïve teenager, doesn't know what you, the reader, has already ascertained: Arnold is no friend. He's a demon (metaphorically and, perhaps, literally).

Deciding on POV

Writers choose their POV carefully and deliberately, sometimes trying out versions of a story using different POVs to see which works best. I once wrote an entire novel in third person, then switched to first person, then switched *back* to third person.

Why does it matter so much, and what is the writer looking for? It comes down to voice, tone, and narrative distance.

A first-person POV is voice-driven and close—sometimes almost claustrophobically close—and can bond the reader with the main character. The third-person omniscient POV ("God mode") is more distant and authoritative, which can work well for a philosophical novel about the world. The standard third-person limited POV still allows for character and voice to come through, but is unobtrusive and fades into the background—making it a great choice for when the story is the main point. In fiction, a second-person or first-person plural POV can call attention to itself the same way a first-person POV would in a movie, but it can work when done well and for the right reason.

Like we discussed earlier, a communication reads differently when it is coming from "I" (the manager or representative of a company) versus "we" (the company itself). Consider a company privacy policy written in first-person plural versus third-person:

We collect data for internal marketing purposes. (First-person plural)

Versus

Mandel Marketing collects data for internal marketing purposes. (Third)

Even the tone of a simple email can be altered dramatically between first-person and third-person:

I need everyone to stay late on today. (First)

Versus

Mandel Marketing needs everyone to stay late today. (Third)

Maybe it's just me, but in both cases third-person feels colder and more distant.

Empathy in Point of View

Being deliberate about point of view forces you, as a writer and businessperson, to remember that everyone has their own POV. By practicing writing in the limited POV, you learn to separate what *you* know about the world from what *your character* (or customer) knows. Despite what Tolstoy or Dickens may present with their omniscient narrators, nobody knows everything.

This means you need to anticipate, and heed, what other people may think and feel about the work you're doing—not just what *you* think and feel about it. People will *legitimately*, honestly, and in good faith feel differently and have different knowledge about things than you do.

That's why the Rashomon-style POV story is both instructive and entertaining—it depicts different points of view of the same event, and shows how each person is the star of their own movie. I don't know how many times I've left a sales meeting with a colleague and we've taken away two opposing conclusions about how it went and next steps. *We have to get them a proposal right away*, my sales-friend will say, and I will reply, *But they just slashed their budget and aren't buying until next fiscal.*

Consider, when you tell your employee to go do some menial, boring, but important task, how it feels when *your* boss tells you to do some menial, boring, but important task. If you don't know how important the task is, you might resent having to do it. If your limited POV doesn't gain the knowledge (by your boss telling you the context of the task), then an unnecessary conflict is created. This may lead to you spending an extra five minutes ensuring the employee knows *why* they've been asked to do the task in the first place, and they'll complete it with more gusto and care. This extra communication is time well spent.

This may seem like more of an empathy lesson than a writing lesson, at first. But good writing comes from good thinking, and good thinking requires empathy. A deeper aspect of point of view is to try to imagine your words or presentation from the point of view of your reader.

If you relate a story about someone in the third person—for example, you're explaining to your manager why your prospect didn't return your email—do you simply say, "John's an asshole" and leave it at that? You could get into John's perspective and say, "John's busy and probably inundated with sales emails right now. He would respond to a better-written and more engaging email."

If you were to narrate a scene from someone else's point of view—the client to whom you are presenting, or the colleague who will receive your email—what would they think? What knowledge and context do they already have? How will they take what you're trying to say?

Unreliable Narrators

The term "unreliable narrator" gets used more often in an MFA program than it should. It refers to narration from the point of view of someone whose words you can't fully trust.

An unreliable narrator might be fun to read because the reader begins to wonder what's true and can start to "look around" the character, to see what's "real." One of the pleasures of reading is figuring things out, so when you discover a narrator is unreliable, it becomes a bit of a game trying to understand what's true in the world. Holden Caulfield from *The Catcher in the Rye* is in some ways unreliable because he's a young kid, and doesn't really understand the world the way the adult reader of the novel does. Humbert Humbert from Nabokov's *Lolita* (1955) is unreliable because he's a sociopathic pedophile. Patrick Bateman from *American Psycho* (1991) by Bret Easton Ellis is unreliable because he's a criminal psychopath.

An unreliable narrator is also very human. When Bruce from Accounting rushes breathlessly into the break room to tell everyone how "This guy in a Corvette came out of nowhere and gave me the finger as I was minding my own business," we know there's more to the story, like when Bruce cut off the guy in the Corvette first. Trust me, I've been in the car with Bruce, and he's a terrible driver.

In creative writing, an unreliable narrator is a deliberate choice. The narrator is dissembling for a reason, not making mistakes accidentally. For example, if in Chapter 1 the narrator says, "My boyfriend had beautiful blue eyes" and then in Chapter 2 says, "My boyfriend stared at me with those gorgeous big brown eyes," then we probably don't think the narrator is unreliable or color-blind. Rather, we think the author made an error. On the other hand, the phenomenal book *Life of Pi* by Yann Martel (2001) features an unreliable narrator whose story becomes even more resonant when the reader fully understands it at the end.

Some literary theory suggests that all narrators are, in a way, unreliable, because nobody in real life can report all things with perfect accuracy. Research has proven that eyewitness testimony is notoriously unreliable. People remember events incorrectly or can unintentionally be implanted with false memories.

Nevertheless, in the world of business communication, you want to try to avoid being an unreliable narrator. There is typically no room for this kind of literary device because it simply leads to confusion, vagueness, and interrupted work. *Life of Pi* is a beautiful meditation about truth and reality. But you don't want your team, colleague, or client to spend any time wondering if they can trust what you wrote in your email.

There are a lot of great films, books, and other stories that feature skillful use of an unreliable narrator. My recommendation is now that you know about it, you leave it there.

Writing Exercise: Rashomon

Part I: Describe something that happened at work, in your business, or in your entire career that involves more than one entity (people, animals, or things—but preferably people). Write 250 words—standard, realistic, straight narration—from your perspective. Use first-person POV ("I was talking to my client on Zoom, when...") or third-person POV ("Phillip Mandel was talking to his client on Zoom, when...").

Part II: Now, write 250 words on the same incident, but change the POV to someone else in the scene. This can also be first-person POV ("I was talking to my marketing guy, Phillip Mandel, on Zoom, when..."), or third person ("Joey Donuts was talking to his marketing guy, Phillip Mandel, on Zoom, when..."). Reflect on how the same event can appear to different people.

If there's a third or fourth entity in the action, keep going. ("I was watching my human talk to another human on that stupid screen again for an hour, and I couldn't understand why he wouldn't give me any pets or why he wouldn't give me a treat.")

Part III: Review anything you've written recently and consider what POV you're using. Is it mostly first person, where you're writing about yourself, or second person, where you're telling someone what to do? How often do you write in first person plural, representing your company as "we," and how often do you write in third person about someone else?

12: CHARACTER

That's what a thirty-one-year-old drunk woman did in one of the episodes [of *Intervention*] I watched as I signed blank sheets of paper: pulled down her pants, positioned herself just so, and defecated on the rear bumper of a parked Audi A4. As she went at it—a diamond shape blurring her from the waist down—I thought of my mother, in part because she was a lady. By this, I mean that she never wore pants, just skirts and dresses. She never left the house without makeup on and her hair styled. Whenever I see a young woman boarding a plane in her pajamas, or a guy in a T-shirt that reads YOUR HOLE IS MY GOAL, I always wonder what Mom would think.

— David Sedaris, "Why Aren't You Laughing?"
from *Calypso* (2018)

Characterization

In the quote that starts this chapter, David Sedaris plays a brilliant trick on the reader: he uses gross-out humor to paint a lovely picture of his mom. The lead-in is a convincing, deadpan description of a woman taking a dump on a car, which is then contrasted with his mother's traditional feminine manners. He furthers the characterization by contrasting her with modern slobs: people who wear pajamas on a plane (implying his mother would think it proper to wear suits and dresses on planes) or sport vulgar phrases on their clothing.

The essay is actually about his mother's alcohol abuse. As a pro, Sedaris eases the reader into serious and emotional material using his familiar, dry brand of humor. He paints an extraordinarily complex picture of his mother using comparison. He describes his mother physically by what she wore and how she did her makeup and hair. But the reader gets a more thorough and complicated view of his mother as a human, beyond her physical appearance, by imagining her judgment and horror of "slobs." Incidentally, this is also a spectacular use case of the old writing adage, **"show, don't tell"** (see Figure 27).

Characterization goes beyond physical description; in fact, it's not *much* about physical description at all. Picture two bodybuilders, or two fashion models. They're all physically beautiful, so what makes them different as people? Hairstyle? Eye color? No. It's their childhoods, their politics, their food allergies. Their hopes and dreams. Humans are endlessly complicated, and it's all about detail.

For example, perhaps instead of warning your new account manager that "This client is a nightmare," you can elucidate with more detail: "This client likes to request revisions on the

The common writing advice **"show, don't tell"** instructs a writer to describe or evoke a scene, instead of simply narrating it. In the David Sedaris quote above, he doesn't tell the reader that his "mother was prim, proper, and judgmental." He does say "She was a lady," which is open to interpretation, but then shows what being a lady means by offering the comparisons between his mother and the other "slobs."

However, "telling" is often a more expedient, direct, and straightforward—if less entertaining—way of communicating information and is preferable in situations where time is constrained, or brevity is required (such as in an email). That's why "show, don't tell" is not included as a lesson in this book, which focuses on business writing. But while you may never need such sophisticated, extraordinary, and literary use of indirect characterization in your day-to-day professional career, it is nevertheless instructive to explore what Sedaris is doing in the way he communicates his mother's personality.

Figure 27. Show, Don't Tell.

weekends and never shows up to appointments," or "This client orders two meals every time we take them to lunch."

Characters in stories (even those we tell at work) are also complicated, if less so. Peter Mendelsund, in his brilliant book *What We See When We Read* (2014), explains:

> Though we may think of characters as visible, they are more like a set of rules that determines a particular outcome. A character's physical attributes may be ornamental, but their features can also contribute to their meaning.

As a businessperson, take a moment to reflect on the people you've come across in your career: Who are the people you work with? Who are your supervisors, colleagues, and direct reports as humans? What about the other people who work in your office? The office manager, the front desk security guard, the guy who makes the sandwiches in the deli? Who are these people, as people? I guarantee this will make *you* a better person and a better communicator if you stop to think about them for a minute and try to understand them more deeply, then adjust how you communicate with them accordingly.

Lawyers, for example, seem to have a tough time turning off the "legalese." I've seen lawyers sign their emails "I trust you will find this sufficiently satisfactory," which is technically fine, I guess, but also, like, what's with the formality? I run an ad agency, not a courtroom.

PERSONAS

Another great use of characterization is to think about an ideal customer, or one segment of your customer base, as represented by a person. If you're in marketing, you've probably done a ton of consumer profiling, or creating a "persona" of your ideal customer. In this application, you may try to come up with a story about who will use your product, how they'll find it, or why they'll choose yours over the competition.

So how do you describe this person?

It's all about characterization.

Our customer is female aged 25-54, lives in the suburbs, and makes \$75–\$100K per year doesn't offer much beyond demographics. Even adding some psychographic and behavioral information only gets a bit closer to human: **Our customer is aspirational, likes to go to the movies, and has, on average, two children.**

But what if we invent a few specific characters:

Jennifer is 39 and lives in White Plains, a suburb of New York City. She's married to Martin (41) and they have two children, Mike (6) and Donna (11). She met Martin in grad school at NYU, where she was studying linguistics and he was at Stern Business School. She knew she was in love when he took her to see a showing of *Oldboy* at the Angelika Theater, and they got engaged on a hike to Kaaterskill Falls in upstate New York. She remembers those as some of the best days of her life, even though she loves her children dearly and spends most of her free time on their activities. Every morning she looks in the mirror and thinks she sees wrinkles—the beginning of crow's feet, smile lines, and new freckles. Though they are not struggling with money, they are trying to save as much as possible for a new car and for their kids' college funds. However, she is willing to spend upwards of \$200 on a new face cream—if she can be sure it works.

Now we know this person. Jennifer will buy our face cream if we use targeted advertising to reach her with a message that shows how effective our product is and plays into her nostalgia for "the good old days."

Is this manipulative? Not really—as long as the product works.

Personas and characterization can also be effective devices for storytelling, especially when your product or service is complicated, uncommon, or new (see Figure 28). Since so much of this book is about clarity and communicating information, anything that helps convey meaning is a worthwhile tool.

Characterization and **personification** allow you to demonstrate complex ideas and concepts to help people understand what you're talking about. Recently I was editing a book about the insurance industry that contained a lot of terminology and numbers. Needless to say, it was difficult to follow, and the author's intended readers were not insurance experts.

We decided to create a series of "asides" in the text wherein the author demonstrated these insurance terms in practice by describing example real-world scenarios with characters as business owners and insurance agents. Kind of like what I'm doing now.

Figure 28. Personas in Asides.

EMPATHY

As discussed with regard to Point of View, one of the most important concepts in good writing is having extreme, radical empathy for your characters. Sometimes you'll be making up characters and situations (if you're writing fiction), but they're usually, typically, in some small way, based on a nugget of truth.

This may seem like touchy-feely kind of advice, and that's because it is. But it is based on sound principles. Have you ever read a novel or story that feels like a didactic slog? This is because the author has a *message* they want to get across, and they don't think about their characters as real people. Instead, the characters are just vehicles to depict their worldview. The characters do things no rational human would ever do, and they think or say things that are unreasonable or hard to believe. It makes for bad fiction and is doubly unconvincing in business.

In addition, empathy is crucial to making a sale. It doesn't matter if you're cold calling a business to sell them a new air conditioning unit or you're "selling in" a new corporate initiative to employees or upper management. Maybe you don't "do sales," but you find your job is trying to convince your client why a certain process is the right one. At the end of the day, you're selling.

I can't believe how many times I've seen a salesperson—or any other businessperson—take the route of most resistance, which is to bulldog through what *they* want. *Buy my thing, buy my thing*, they say. They don't ask any questions, or even try to understand where the other person is coming from.

I don't think you can consistently make "sales" unless you understand the mindset and worldview of the person you're selling to. Sure, you'll get a win here and there out of luck or tenacity. Eventually *some* people will just give in to your demands out of politeness, but they won't be repeat customers. To get consistent acceptance of your ideas, products, and initiatives, you must understand where your stakeholder is coming from. What do they want and need? Why would they benefit from whatever it is you're pitching to them?

You can learn a lot by asking questions. It's easier than writing fiction, because when you "interview your characters" (a great exercise for anyone writing a novel, by the way), you have to come up with both the questions and the answers. In business, you need merely ask, nicely, and most likely the person sitting opposite you will tell you what you need to know. People love talking about themselves.

Sometimes you'll get resistance, and people won't want to open up. This is an opportunity for more empathy. Try to understand what is blocking them: Do they not have any time to talk right now? Then reschedule. Are they skeptical of you, your product, or your initiative? Try to understand why, without taking anything personally. What kind of prior experience has this person had with you, your product, or your initiative that would make them hesitant? Perhaps they are just careful, not a risk-taker, and don't want to rock the boat.

That's fair. It may be frustrating to you, but it's fair to them. Armed with this knowledge, however, you can devise a kind way to respect their risk aversion while still making them excited to hear your pitch.

Ideally, a successful negotiation ends with *both* parties feeling satisfied. Odds are you know what you want to feel good about the deal, but there's no way you can know what the other person wants unless you ask a lot of questions, actually listen to the answers, and think deeply about what they're saying. You truly need to put yourself in their place.

EMPATHY WITH EMPLOYEES AND EXPERTS

You must have empathy to succeed in business. Not only for your customers, but for your employees and colleagues as well. Sometimes entrepreneurs come up with an idea for a product or service but haven't really taken the time to think about and understand why people would want it.

Understand why your employees work for you. What do they get out of the job? Is it only money? Is there a different sort of satisfaction your workers derive from making your widgets all day? If not, can you make one?

And this goes *way* beyond putting a foosball table in the break room (which is merely a distraction, and an insulting one at that). It's about finding a purpose: How can you make each employee feel good about the work they do every day? Consider the rise of the Chief Purpose Officer or Chief Impact Officer role in many well-run companies these days. This has come from a mass rethinking of the meaning of work and how it fits in with human life and flourishing.[17]

Another benefit of radical empathy is getting expert answers to your own problems or perhaps advice on problems you didn't even know you had. If you think you know everything, you'll learn nothing. But if you admit to yourself that you will be wrong, and that you will fail, at least sometimes, you are opening yourself to the possibility of seeing how *other* people—perhaps people who are smarter or more experienced or more skilled than you in that one field—get it right.

But you have to be humble—you have to be open and willing.

MOTIVATION

> Every character should want something, even if it's only a glass of water.
>
> — Kurt Vonnegut

Character motivation is not Level One characterization, which consists of picking out a name or ensuring your character isn't a one-note stereotype. But once you've given them depth and a backstory (Level Two), you can start on Level Three characterization: finding their motivation. Why do characters do what they do in the story? What do they want? And why do they want it?

Sometimes I find this difficult in my writing because I like playing God and having characters do what *I* want them to do. Why did Sandra just hit Morgan across the face with a broom? Because it was funny! Because I *wanted* her to do it!

The risk of writing willy-nilly like this without considering the character's motivation is that the story will feel unrealistic. It's hard to find examples of movies or bestsellers where characters are not motivated, because they don't get made or do well, as motivation is such an elementary part of storytelling. However, comic book movies can sometimes feel flat because superheroes and supervillains are wooden: they are just "good" and "evil" and therefore act "good" and "evil." This is why writers give them interesting origin stories that explain why they do what they do, such as Batman's parents being murdered, or Black Panther's commitment to protecting Wakanda.

In the movie *Uncut Gems* (2019), the motivation behind Howard's actions—as despicable, foolish, and tragic as they are—is clear: he is a gambling addict.

Addiction is as strong a motivation to see as it is tragic. A person doesn't *want* to be an addict, but the addiction forces them to do things they don't want to do.

The seven deadly sins—lust, sloth, greed, envy, gluttony, pride, wrath—are all good motivators. However, sometimes it's not compelling enough just to know *that* a character is greedy (which motivates the attempted bank robbery, for example)—the audience also wants to know *why* a character is greedy.

In *Breaking Bad* (2008–2013), Walter White's motivation is clear at the beginning of the series: he's a brilliant but not affluent high school chemistry teacher, and when he gets a terminal cancer diagnosis, he decides to figure out a way to make a lot of money quickly so his family will be secure when he dies. Motivation is clear.

But then the motivation shifts. Mid-series, Walter White already has more money than he knows what to do with. His family will be fine when he dies. But he can't help going after more money. He's not greedy for money, though; he's greedy for power. He now *enjoys* what he does. It's what makes White go from a sympathetic hero to an evil antihero. In the final season, the story absolves and redeems him, in a way, by giving him a villain even more reprehensible than he (Nazis), but that's neither here nor there.

From a business perspective, the MFA lesson here is that you should look for the motivations behind what your clients and colleagues do.

Maybe your supervisor didn't bring you to the meeting because they think you don't need to be there and they sincerely don't want to waste your time (at least, that's what they told you). But maybe they're afraid you'll take their job, so they don't want to share the limelight with you. Well, why would they be so insecure? Maybe they just got a bad performance review. Maybe they're going through a divorce. Maybe they aren't insecure, but they think *you* are incompetent and don't want you to mess up their meeting.

Could it be true? *Are* you incompetent? Are you gunning for their job? Be honest.

Salespeople find the motivation behind what will make their prospect say yes. In some cases, the prospect wants to do right by their company; for example, maybe a product saves their company money, or maybe a product is more expensive but the quality is superior to the competitors. Alternately, maybe the prospect doesn't really care what the best option is, but they want to look like they're competent and forward-thinking, so they will choose a product because it's new to market and has a cool tech-heavy brand. This prospect wants to be seen in the industry as the kind of person who takes risks and is always at the cutting-edge. Or maybe the prospect enjoys being wined and dined and feels comfortable doing business with people they trust and know well.

While an author *creates* motivations for their character, in business you must *discover* the motivations of others. Sometimes it's as simple as asking.

PERSONIFICATION

Personification, as a craft tool, isn't a common topic of discussion in the MFA program—maybe it's too basic. Nevertheless, it is a useful, creative, and pervasive literary technique that allows writers to build a world and describe what's going on in it using figurative language that conveys meaning outside of the literal reality. The technique—which should be used sparingly—is when an author ascribes human characteristics to something that is not human, such as:

My phone screamed bloody murder that it was time to wake up.

First, "bloody murder" is a cliché. Secondly, my phone does not "scream" at all, and it certainly does not scream "at" anyone. It is simply programmed to beep at certain times. But this poorly-stylized sentence conveys that I, the character, felt as if my phone was screaming at me, and thus my day started out in a frenzy, full of angry emotions.

When we say Siri or Alexa is being a bitch, we're using personification.

The technique must be used sparingly and wisely, however, because it may be confusing and inaccurate. For example, a subset of personification is the *pathetic fallacy*, where you ascribe human feelings to an animal or something else in nature:

The dolphin smiled at his handler, Jennifer.

Dolphins aren't actually smiling. But their almost sinister-looking mouth, with its *terrifying* row of teeth, makes it *look* like they're smiling. So, are we conveying that this dolphin is *happy* to see Jennifer? Or are we conveying that Jennifer *thinks* the dolphin is happy to see her? The dolphin might be happy to see Jennifer, but unless the dolphin is a major character in the story—which outside of fables, Disney movies, and the occasional oddity such as Mr. Ed, anthropomorphized animals are *not* often the protagonists of human-told stories—we must assume that the writer wants to say that Jennifer is seeing the dolphin as smiling. Except Jennifer is the dolphin's handler, not a tourist visiting the aquarium for the first time—so to be true to her character, she probably knows dolphins don't smile.

In business, personification can be used to help humanize a product or brand. So much of the business world is cold and emotionless, and when it comes to making decisions or working with money, this is often a good thing. But businesses are, in fact, made of people, and humanizing your company, product, and brand—to the extent you can—will help your clients, customers, and prospects form a more meaningful connection.

Brand positioning often includes a lot of personification talk. For example, Brand X is warm, loving, open, curious, playful.

No, it's not. Brand X is a name, a logo, a color scheme, and an idea that people have about a certain product, company, or service. And the people *working* for Brand X may or may not be warm, loving, open, curious, or playful. It's actually irrelevant. The people working for Brand X may be cold, calculating, serious, astute, or hateful. But the marketers working on Brand X want customers to associate warmth, loving, openness, curiosity, and playfulness with said brand to sell more of it.

Using personification, they may say that Brand X—let's call it Dove soap—is "generous" and "welcoming to all body types." This is untrue. "Dove" is the brand name given to a product made of sodium lauryl isethionate, stearic acid, and a whole bunch of other ingredients people know nothing about (though we trust are safe).

Dove is a marketing concept and therefore cannot care whether the body being cleaned by it is fit or fat. Neither do most of the people who own shares of Unilever. Rather, these shareholders care that people are buying and using a lot of Dove soap to clean their bodies, and that Unilever continues to make a profit. If the brand managers identified a market segment of consumers who were not being targeted by other personal hygiene products because, historically, "beauty" care products were all about either aspirational beauty or making people—women, mostly—feel horrible about themselves, and were therefore a prime audience for marketing messaging, then so be it. Throw a diverse group of women in their underwear—still mostly white, mostly young, and all fairly attractive if not downright beautiful—into a print ad and call Dove soap open to women of all ages, shapes, and sizes. Sure, sure, if it moves units, great. Dove represents "all bodies."

Once it stops moving units, I'm certain "Dove" will no longer care about women of a certain size. And by the way, that's not to say I don't admire the Dove "Real Beauty" campaign or think it's a remarkable and positive thing for the world. But let's not pretend it's much more than a marketing ploy to drive sales:

This year marks ten years since Dove launched its revolutionary "Campaign for Real Beauty." Dove was looking for a way to revive its brand, so they had its PR Company, Edelman, conduct a study involving more than 3,000 women in 10 different countries to learn about women's priorities and interests. After the study reported that only 2 percent of women considered themselves beautiful, the executives at Dove saw a great opportunity. Because they were recently beginning to introduce beauty supplies, other than soap, into their product line, they thought maybe they could start a conversation about beauty.

The aim of the Dove Campaign for Real Beauty is to celebrate the natural physical differences personified by all women and to encourage them to have the confidence to be comfortable and happy with themselves. This campaign has won a handful (or two) of ad awards and has sold an enormous amount of product. Sales have increased to $4 billion today from $2.5 billion in its opening campaign year.

Not only has this campaign helped Dove successfully increase its sales (and number of awards), but it has also increased women's confidence. Research from a Harvard psychologist, Nancy Etcoff, examining the campaign then and now found that more women today describe beauty on a wider variety of qualities outside of just looks, such as confidence.

– "A PR Case Study: Dove Real Beauty Campaign," by Kiley Skene (April 2014)[18]

WRITING EXERCISE: CHARACTER

Part I: This is your chance to bring out your most wicked demons. Write about someone from your career or life you despised. Excoriate them. Describe them in all their awful glory—every stupid thing they said, everything horrific thing they did. This should be in third person, and should be about someone you no longer have to see every day:

> Joe, our Senior Engineer, was a lout. He came to work drunk every morning and his clothes looked like a toilet that hadn't been flushed in a decade. His teeth were rotting and his breath smelled like permanent fart.

Part II: Do a character interview. It can be the person from Part I, or it can be someone else from your life. You can make this all up, but ask and answer questions such as: *What are your hobbies? What is your favorite food? Who was the first person you kissed? What's your favorite color, and why? How did your parents meet? What was your mother like? What is your darkest secret, and what is your secret shame? What makes you happiest?*

Part III: Now switch to first person and write a monologue from the perspective of the person you wrote about it in Part I. Humanize this person with radical empathy. Find their motivations. Describe their day:

> My name is Joe. I've been at Mandel Marketing for nearly seven years, and though I started as a mid-level engineer, I was promoted last year to Senior Engineer. To be honest, I'm out of my depth. I suspect my wife is having an affair with her boss, and it's leading me to drink again. Things are spiraling and I know it. Yesterday, as I was tucking in my daughter, I started crying. She put her sweet baby hand on my head and said, "Daddy, why are you crying? It'll be

okay." And that only made me cry harder.

Part IV: Consider that you are writing about the same person. Were you able to find sympathy and make them, if not likable, then at least more relatable? What different muscles of your mind did you have to exercise to do this? Have you ever had to do this at work or on a project?

Now here's the *really* hard part, since it has to do with someone you're *currently* working with. Take a look at some recent communications you've had with colleagues, partners, or clients: Are you offering the same level of sympathy and empathy to them as you did to your old nemesis? See if you can revise how and what you're saying after you've looked at the project or event from the other person's perspective.

13: STORYTELLING

Writing is like driving at night in the fog. You can only see as far as your headlights, but you can make the whole trip that way.
— E. L. Doctorow, *Writers at Work: The Paris Review Interviews* (1986)

The Narrative Story Arc

Almost all good stories, at least in the Western tradition, have a story arc that follows this pattern:

- Beginning
- Middle
- End

This may seem obvious, but it's not. You wouldn't believe how many stories I read in the MFA workshop that started out strong, then petered off until the author finally just put the damn thing out of its misery by typing "THE END" after the last paragraph.

Now, yes, technically, the story did "end," but it did not have an *ending*. Nor did it have, in many cases, a middle.

How is this possible?

Maybe the writer went off on a tear with a great idea, but never fully fleshed it out in their mind. They didn't develop the characters or the plot, so instead they were left with a concept and a beginning. This also happens when a story bloats and becomes convoluted and unwieldy, like when a great show gets picked up for too many seasons and doesn't know how to end (looking at you, *Game of Thrones* and *Lost*).

To generate a satisfying sense of completeness in a joke, anecdote, story, email, or business plan, you should start with the beginning and end with the ending. Everything in between is your middle.

Sounds easy, but it isn't. It takes forethought and revision.

It doesn't mean you need to *know* the ending when you start out, but it does mean that when you ultimately press "send" or "print," or say "thank you" after your presentation, you should have arrived at a place predicted by and relevant to where you started.

Some people arrive there by discovery, as E. L. Doctorow describes in the famous quote that begins this chapter. This type of writing is also called "pantsing" because a writer starts writing a story and "flies by the seat of their pants" (cliché alert!) as they go along. Writing this way offers the freedom to make stuff up and have fun. However, it also entails more editing and rewrites, such as when you realize one of your plot lines or characters isn't working.

Other writers create long and detailed outlines that plan the story from beginning to end before ever touching pen to paper. This is difficult work but can save you headaches later.

Sometimes, writers start at the ending and work backwards.

However you choose to write, there is more to storytelling than a compelling setup or a funny punchline. The beginning and the ending should tie together thematically, and this is especially difficult to do in a first draft, because you may not know where the story is going or how it ends.

And the middle, well—the middle is where much of the good stuff is. Think of it this way: every human life story, in real life, begins and ends the same way—birth and death, respectively. What happens in the middle is the difference.

Again, this may seem obvious, but sequence is important to both the story you tell and how you tell it. And though it varies, there are a few guidelines.

Just as you wouldn't normally tell a joke by starting with a punchline, you don't, usually, want to present the ending of your story first. We all know this because 99 percent of everything we've ever read, said, or watched doesn't give away the ending in the first line. But as with all rules, this can be broken. If you need to report to your manager how the meeting went, you may skip to the outcome first, and then proceed with the details of how it all transpired.

The narrative of the novel *Time's Arrow* (1991) by Martin Amis proceeds backwards, as does Harold Pinter's play *Betrayal* (1978) and the movie *Memento* (2000). However, this technique is rare and, frankly, any kind of storytelling device like this can feel gimmicky or trite. As with second-person POV, you should have a good reason for using it, something that has thematic resonance.

You also typically don't want to start at the beginning of time, either. Otherwise, every story about a person would begin with their birth—no, their conception, as *Tristram Shandy* (1759) by Laurence Sterne does. Actually, it would have to be their *parents'* births; no, their *grandparents*...and so on and so forth until every story starts with "In the Beginning," which is, depending on your preference, the Big Bang, the Word of God, or turtles all the way down.

This would be equivalent to starting every sales presentation with Adam Smith and *The Wealth of Nations* (1776) or listing where you went to kindergarten on your résumé.

Most well-told stories, in fact, start somewhere in the very early middle, when things are already happening. This is known as "*in media res*" and allows for expository backstory to come through naturally in the storytelling. Don't get confused, however, by a movie such as *Pulp Fiction*, where the story is told *out of chronological order* (not backwards, like in the examples

> An **inciting incident** is the action or event that happens to the main character (protagonist) of a story that sends it in a new direction. It's the reason the story is being told and is the point from which the rest of the plot unfolds. Katniss Everdeen volunteering for the Hunger Games, Walter White learning he has cancer, and the sales contest in GlenGarry Glen Ross (1992) are inciting incidents.

Figure 29. Inciting Incidents.

above). The plot of the movie still begins "in media res" with an **inciting incident** (see Figure 29) that kicks off the story: when the boxer Butch (played by Bruce Willis) decides not to take a dive for Marcellus Wallace (Ving Rhames).

Consider a pitch deck, where a startup is trying to raise funds. Should we start with a slide discussing where the founders went to college? Too far back. Should we start with how much money we're asking for and what marketing strategy we'll pursue with it? Too far forward. How about we start with the inciting incident: where is the company right now, and how we imagine our future? We then talk about our patents, headcounts, and goals. *Then* we ask for the money. Beginning, middle, end.

Now consider a simple email from one colleague to another requesting help on a project. Do you start with a recap of what you had for breakfast this morning? Too far back. Do you start with when you need the deliverable? Too far forward. How about you start with a quick summary of where you're at right now and what brought you to ask for their help (the inciting incident, as it were)? Then ask for what you need, and when you need it. Beginning, middle, end.

WHAT'S AT STAKE?

An enormous part of good storytelling hinges on knowing what's at stake.

There are several components to this: *First*, what is at stake for the characters in the story? What do they stand to lose or gain? If the answer is "nothing"—or very little—then it's going to be hard for readers to care about what happens. If the answer is "everything," then it'll be hard *not* to care about what happens.

In MFA workshops, writers are often told to "raise the stakes." In many action movies, the stakes are life and death (*Die Hard, Jurassic Park, Terminator 2*), while in dramas the stakes are more emotional.

Physical stakes—dying, getting hurt—are easy to understand. Emotional stakes—happiness, jealousy, satisfaction in life—are more subjective, but just as important.

In a well-told story, there are stakes for the audience as well, as they develop emotional attachments to the characters. It can be devastating when one of your favorite characters dies, and you might even feel real grief even though the story—and the character—is fake. In fact, Hollywood is famous for changing the endings of movies that don't test well with unhappy, downer endings. The thinking is that if the audience doesn't feel satisfied or doesn't like it, then it probably won't do well in the box office.

The corollary to work is that much business communication tries to influence others and get them to take an action, whether it's to meet with you, buy your product, read your report, or understand the data you've presented.

Determine what is at stake for the person whose behavior you're trying to influence.

You know what's at stake for *you* if they don't do what you want, right? You'll lose your job. But what about them? If a potential client doesn't meet with you, perhaps they will lose out on the opportunity to learn how to reduce company expenditures, improve productivity, reach new potential consumers of their own, buy a great house, lock in a great rate on a loan. If your team doesn't read your email, maybe they will come in on Friday when the office is closed and lose out on the opportunity to sleep in. If the publisher doesn't publish Mandel's new book, the world will lose a cultural gem.

When you've figured out what's at stake, you will be better prepared to make sure your communication addresses it directly.

WHY TODAY?

Another crucial question for which a story must have an answer is "Why today?" or "Why now?" This is more tactical and grounded than "What's at stake?" because it investigates why the story takes place *when* it does, even though the answer will be informed by what is wholly at stake.

As we already discussed, no story starts at the *absolute* beginning. But it has to start somewhere, and usually the best place is as close to the action as possible.

This action is the *change* or *conflict* that's happening in the story.

So why now? Because *now* is when the change is taking place.

The original *Star Wars* trilogy (episodes IV-VI) follows Luke Skywalker's journey from country bumpkin to Jedi Master, but the movie's *storytelling* begins weeks before Obi-Wan starts training him on the Force—not when he is born.

"Why today?" is important to ask with any piece of writing. Sometimes the answer is obvious: My boss emailed this morning, so I need to email back by lunch. Our firm has a twenty-four-hour turnaround time on client deliverables. The house gets listed next week. Reports are due at the end of every month so we can forecast accurately.

But within each piece, think about the chronology of events and your scope; in other words, how much time should I cover? Does my sales report need to go back four years or four weeks? Does my client need a plan for the next six days or the next six months? Should I email my boss a summary of the entire meeting or just the part where the prospect signed the deal?

This question is also applicable to any task you're doing at work, and for your entire career. For example:

- Why am I working on this particular project today? Why am I calling on these specific businesses today? Why did this client decide to say yes to meeting with me today?

- Why do I have this particular job, at this point in my career? Am I ahead of where I thought I'd be, behind, or exactly at the right place?

The answers to questions like these will give you a renewed sense of purpose and direction with your work. If you can explain to a client why they made a good decision meeting with you today, you'll have a better chance of closing the deal. If you can give yourself a good reason to send a certain email today, then you'll get it done. Or maybe you'll realize that you *don't* need to do something today—such as clean out your inbox—because something else is more pressing.

But I also encourage you to ask yourself why you picked up this book. Why are you reading it today?

If your life was a novel and the story began today, what would happen next?

PLOT

Put simply, a plot is what happens in a story. It's the sequence of events, and just as we saw in the story arc, there is an inciting incident in the beginning; the middle, where all the things happen; and the end, when everything is resolved. (This also goes for stories that are narrated out of chronological order.) For example:

1. A hero goes questing for a magic object (a ring, a lightsaber, infinity stones).

2.   The hero encounters many trials and tribulations on his journey.

3.   The hero fights and defeats the "evil one" and comes back victorious.

The reality is more complicated, of course, and every plot has its own specific characters, setting, and timeline. But generally speaking, a main feature of a successful plot is that it keeps the story flowing and draws the reader or viewer along. This is done by raising the tension until the climax of the story, shortly after which the story ends.

In most business communication, there isn't usually a "plot," in a classical sense; however, in the examples from the previous section we can see that there is, indeed, a setup and a denouement:

1.   **We started a company.**

2.   **We are building a company and have hit a wall.**

3.   **We need money to climb over that wall.**

Or

1.   **A project landed on my desk that I can't do alone.**

2.   **I've considered all possibilities and identified you as someone who can help.**

3.   **Please help me on my project.**

Another important element of a good plot is that it does not contain events extraneous to the story. Let me reiterate: if a detail or anecdote is not pertinent to your project, leave it out. Thus, in the first example above, we don't have part 2.5 where we discuss how the original founder left the company for two years to learn how to make boats and came back after he realized that boat-making doesn't pay well.

Conflict and Solving Problems

Drama and tension arise in a good plot when a character wants something (see "Motivation" in Chapter 12) but doesn't get it, and they have to continually struggle. A character wants to have a happy marriage? Throw in a cheating spouse or a drinking problem, or a narcissistic ambition to be a movie star, and boom—achieving the happy marriage becomes very difficult.

Big, obvious conflicts appear in epics, myths, and Hollywood blockbusters. In *Lord of the Rings*, Frodo Baggins wants to throw the One Ring into the fiery pit of Mordor. It takes thousands of pages of drama and conflict for him to get there. In the aptly-titled Sylvester Stallone vehicle *Cliffhanger* (1993), Sly wants to hang on to the cliff. He does not want to fall. The entire movie, we are waiting to see if he falls. In *Star Wars*, the Rebels want to throw off the yoke of the oppressive, Sith-controlled Empire, and they enlist the Jedi to help.

There are also more quiet conflicts that appear in the internal and emotional lives of characters, and these are just as—if not more—powerful than external conflicts. In the movie *Joker* (2019), the *external* conflict of Arthur Fleck's dealings with his job, love life, and society is eclipsed by the *internal* conflict of his descent into depravity.

Fight Club (1999) is an explicit intermingling of the two: there are literal physical fights (external conflict), but the narrator's internal, mental conflict manifests in the form of Tyler Durden (spoiler alert).

Much "genre" fiction, such as murder mysteries, spy thrillers, fantasy and sci-fi, focuses on external conflict. This doesn't make it any less artistic or worthy, by the way. But because fiction, as an artistic form, uniquely allows an author to get into the head and heart of their characters in a substantial and effective way, internal and emotional conflicts can be showcased in a novel better than in any other medium. In *Crime and Punishment* (1866) by Fyodor Dostoevsky, the murder takes place at the beginning of the novel, but the next five million pages are about Raskolnikov's guilt, madness, and inner turmoil.

So now that we've agreed that a story and a plot have a beginning, middle, and end, let's look at how this applies to solving the problems that create conflict:

- Beginning: Identify problem

- Middle: Work on problem

- End: Execute solution of problem

In this book, I've identified a problem: the soul-sucking and enervating crisis of artlessness that permeates the modern business landscape. It reinforces a culture that treats workers like machine parts and grinds anything colorful and interesting into a smooth and boring grey widget.

Let's work on this problem by conceiving of a business book that utilizes graduate-level writing techniques to help folks improve themselves and their professional communication.

The solution: Write a book that applies the principles of an MFA in Creative Writing program to business.

Backstory and Flashback

Backstory is everything that happened before your story (or plot) begins. In the original *Star Wars*, the backstory to Luke becoming a Jedi is that his father, Anakin Skywalker, was a Jedi who became Darth Vader. The movie doesn't start with Anakin becoming a Jedi, though. We start *after*, "in media res," when Anakin has already become Darth Vader and Luke is about to do his Jedi thing. (And yes, it's *technically* true that Episodes I-III tell this story, but those movies came out decades after Episode IV.)

The first problem a storyteller must solve is determining

what backstory knowledge is necessary. Han Solo is an exceptional character, but we never learn much about his parents, because, ostensibly, that information is not necessary for the audience to understand and enjoy *Star Wars*.

The second problem is finding a judicious and interesting way to communicate backstory without boring the audience or interrupting the narrative flow.

One way is via narrative summary: *this happened, then this happened, then this happened.* Summary is fine in small doses but gets boring quickly and can sound like an encyclopedia article rather than a story.

Another way is in "scene," as if it's happening now, with characters, dialogue, setting, and action. This is called a "flashback."

Flashbacks get a bad rap among the writing community, but are sometimes necessary. They can provide context as well as deepen the theme and overall arc of the story—so long as they don't break the continuity of the narrative. That's the trick of successful flashback: being able to jump out of the *current* story and into a side branch of another story without interrupting the reader's flow.

The TV show *Game of Thrones* uses a mix of both. There is a huge backstory that needs to be communicated for the viewer to recognize the hundreds of characters and understand what the hell is going on. Sometimes they used dialogue, but to make it more interesting they would dress up the narrative dump with a sex scene, a joke, or a fight. For example, we learn Jamie Lannister killed the old king because of his nickname, "Kingslayer," and from the many, *many* conversations every other knight in Westeros feels the need to have with him about it—even though it happened two decades earlier.

Bran's telepathy, however, is a device that allows the audience to "see" flashbacks. We actually witness the king-slaying itself, in "real time," as a scene, in Episode 6 of Season 6, when Bran has a series of historical visions (which are flashbacks).

Flashbacks should be used with caution. Regardless of how

interesting, suspenseful, or funny it might be, a flashback must serve the current story. Otherwise, it is simply an interruption, making the story longer than it needs to be (see Chapter 9 on Brevity).

For example, while the story of the founding of your company may be serendipitous and charming, it doesn't need to be included in a pitch deck unless that information is necessary to illuminate some aspect of your product or service or helps close the deal by weaving a magical company mythos.

Branding

Anyone in marketing will tell you that storytelling is an essential part of branding, and this is true for products, companies, and individuals. It's even true for nations and ideas.

Consider the inspirational and unique story of a now-huge and successful company that was started in a garage by plucky founders who wouldn't give up. Let's see, there's Microsoft, Google, Amazon, and Apple—to name a few.

Not so unique, I guess.

What about the brilliant genius who dropped out of college to start a now-huge and successful company? Bill Gates and Mark Zuckerberg both dropped out of Harvard. Michael Dell dropped out of UT Austin. Steve Jobs dropped out of Reed college. And speaking of Steve Jobs, he took personal branding as seriously as he did that of his products, becoming instantly recognizable in a black turtleneck and jeans—though that's more about appearance and style (see Chapter 6) than storytelling.

The point is not that one needs to drop out of college and start a company in a garage to be successful, but that these are stories that have become part of company lore. Indeed, Steve Wozniak debunked some of that garage myth in 2014, noting that he and Steve Jobs never did any designing, prototyping, or manufacturing there. The Google garage is also not what it seems, either. They had already been in business for some time and received over a million dollars of venture capital funding before renting said magical garage.

The story of Facebook, too, is so mythical that it was made into a movie, *The Social Network* (2010), which stretches truth in all directions.

What about the founding of the United States? The writers of *The 1619 Project: A New Origin Story* (2021) tell a different narrative than what most people may learn from history textbooks. The stories people tell about anything from communism to capitalism to democracy, pluralism, and liberty will all affect what people think and believe about these ideas, regardless of the historical veracity.

Storytelling is, indeed, quite powerful. Use it wisely.

Writing Exercise: Telling A Story

Part I: Spend 500 words (two pages) telling the story of either your career or your company. Before you begin, decide if you prefer to start writing and see where it goes (pantsing) or plan out your story ahead of time (outlining). Or start at the end—where you are right now—and work backwards.

Part II: Reread your work. Do you have a clear beginning, middle, and end? Does the end relate to the beginning somehow? Does the beginning lead inevitably to the end? If not, what did you miss, or where did you go wrong?

Revise your story so that the beginning and end tie together.

Part III: Take a look at some recent projects you've done and create an outline of the "story" you told, including the beginning, middle, and end. Note where you started the communication and note what is backstory. Where, if at all, did you stop storytelling to jump into a flashback? What parts of the story did you leave out?

Also, where is the conflict? Did you solve it? How?

14: FIRST LINES AND SECOND PAGES

One morning, when Gregor Samsa woke from troubled dreams, he found himself transformed in his bed into a horrible cockroach.

— Franz Kafka, The Metamorphosis (1915)

WILLING PARTICIPANTS

You cannot force a reader to turn the page. This is a fact, no matter how much we writers wish otherwise.

You can't force people to stream a television show, go to a movie theater, or look at a painting.

In the MFA program, I read a lot of great literature—novels and stories that were funny, exciting, poignant, and gripping. I couldn't help but turn the page to see what happened next. There are many ways authors accomplish this, and these tools have their basis in all the craft techniques discussed in Part II of this book.

I also read a ton of awful, putrid, half-formed goblins that I had to *force* myself to finish because they were workshop stories. And I took comfort in knowing these were first drafts and would be revised into great pieces.

So how do you keep the reader *wanting* to turn pages?

You can't *force* them to. Especially not now, in the age of social media and constant messaging and extreme attention diversion. Just look at how many apps you have on your phone.

The same goes in business. You have limited opportunity to gain the attention and mental energy of your potential clients, your current clients, your employees, your colleagues. Sure, in some instances you can *compel* people to listen to you. If you're the boss, they'll laugh politely and obsequiously at your jokes, whether or not they're funny, and if you call an all-hands, they'll probably show. But how many will even be listening?

And what if you're *not* the boss?

I learned this lesson early in my career. It was my first big presentation in front of my client, which was an enormous, global CPG (consumer packaged goods) firm that made delicious cookies and other snacks.

This company was constantly "innovating" (a word I don't love), as their research showed any new SKU would generate sales simply because a certain number of bored, unhappy people would buy the product just to try it out, regardless of how gross it was, just to have a diversion from their daily ennui. Under their world-famous peanut brand they released a line of deep-fried peanuts that performed so dismally they were discontinued as quickly and wholly as if they were poison. My colleagues found them "disgusting," "unsettling," and "too chewy to be natural." I thought they were delicious, though, and because we were allowed to buy product from the company store at discount, and because I had no money, I bought bags and bags of these repellent, tasty little abominations, these "nut poppers" (even the name sounds vaguely obscene), and I couldn't stop "popping" them, until one afternoon my guts finally erupted and I sprinted from my cubicle to the bathroom, alarmed and horrified at what sin I'd committed upon myself.

In any event, my company had a learn-by-doing approach that allowed me and the other lowly assistant on the team to each take a handful of slides to present to the brand managers.

On the drive back to the office, one of my supervisors (I had seven bosses at the time, just like in the movie *Office Space*) told me and the other assistant we were "rock stars," presumably for having just presented—too quickly and in muttered, half-terrified murmurs that were near-indistinguishable from a child's cry—a handful of meaningless competitive market research slides. Being called a rock star for this was almost insulting—like she was being sarcastic.

But I choose to believe she was being sincere. She wanted to boost our spirits because she, as well as everyone else on my team, saw what I saw as I was standing in the darkened conference room in front of the projector: all five MBA-toting brand managers staring at the floor, faces bathed in the cold blue light of their Blackberry screens, presumably checking their email. The odious, muted *tap-tap-tap* of their grubby fingers typing on those stupid little keyboards still haunts me, not unlike infantry veterans hearing echoes of the *rap-rap-rap* report of M-16 fire in the Vietnamese jungle.

Anyway. I resented those asshole clients for looking at their phones for the entirety of my first client presentation ever. Who would do such a thing?

Well, everyone.

Because that shit was boring. It was boring research, it was a boring presentation, and it was presented in a boring way, despite my attempts to sound enthused.

In retrospect, I shouldn't blame them for looking at their phones, despite the lack of manners. But this was 2004, *before* apps. Before Instagram and TikTok and SchmikSchmuck and FartFuck, and whatever other addicting software was invented to steal your attention and siphon your brain juice.

Nevertheless, our presentation was *so* boring, so corporate, so full of cliché and logorrhea that these people would rather do anything but listen to me present those dumb slides.

The point is: you cannot force people to pay attention to you. Not now, not ever. You have to make them *want* to pay attention. That means you have to keep the boring stuff to a minimum. You have to use humor (if you can—and if you can't, find someone who can help you), shock, awe, surprise, intrigue, suspense—anything that makes a person lift their face from their phone, look at you, and go, "Huh? What was that?"

THE FIRST LINE

Oceans of ink have been spilled about first lines already, because they are so important. Here is just a puddle's worth more, because it applies to business as much as it does to literature. How you start will often dictate how the rest of the voyage will go (see Chapter 17 for more on "flow").

The first line must grip a reader's attention and entice them to keep reading.

Do research and you'll unearth countless lists of great first lines, so I need not repeat them all here. But a few examples are worth examining. The first line of *One Hundred Years of Solitude* (1967) by Gabriel Garcia Marquez brings chills:

> Many years later, as he faced the firing squad, Colonel Aureliano Buendía was to remember that distant afternoon when his father took him to discover ice.

So much is happening: we have a character and a firing squad; we have memory, discovery, and a *very* strange timeline. An entire universe is adumbrated in a few words, piquing enough interest to find out what is going to happen in the rest of this story.

Another great first line is from *The Metamorphosis* (quoted at the beginning of this chapter). Kafka jumps right into a strange world and presents conflict: dude wakes up as an insect (also translated as "vermin").

The first line of *Confessions of an Indian Woman Eater* (1971) by Sasthi Brata contains an interesting hook and an evocative, original metaphor:

I now realize that leaving home was a gesture, like goodbye notes from failed suicides.

Great first lines invoke mystery, such as Margaret Atwood's *The Handmaid's Tale* (1985):

We slept in what had once been the gymnasium.

The reader jumps directly into this novel wondering who was sleeping in the gymnasium, and why it is no longer a gymnasium. What happened to the gymnasium?!?!?!

George Orwell creates similar mystery in *1984* with one simple line of world-building:

It was a bright cold day in April, and the clocks were striking thirteen.

On the other hand, *bad* first lines also abound, though in these cases most people never make it to see if the rest of the book is just as bad. Perhaps the most famous is from Edward Bulwer-Lytton, who began his 1830 novel *Paul Clifford* with this:

It was a dark and stormy night; the rain fell in torrents— except at occasional intervals, when it was checked by a violent gust of wind which swept up the streets (for it is in London that our scene lies), rattling along the housetops, and fiercely agitating the scanty flame of the lamps that struggled against the darkness.

At this point, the phrase "it was a dark and stormy night" is a cliché to rival clichés, but the point is that starting a story with a clunker of a sentence like this does not invite further reading.

When you're starting your business communication—emails, sales presentations, competitive reports, meetings, whatever it is—try to be interesting and evocative with your first line. So often I've known from the beginning of a meeting that what followed would be terrible. It's hard to concentrate when you're already thinking, *Damn, I'll never get this hour of my life back.* Starting a meeting with five minutes of trying to get your computer to work or rehashing everything that was said in the last meeting—these are good ways of failing before you've begun.

You might be at this point thinking, *Sure, Phil, that's all well and good when you're starting a* novel. *But I'm starting a business communication, which is, in its very nature, boring.* Possibly—but nonfiction doesn't have to be boring. Consider the opening of *Our Band Could Be Your Life: Scenes from the American Indie Underground 1981–1991* by Michael Azerrad (2001):

> On September 24, 1991, an album called *Nevermind* by a band called Nirvana came out, went gold in a matter of weeks, bumped Michael Jackson off the number one spot on the *Billboard* album charts soon afterward, and prompted music journalist Gina Arnold to proclaim, "We won." But who was "we"? And why were "we" so different from "them"?

He states the questions that his book will answer: What was the "indie underground" music scene of the 1980s, and what made it so exciting and different from mainstream pop culture?

Wait! You're not saying. *That book is about music, which is inherently interesting! The story I have to tell is about corporate governance!*

Fair enough. And truth be told, it's easy to fall into the trap of echoing your boring material with a boring beginning. The preface to *Book Collecting: A Modern Guide* (1985) begins thusly:

> There are many people who read and accumulate books, but who can in no way be considered collectors, because their book buying is without direction.

That's just the preface, however. In the *introduction* to this miserable tome about book collecting, Frederick B. Adams, Jr. tries to be more interesting:

> The age of luxury in American book collecting ended with the spectacular fireworks of the Jerome Kern sale in 1929.

Adams is at least *attempting* to "spark" some excitement with the phrase "spectacular fireworks" (though you still might think it's a "dud").

Economics is called "the dismal science" for a reason. Consider the snore-inducing first line of the weirdly titled book *Economics, Peace and Laughter* (1971) by John K. Galbraith:

> In this article, I suggest the social problems, and therewith the political tasks, which become most important with a relatively advanced state of economic development.

You have to read this terrible sentence several times just to figure out what he's saying. Don't write like this, please—and definitely don't write *emails* like this, if you ever want them to be read.

As a counterpoint, though, let's look at the remarkable first sentence of the Introduction to Ray Dalio's *Principles* (2017):

> Before I begin telling you what I think, I want to establish that I'm a "dumb shit" who doesn't know much relative to what I need to know.

Dalio is a billionaire, but establishes an approachable, no-nonsense voice and tone for his book—even if it's a persona—with the phrase "dumb shit."

WRITING MANY, MANY FIRST LINES

So how does one create a great first line?

Truthfully, nobody knows. There's no secret to it. But it's helpful to know that writers spend countless hours revising their first lines. They probably spend more time on the first and last lines of their books than anything else. They take everything and put it into that first line. It sets the tone for the piece; it needs to arouse the reader's curiosity, create tension, suspense, interest, and mystery, and be beautiful. It sets up a series of promises that the book will fulfill.

You want to demonstrate that you, as an author, know what you're doing and that the reader is in good hands. You are establishing your authoritative voice and making a promise to deliver something: entertainment, knowledge, information, emotional release. You are assuring the reader that however long it takes to read the rest of the work (from twenty hours for a novel to ten minutes for a poem to ninety seconds for an email) will be well spent.

Unfortunately, the creativity evinced in creative writing is not always taken to the business book world, though the promise of the first line is. I find it surprising anyone would continue reading past the wooden first line of Stephen Covey's bajillion-selling book *The 7 Habits of Highly Effective People* (1989), but surely they must have. Probably because the promise of solving these common problems is so compelling:

> In more than 25 years of working with people in business, university, and marriage and family settings, I have come in contact with many individuals who have achieved an incredible degree of outward success, but have found themselves struggling with an inner hunger, a deep need for personal congruency and effectiveness and for healthy, growing relationships with other people.

Contrast this with the bold opening of *Built To Last* (1994) by Collins and Porras, which is more voice-driven and stylish:

> This is not a book about charismatic visionary leaders. It is not even about visionary product concepts or visionary market insights. Nor even is it about just having a corporate vision.
> This is a book about something far more important, enduring, and substantial. This is a book about **visionary companies**.

There are no rules for starting a novel, though one common guideline is to *not* start with dialogue (I'm sure great examples can be found). This is because dialogue, in a vacuum, has no context. The reader doesn't know who is speaking, or to whom, or where, or why. And while novels have creative license, business communication has much less leeway. So don't start an email,

And that's why we're doing it this way.

Rather than arousing a reader's curiosity, you're creating frustration. Note how in the examples above, the reader is given the information they need to keep reading. Covey begins with a very explicit announcement of what his book will be about—and clues as to how dry and boring it'll be, while Collins and Parras get there by the fourth line (but by using nine fewer words).

If the first sentence—or first page at most—doesn't launch the flow of reading for your reader, you'll have a difficult time convincing them to turn to page two.

THE PLEASURE OF READING (OR MEETING YOU HALFWAY)

After that remarkable and brilliant first line you spent three hours formulating, know that people will only keep turning your pages willingly if they continue finding it worthwhile.

For nonfiction, the reward might be knowledge about a subject, or wisdom about life—even if the prose is dull, and with a novel comes the emotional experience and pleasure of reading it.

The process of imagination is what makes reading pleasurable. The reader actively participates in creating the story, as the author can only provide so much information in words. In fact, being deeply absorbed in a good book (good to *you*) can be a more pleasurable experience than watching a good movie, because the former is an active experience, while the latter is a passive one. To be fair, however, movies have more to play with beyond just plot and dialogue, such as the score, the setting, or the colors, and I have watched certain movies (*Terminator 2* and *Goodfellas* come to mind) far more times than I've read any single book.

But I'm not sure I've ever felt as connected to a character in a movie as I have in a novel. I've also never spent weeks of my life and hours each day watching the same movie, as I have with great books.

Discovery is another aspect that makes reading fun. Good writing has clues that pay off later in the book, and this goes for more than just mystery novels. The audience loves to figure things out right before they're told, and then, even if they're right or wrong, it's still a thrilling experience.

It's because readers actively participate in the story. In essence, the author only presents half the story, and the reader, by necessity, fills in the rest. One of the first novels ever written (and still one of the most experimental) is *Tristram Shandy* by Laurence Sterne, who wrote:

No author, who understands the just boundaries of decorum and good breeding, would presume to think all: the truest respect which you can pay to the reader's understanding is to half this matter amicably, and leave him something to imagine, in his turn, as well as yourself.

So how can you make your business writing more pleasurable for your coworkers and colleagues? Simple: invite and allow them to participate.

Take the cue from Stephen Covey and Collins / Parras: let people know what to expect and provide a compelling reason for them to continue reading (or listening). Allow for your audience or reader to put themselves into the world you're creating by relating it back to them—what does your information mean to their life or career, and what is the reward for sticking with you until the end?

Perhaps add some humor to lighten the tone, vivid anecdotes or creativity to make things more interesting, or foreshadow how what you write will make their life or job better.

If there are details your audience can fill in, or information they already know, then don't bore them with it—let them meet you halfway by helping you create the world of your communication.

No matter what you do, though, don't be vague or confuse your audience. Don't bore them. And for God's sake, for the one-millionth time, don't interrupt the flow of reading.

Trust Your Audience

There's another corollary to audience participation that relates to business, and it's about trust.

The author must trust that their reader *will* meet them halfway. That they will get it. This error of judgment on behalf of the creator happens all the time:

- A joke explained in a movie

- A reaction shot from another character to make sure the audience knows they're supposed to laugh

- A laugh track in a sitcom

- A swell of cinematic orchestral strings accompanying an obviously emotional scene

This is why, though I've defined a couple of terms in this book, I trust you will look up words don't you know if you feel compelled to.

Micromanaging your audience is just as bad as micromanaging your staff. Managers should trust that their employees can and will accomplish the tasks they've been hired to do. If you don't think they can do the work, then let them go (euphemism alert!). But don't spend all your time tracking every minuscule detail of it, or worse, doing it for them. There's no pleasure in that. It's miserable. It's no way to live.

WRITING EXERCISE: FIRST LINES AND SECOND PAGES

Part I: Gather a dozen or so pieces of communication from the past week or so—emails, reports, memos, anything—that you have both written and received. Look at the first lines of each: Do they make promises, establish authority, or induce you to keep reading? Why or why not?

Do the same for some articles you've read recently. Notice how journalism should, if written well, have both compelling headlines (that make you click) *and* compelling first lines (that make you read the rest of the article).

Now think back to some of your favorite books. Think hard. What made you enjoy these books? What stuck with you, and why did you enjoy the experience? Was it what you learned? Was it exciting? Was it emotional?

Part II: For anything you have written recently, try to come up with a better first line.

Part III: This is an ongoing exercise. The next few times you have to write anything—emails, presentations, reports, text messages—come up with a half-dozen first lines before sending it out. See what you get, and then pick the most enticing one.

15: THEME

That which is hateful to you, do not do to another: This is the whole Torah. The rest is commentary. Now go study.

— Hillel

WHAT IS THEME?

You needn't be a Talmudic scholar to appreciate Hillel's distillation of one of the most important books in human history into a single pithy theme ("Don't be an asshole"). You just need to be human. Hillel isn't saying that the rest of the Torah doesn't matter, he's saying it builds on this theme and is worth spending one's life studying it.

At first glance, the concept of "theme" might seem kind of squishy, as it can feel subjective, open to interpretation, and vague. And while the theme (or themes) of a single novel or movie might be ambiguous, the concept of theme itself is not.

Most people kind of "get" theme inherently because we've all been exposed to so many stories since childhood. Theme is the underlying subject, or what a story is "about," beyond the plot or premise. For example, the **virtue of persistence** figures in "The Itsy Bitsy Spider," Aesop's tortoise and hare, Disney's *Homeward Bound* (1993), and Marvel superhero Wolverine.

Typically, there is more than one theme in a given story. In *Star Wars*, "Good vs. Evil" is one overarching theme of the series:

- Jedi & Rebels = Good

- Sith & the Empire = Evil.

It's so black and white that characters who blur the lines, such as Darth Vader, Han Solo, Kylo Ren, Luke, and Rey are so compelling. Yoda and Emperor Palpatine are fun, but they don't have a ton of nuance.

But another, deeper theme in *Star Wars* is free will and personal choice. Does Anakin Skywalker have control of his destiny, or must he inevitably join the Dark Side?

When I was growing up in the '80s and '90s, sitcoms had "Very Special Episodes" that contained a "life lesson" as their one-time theme. An example is the notorious "I'm so excited" episode of *Saved by the Bell*,[19] in which Jessie Spano is not, in fact, saved by the titular Bell, but instead saved by blond-Jesus Zack Morris after getting addicted to caffeine pills in an effort to keep up both her high school studies and her new singing group, "Hot Sundae." If this grotesque and nonsensical premise hasn't already turned you off, the acting certainly will. Besides, I've been addicted to caffeine since I was fifteen and I'm no worse for wear. Anyway, the theme of this episode was that you shouldn't put so much pressure on yourself to succeed that you unintentionally harm yourself in the process.

Something like that.

The theme of any piece of writing isn't accidental, though when a writer begins they may not know what it ultimately will be. For example, you may start writing a story about surviving the zombie apocalypse but end up depicting how humans in anarchy are a much more dangerous and scary enemy (see *The Walking Dead*).

It all depends on the questions you're trying to answer. It's a bit nebulous, but the questions can range from very specific:

- What would the Wars of the Roses look like in a medieval-style land called Westeros, with all of the political intrigue, military strategy, and noblesse oblige, but also with dragons, dark magic, and a zombie army invasion? This is the plot of *Game of Thrones*.

to the very general:

- What is the point of life? Asked in Somerset Maugham's *A Razor's Edge* (1944).

- Can a woman be happy in a bad marriage? Gustave Flaubert tackles this in *Madame Bovary* (1856).

- Can money make you happy? See F. Scott Fitzgerald's *The Great Gatsby* (1925), *The Sound and the Fury* (1929) by William Faulkner, or *Money* (1984) by Martin Amis (though the full title of Amis's book spoils his answer, which is *Money: A Suicide Note*).

Maybe you just have an interesting idea or premise: *A struggling writer takes a trip around the world in the wake of his ex-boyfriend's impending marriage*—the award-winning and marvelous novel *Less* (2017) by Andrew Sean Greer. Or *killer robots and artificial intelligence* (pick one of many).

The process of discovery is in the writing, and this is the thrill of art-making.

Similarly, in business you may think you're writing a simple status report of recent sales, but end up with a wide-ranging blueprint for boosting the entire team's performance. Each piece of business communication has a set of specific questions it's trying to answer:

- How much profit did our company make last quarter?

- What project should you, my employee, take on next?

- How can my software skills help you, the prospective customer?

- What are the advantages of this house and property at this price?

Resonance

As we discussed in Chapter 9 (on Brevity), all elements of a well-told story must have thematic resonance, or they should be cut.

If a character has only one eye, there should be a reason for it, such as the character's other eye was pecked out by a raven on a midnight sojourn to the Wishing Well. Whatever it is, if the cyclopticism doesn't somehow relate to the story at large, it'll be distracting, fall flat, and seem false to the audience or reader. Something will feel "off."

Similarly, if your sales report suddenly digresses into what type of coffee should be in the break room, it better be because the sales team prefers that kind of coffee and will drink more of it, thereby getting amped up on caffeine and making more cold calls.

If your "Digital Security Tip of the Week" references a *Seinfeld* episode, it better be because Jerry left his apartment door unlocked too much, and this is why you need a VPN or to change your password.

Speaking of *Seinfeld*, the show was ostensibly "about nothing," but in fact every episode is so tightly plotted that no scene, no action, no line of dialogue, and no joke appears in the show that does not tie back into something else in that episode. It's as cohesive and organized as the molecules of a diamond.

In business, you should make sure you understand the theme of your work, and make sure all elements of your work contain resonance with that theme.

Identifying Theme

So how do you figure out what it is you're talking about? Well, this takes some deep thinking, but isn't all that *difficult*. Start by answering some questions:

- What are you trying to say?
  - Are you teaching a skill to someone or educating a team about a product or service?
  - Are you trying to convince somone of something?

- Why are you writing?
  - What do you get out of this document, and what should your audience get out of it?
  - Could this email be a phone call instead, or this presentation be a memo?

- What are your goals?
  - Are you trying to change a mindset throughout the company?
  - Are you helping define process or operations for a specific team?

- How does this apply to your audience's life, both in and out of work?
  - Does it affect daily work life, or a once-a-year decision-making process?
  - Does it affect everyone in the company, or just a handful of people?

Unlike in the rest of the book, here I don't want you to overthink. There are usually several themes in a story, just as there may be several themes in a project at work. For example, the themes of a marketing presentation might be:

- Social media marketing will help your company grow because of X.

- We have the expertise to help you do social media marketing because of Y.

- Here are specific elements of social media marketing and how much they cost.

- You should work with us because of Z.

It doesn't have to be complicated. Here are some themes of *An MFA for Your MBA*:

- Business communication is essential to everyday life, especially for knowledge workers, and getting better at it will improve both their working life and their careers.

- Writing, public speaking, and interpersonal speech are the most common forms of business communication.

- Writing skills can be learned.

- While the quality of professional communication—especially business writing—is often putrid and/or deteriorating, it can be improved through several specific tactics.

- Through my personal experience and erudition, I, Phillip Mandel, have the knowledge and expertise to help businesspeople become better writers.

Despite my many (hilarious) digressions, nothing in this book appears that isn't relevant, in some way, to those themes. I don't have any asides about the New York Jets, for example, or my favorite pastime, *Magic: The Gathering*.

Much of the work of identifying theme will be done after your first draft is complete, as you're starting to revise. This is because you may not know, definitively, what your theme is (or should be), and what to look for, until you've finished writing.

And the theme may change. You might start a blog post about VPNs but end up discussing password security and phishing scams as well. The sales presentation that goes into every service your company offers may eventually be honed into a few specific slides about one product. A real estate listing that relies heavily on a description of the above-ground pool may end up focusing on the neighborhood and school district.

After completing your first draft, go back and review every element. Every paragraph, every line, every slide, every statistic, chart, and image. Even for a five-minute email, ask yourself: How does this sentence or word relate to the topic and theme at large?

If it doesn't, then figure out a way to make it applicable to your theme, or cut it.

Be honest with yourself. The value of brevity is a key theme of this book. Just as with cutting clichés, you should try to cut anything that doesn't have thematic resonance.

WRITING EXERCISE: THEME

Part I: Find two pieces of communication you've written recently, in different modes (one email and one slide presentation, or one TV script and one letter). Read through and identify the main theme of the piece, as well as any other themes. Write these down.

Part II: Re-read your pieces and highlight any details or elements that were not on theme. Hopefully, much of what you wrote was on theme, but there may always be a few lines that slip by—especially if you're not in the regular habit of revising carefully before sending out work.

Now ask yourself, why did you include these lines? Were you perhaps trying to pad the document so it was longer and seemed more important? Should you have written a follow-up document that included these points, or perhaps made the current document larger in scope? Could you have rewritten these lines so that there was more thematic resonance? Or should you have simply cut them?

Thematic resonance is sometimes recognizable only *after*

the initial draft of a work is completed. You may not know exactly what you're trying to say—or every part of what you're trying to say—when you set out, which is why the process of writing is also the process of thinking. Only in revision will you be able to identify and cut (or edit) elements that aren't on theme.

16: ADVANCED BASICS

If you want to make an audience laugh, you dress a man up like an old lady and push her down the stairs. If you want to make comedy writers laugh, you push an actual old lady down the stairs.

— Tina Fey

DIALOGUE

Entire books have been written about dialogue, so I'll be brief. Writing dialogue is difficult. It must be interesting as well as move the story along, whether plot-wise, thematically, or by developing character. Any line of dialogue that doesn't accomplish one of these three is superfluous and can be cut.

In a first draft, you might see a boring, straightforward conversation with obvious and stupid lines being said by characters, making the writing clunky and difficult to read. It's a hallmark of amateur writing and needs to be fixed for someone to have any chance at publication.

See how boring dialogue is with no tension or conflict:

"It is sunny outside."
> **"Yes, it is sunny, and I like when the sun shines."**
> **"I like when the sun shines, too."**

Another characteristic of bad dialogue is when characters tell each other things they already know. This is sometimes used as a way for the author to communicate information, because long narrative exposition can get boring and feel like an "info dump." However, wedging information into conversation rarely reads well:

> **"Hello, my cousin Dirk. How fares your younger brother Jason, also my cousin, at the medical school in Ohio which he got into last year?"**
>
> **"Hi, my cousin Amy. Dirk is doing well. He is still driving the Mitsubishi Eclipse from 1995 with the dented door and cracked windshield that you gave him last year for an even swap of his baseball card collection."**

Much of what each character said, the other would have already known (even if the reader didn't). This is clunky dialogue—even though it's chock full of details and information—and feels "off." It doesn't feel true to how people would talk to each other.

The lesson for business communication is simple: don't waste time with superfluous details or by telling people what they already know. It's boring. It's uninteresting. You have a limited amount of people's time and attention, so use it wisely. Make sure everything you write moves your story along.

But maybe you *do* have to recap or summarize where things stand, even though the other person may know some of that information already. Or perhaps you need to set up what comes next. That's fine, just keep it brief. Or find a way to make it interesting, such as with a non-lame joke, a vivid detail, or an evocative comparison.

Subtext

Dialogue can be also uninteresting when it lacks subtext. This is the information that is conveyed without being said explicitly. It occurs constantly, in both interpersonal communication and business, through body language, tone, and in conversations such as this:

> **Amy cornered her cousin Dirk at the bowl of potato chips. "How's Shithead?" she said.**
>
> **Dirk raised an eyebrow.**
>
> **"I mean Jason."**
>
> **"He's fine."**
>
> **"Fine?"**
>
> **"You suddenly having hearing problems?"**
>
> **Amy crunched on a particularly salty chip. "Is it difficult? First year is supposed to be—"**
>
> **"I can barely get him on the phone," Dirk said.**
>
> **"How about my old Mitsubishi Eclipse?"**
>
> **Dirk thought about that deathtrap his brother was driving around Ohio, with the dented door and cracked windshield. "Still runs," he said. "Though I'm glad the med school is attached to a hospital. You still have his baseball card collection?"**
>
> **Amy shook her head, unable to repress a smile. "It was more valuable than either of you thought."**

What we see here is called *subtext*. Nowhere in the conversation do they actually say it, but it's clear the cousins all hate each other, and Amy screwed Jason over. And for those of you keeping score, this is an example of omniscient POV, as we are in both Amy's and Dirk's heads.

Subtext is a powerful tool for communicating information without saying it. We use it in business all the time, probably unintentionally. In the email below, there is a very un-subtle subtext coming through:

> **Dear Team,**
>
> **Sales managers from corporate will be going out on calls with all of you next week and will be reporting on**

the performance to senior management. Have fun and make sure you've set up a bunch of great meetings!

The text of the email is simple, but the underlying subtext is clear: don't perform well, and upper management will know. The subtext of them knowing further implies that poor-performing salespeople may face some kind of punishment and/or get fired.

Sometimes people take subtext too far. Have you ever read a novel or watched a movie where none of the characters seem to be having the same conversation? People talking past each other happens in life all the time, but most people I know take pains to at least *try* to be straightforward with each other. Yet I've seen MFA workshop stories with dialogue like this:

Amy cornered her cousin Dirk at the bowl of potato chips. "How's Jason?" she said.

Dirk looked at her. "These chips are too salty."

Amy nodded. "First year is like a swimming pool full of shark blood."

"I can barely get him on the phone," Dirk said.

"How about the old Mitsubishi Eclipse?"

Dirk thought about that deathtrap his brother was driving around Ohio, with the dented door and cracked windshield. "I ripped out all the pages in my old copy of *The Catcher in the Rye*," he said. "You still have his baseball cards?"

Amy shook her head, unable to repress a smile. "My eBay password is RQ!45MN-OX&-LO3$4," she said.

What the fuck are they talking about?

Vague and subtle subtext can get overdone quickly, and the lesson for business writing is this: stay on subject. Don't be overly confusing, mysterious, or clever. Don't be so obvious that you're telling someone something they already know, but also don't be so coy as to leave people wondering what you're talking about.

Humor

Humor is as difficult to explain as it is to do. This is the German philosopher Arthur Schopenhauer's definition in *The World as Will and Representation* (1818):

> The cause of laughter in every case is simply the sudden perception of the incongruity between a concept and the real objects which have been thought through it in some relation, and laughter itself is just the expression of this incongruity.

I mean, he really gets it, huh?
Perhaps Mel Brooks can describe it better:

> Tragedy is when I cut my finger. Comedy is when you fall into the sewer and die.

Some people say comedy is simply tragedy plus time, but I find that reductive. In any case, whatever humor is, or however it works, it's an element of writing that can be devastatingly impactful when done well. Making your reader laugh puts them in a good mood and disarms them. It prepares them to receive whatever information you need to impart.

Still, humor has a rather modest place in business communication. If you're not careful, too much humor can border on silliness and undermine what you're saying. But one surprise joke can be wonderful in an otherwise serious and formal situation.

Humor isn't really taught in the MFA program. Being funny can't be taught, though like everything else, joke-telling, timing, and creative thinking can be *practiced*. You can get better at reacting quickly, but you don't suddenly become a comedian. Serious folks say funny things now and again, but if it's not one of your strengths (and be honest with yourself), then don't force it.

Writing funny is extremely difficult. I know this because I'm sometimes a funny writer (though not everyone thinks so), and I've read widely enough to know how rare this is. And I'm not saying this to brag—some of my work is funny, some of it isn't, and there is a cruel pain when you *try* to write something funny and people don't laugh—but that's just the style I like to write.

However, *forced* humor does the opposite of what you intend: it sets people on edge, it induces cringes, and it makes people unreceptive to your message.

Also, this should go without saying, but humor is subjective. What you find funny might be a sensitive subject and offensive to someone else. The entire TV show *The Office* was based on this premise.

BEING CLEVER VS. BEING PROFOUND

Just as being funny is difficult, being clever is no small feat either. But sometimes people mistake something clever for something "profound." The two aren't necessarily connected.

These two examples from my ad agency days were meant to be profound, but were instead just sort of clever:

- A branding agency bragged how smart they were for telling Burger King executives the "Have it your way" campaign wasn't reflected in the actual experience of going to Burger King—even from the outset, because the door only opened one way. The door should open by pushing *or* pulling, they said, so that the customer truly "has it their way." This is a clever idea—but also pointless.

- Ad lore features an oft-repeated story of how a car named "Chevy Nova" didn't sell in Mexico because in Spanish the words "no va" means "no go." I've heard this same anecdote repeated at least a dozen times, and the first time I heard it was like, "huh." It just didn't *feel* true. It seemed too clever, too ... perfect. And it isn't true.

The lesson is to be judicious with being "clever." A snide remark can come off offensive, and a sharp witticism doesn't necessarily mean anything. Worse, being too clever can feel inauthentic, or like you're trying too hard. It can also feel cagey, leading to suspicion or mistrust in your reader. And despite your own self-satisfaction at your savvy remark, this will only serve to make your job of communicating information more difficult.

Satire and Parody

"Surely you can't be serious."
"I am, and don't call me Shirley."

— Airplane! (1980)

Satire is when you make fun of something to produce a didactic effect (to "teach"). It uses irony, sarcasm, ridicule, humor, exaggeration, hyperbole—all things I love to put in my writing—to expose and criticize, usually an aspect of the contemporary public consciousness, politics, or recent history.

Mike Judge wrote many satires, including the movies *Office Space* (1999) and *Idiocracy* (2006), as well as the TV series *Silicon Valley* (2014–2019).

Sadly, satire doesn't have much of a place in everyday business communication, except for perhaps the rare oddball corporate video HR produces for a team-building exercise. We often need to be more forthright and sincere in our language. But as a fan of satire, I didn't want to skip at least mentioning it as a literary device.

Parody can sometimes be confused with satire because it also pokes fun. The difference is that parody mimics the original, often exaggerating for comedic effect, but doesn't really make a commentary on it. *Airplane!* Is a parody of Hollywood disaster movies, especially the 1957 film *Zero Hour!*, with which it shares a similar plot and character names (Ted Stryker), just as *Scary Movie* (2000) is a parody of slasher films. As far as I can tell, however, neither parody makes any kind of critique on the human condition; the gags are all just in the name of getting a laugh. (And making money: *Scary Movie* grossed $278 million at the box office on a $19 million budget, while *Airplane* made $171 million on a $3.5 million budget.)

IRONY

It's like ten thousand spoons when all you need is a knife. It's meeting the man of my dreams, and then meeting his beautiful wife.

— Alanis Morissette, "Ironic"

This book is strongly against cliché, and it is a cliché to point out that the song "Ironic" by Alanis Morissette doesn't depict irony, but rather coincidence, paradox, misfortune, bad news, and bad luck.

But I can't help myself. And it's instructive nonetheless.

Irony is hard to define. Most people think of it in the same way old Supreme Court justices thought of obscenity: you know it when you see it. But as evidenced in the above quote, this isn't true. Irony does have a definition. There are three types of irony:

- *Dramatic* irony is when the audience knows something in a story that the characters within the story do not. It adds suspense, because the audience is waiting for the consequences of whatever they know to happen to the characters that don't know.

- *Situational* irony is when something happens that has the opposite effect of what's intended. There is this great O. Henry short story called "The Gift of the Magi" wherein a destitute young couple wants to buy each other Christmas gifts. The dude sells his pocket watch to buy a set of combs for his wife, while his wife sells her hair to buy a chain for her husband's watch. Lo, they can't use either gift!

- *Verbal* irony is when you write or say something other than what you intend, such as understatement and overstatement. In Morissette's song "Ironic," it is *not* ironic that the first flight Mr. Play It Safe ever takes crashes. It is purely bad luck, or coincidence. Or nothing at all—it's just an event that occurs. However, his thought as the plane crashes, "Well isn't this nice," *is* an example of verbal irony (because it *isn't* nice that his plane is crashing). Verbal irony can be used for comic effect, or to make a point. Sarcasm and snark are forms of verbal irony, favored by yours truly, and are meaner and more irreverent, usually intended to ridicule something or someone.

Unintended situational irony pervades modern business and life. For example, it's ironic that the advent of technology—which was supposed to make life easier and free people from the burden of working forty hours a week (at least, according to John Maynard Keynes in his *Economic Possibilities for our Grandchildren* in 1930)—has, despite (or perhaps because of) increasing people's productivity, instead only made people work *more.*

Likewise, it is tragic situational irony that so many people got out of the horrible, back-breaking labor of activities such as farming by hand or mining coal, only to find themselves in a mind-numbing, soul-sucking cave of corporate cubicle drudgery or meaningless, degrading customer service. I guess work just sucks sometimes.

And it's ironic to me that, despite the wondrous improvements to the quality of life for so many people around the world, people don't seem any happier.

A depressing thought.

Thus, just as with satire and parody, irony doesn't have much of a place in modern business communication. It might be a neat trick for a clever ad campaign, but typically you want to communicate your message in a straightforward and easily digestible manner. Irony may obfuscate your meaning or distract from it. And outside of a joke, the verbal irony deployed as sarcasm or snark is usually mean-spirited and counterproductive. If you want to tell someone their report had errors, I suggest you tell them in a straightforward and kind manner with suggestions for improvements, as this will most likely lead to the best and most desirable outcome: they improve and the work has fewer errors next time around. I *don't* suggest you say, "Ohhhhh, your sales report was *soooooo* good" with an exaggerated eye roll. That's just being an asshole—and will result in resentment and even worse performance next time around.

If you have to choose irony or sincerity in business, choose sincerity. Leave irony for the cool kids whom you're no longer trying to impress.

SUSPENSE AND TENSION

Dramatic irony, wherein the audience knows something that the characters do not, engenders a tremendous amount of pleasurable sadness, tension, and emotion. Consider the audience knowing that Romeo is alive while Juliet thinks he's dead. Sorry for any spoilers, but the suspense and tension turn into tragedy and catharsis as we watch her commit suicide.

Alfred Hitchcock explained suspense and tension this way: if you see a bomb go off from under a table and kill two dudes sitting there, then you get ten seconds of shock. But if you *tell* the audience there is a bomb under the table that will go off in five minutes, the audience will be riveted to their seats for those five minutes, waiting to see if the bomb goes off and what happens when it does. (Hitchcock also says you can't ever let the bomb go off and kill the characters in the story, but by that point, our metaphor has ended.)

Use this to your benefit when presenting information. Don't surprise your audience with a bomb of important information out of context. But don't save up all the good bits until the end either, because by then you will bore them so much they won't care.

Instead, tease the information and make them willing participants.

"In the next fifteen minutes, I will show you how to save 15 percent on your printing costs" will attract more interest than "Our company was started in 1955 by a man in a grey flannel suit," and then, fifteen minutes later, "and *that's* how we save our clients 15 percent on their printing costs!"

And just to be clear, you obviously don't want to give away all the good bits at the beginning either, because that doesn't create tension or suspense.

But be smart with this technique. I was on a call the other day with a salesperson who was trying to sell me something. I tried to get off the phone after forty-five minutes, but I'm just too damn polite to simply hang up on the guy. Then, after I kept insisting, he *finally* told me about his prices after about an hour and fifteen minutes. By that point, any tension and suspense for learning his prices were gone—I was merely frustrated, bored, and angry.

WRITING EXERCISE: ADVANCED BASICS

Part I: Transcribe a conversation so you can see the dialogue of everyday speech. What you'll notice is that it's nothing like what you read in books. This is because much of what is said by people in casual conversation is nonsensical garbage, repetition, or throat-clearing such as "like," "uh," and "um."

Part II: In the world of scriptwriting, the term "punch-up" is when you hire professional writers and comedians to make a script better. They take the existing content and add new lines and better jokes. In this exercise, take a look at some recent business communications—emails, presentations, reports, even your résumé—and try to "punch it up" using some of the techniques we've discussed in Part II of this book.

See where you are stopping the reader's flow, or where you can add a good metaphor that would make your otherwise decent, passable paragraph into a memorable and engaging one.

Part III: For your next few emails, reports, or other communications, write a first draft that is punchy, funny, and full of irony, snark, and sarcasm. Don't worry, you won't be sending this one to anyone—it's just to practice some of these techniques.

In your second draft, tone it down to something more sober and professional. Don't get fired on my account!

Part IV: Now think about how long each part of this exercise took to complete. Writing is not only about generating content, but about revision—and if you're going to improve your skills, then you'll need to budget in this extra time for your projects. You may write more slowly, at first—but what you produce will be so much better.

17: THE FLOW

Good fiction sets off … a vivid and continuous dream in the reader's mind.

> — John Gardner, *On Becoming a Novelist* (1983)

A Body of Water

In the famous quote that begins this chapter (and by "famous" I mean a few dozen people—all of them writers—know it), John Gardner coined "the vivid and continuous dream" as a poetic and creative way of describing what happens to someone as they read a story. The artist Peter Mendelsund wrote an entire book attempting to describe this sublime and indefinable experience in *What We See When We Read* (2014), and the immateriality of Gardner's vivid, continuous dream-world is akin to Mendelsund's "synesthesia":

Much of what we experience when we read is an overlapping of, or replacement by, one kind of sensation over another—a synesthetic event. A sound is seen; a color is heard; a sight is smelled.[20]

Throughout this book, I've referred to this state as "flow." Like all qualia, how people experience the process of reading and absorbing text is most likely unique and personal: maybe some people "see" an image in their mind's eye while others "feel" or "hear" a story.

Nevertheless, we can imagine each piece of communication—whether it's a novel, an email, a movie, or a real estate listing—as a way of navigating a body of water, which is the material. For a casual beach read, easy and breezy, perhaps it's an inner tube on a lazy river, while a short email is a plank of wood lain across a puddle on the sidewalk. Some texts, such as the difficult literary theories of Jacques Derrida and Michel Foucault I had to read in grad school, are a kayak in dangerous rapids, requiring much concentration and work to navigate. Blockbuster movies are casino boats with a lot of noise and lights, allowing you to watch the wide, expansive banks of the river as they drift along, doing the work for you. Episodic sitcoms are pool floats: you jump in and have some fun swimming for a bit and then jump out, but you haven't gone anywhere. A well-written real estate listing can be a speedboat taking you from part of the lake to another, while a poorly-written one never leaves the dock.

Regardless of how you explain it, the trick is that as an author, you don't want your word choice, syntax, grammar, or style to interrupt the flow of this journey—the "synesthetic dream," if you prefer—for your reader. If your story is a lazy river, you want to keep your audience in the inner tube.

But it's so easy to dump them into the water, however unintentionally. Using some fancy new word you learned, elaborate and baroque description of scenery, wooden dialogue, characters that act with no motivation, or anything that allows the author to intrude on the writing—this all stops the flow.

My flow was interrupted during the movie *The Last Jedi* (2017) when General Leia Organa Solo (aka "Princess Leia") flies through space. I posit that no human—not even a Jedi—can survive in empty space like a tardigrade. Even for a science fiction space opera known for ludicrous imagery and outlandish plot lines, the story imploded (for me) when a character defied *this level* of physics. As an audience member, I was willing to believe that people could move objects with their minds and shoot lightning from their fingertips. But when your body goes into space, everyone knows you die. Space is like, one degree above Absolute Zero, there's no air at all, let alone oxygen, and your organs would rupture, and, well, it doesn't matter. I love *Star Wars*, but this scene had me punching my tub of popcorn in rage.

This scene made my "vivid and continuous dream" into a living nightmare.

Beyond plot holes, though, there are unfortunately many other stylistic and language blunders that can inadvertently dump your reader from their inner tube.

Consider dialogue tags. As a reader, you probably rarely notice dialogue tags, and that's the point. They communicate who is saying what and appear and disappear without being noticed. At least, they're supposed to:

> **"What are you doing?" Joe said to Mike.**
>
> **Mike looked up. "I'm reading a book about what happens to the human body in empty space without a spacesuit," he said.**
>
> **"What happens?"**
>
> **"It explodes," Mike said.**
>
> **"Not if you're a Jedi!" Joe said.**
>
> **"Well, it damn well should!"**

Authors sometimes mistakenly think "said" is a boring word and try to spruce up their writing with synonyms. This is a hallmark of bad writing, and here's why:

> **"What are you doing?" Joe queried, to Mike.**
>
> **Mike looked up. "I'm reading a book about what happens to the human body in empty space without a spacesuit," he barked.**
>
> **"What happens?" Joe countered.**
>
> **"It explodes," Mike murmured.**

"Not if you're a Jedi!" Joe remarked.
"Well it damn well should!" Mike thundered.

See how annoying the second version is? This is because the conversation is continually interrupted by unnecessary and unnecessarily descriptive dialogue tags. You can't focus on what is being said because you're constantly being told who is saying it, and how.

So, a quick tip: for the most part—like, 95 percent of the time—don't use any dialogue tags other than "said." This word is grammatically necessary, and is sort of unconsciously skipped over by the reader when they're reading. Kind of like how, when you're watching a show, you don't see the edges of the TV.

"Queried," "barked," "remarked," "murmured," and "thundered" are all big stop signs for the reader—like having a big, flashing red border around the screen.

Besides, strong writing should convey *how* someone is saying what they're saying, so if you're doing it right, these kinds of dialogue tags are redundant. If they aren't, you need to polish your dialogue. For example:

"I said Good Day!" thundered Wonka

does not need the word "thundered" because the reader *knows* Wonka is thundering by context. The writer Sol Stein explains in *Stein on Writing* (1995):

> Thou shalt not mutter, whisper, blurt, bellow, or scream,
> for it is the words and not the characterization of the words
> that must carry their own decibels.

This may seem nitpicky, but as you've seen throughout this book, that's the level of detail and precision needed to be a professional writer. Think of it as a measure-twice, cut-once kind of thing.

Any words that allow the author to intrude in on storytelling are annoying and disruptive. In the ideal reading experience, the author disappears, allowing the reader to sail through the story uninterrupted, even if that story is about business or work. But whenever you, the writer, decide to consult the old thesaurus and choose a "fancy" word you don't know, you risk intruding in on your story and dumping your reader into the water. For example:

Please make sure you record your sales calls in the CRM as per the guidelines outlined in our nudiustertion sales meeting.

Wait, what? What the fuck does "nudiustertion" mean? Where have I seen that before? (It was in Chapter 9.)

Now, instead of reminding your sales team to input their sales calls into the CRM, you've got them wondering what you meant by "nudiustertion." Technically, this archaic word means, "of or pertaining to the day before yesterday," so this sentence could also read:

Please make sure you record your sales calls in the CRM as per the guidelines outlined in the sales meeting we had the day before yesterday.

Now it makes sense.

Whether you're presenting a sales pitch to your client or teaching your team how to code, you want to keep your audience engaged. You don't want to confuse them or get them hung up on some strange word you just used. Unfortunately, almost anything can interrupt the flow: a bad joke, profanity, jargon, typos, spilling coffee on your suit. That is why revision, polish, and specificity with language are so important.

Cut All the Boring Parts

I'm sorry this letter isn't shorter, but I ran out of time.

— Attributed to many

Boredom also interrupts the flow. Despite all our talk about John Gardner's "vivid and continuous dream," you don't want your speech, email, presentation, or report to be so dull it *literally* puts your audience to sleep.

In public speaking, one way to engage your audience is to ask questions, so they feel like they are participating in the conversation, rather than receiving a lecture. You might fear this will interrupt your narrative, but it's better to have your audience awake and participating in the flow—and thus not bored—than asleep and dreaming about something else.

People don't like to sit in boring meetings. People don't like to read boring emails.

Yes, sometimes boring shit has to be communicated, but perhaps you can find interesting ways to deliver such boring material. That's why *Game of Thrones* always delivered a massive amount of exposition in dialogue during a sex scene. The audience was too distracted by nudity to notice they were getting an info dump.

I once had a manager, early on in my career, who responded to a meeting request with an email: "Tell me what you want over email or come to my office for a quick discussion."

Annoyed, I went to his office.

"I don't take meetings," he said.

"Of course you do," I replied. "You must."

He shook his head. "Unless I absolutely *have* to, I don't do meetings. What do you want?"

I told him what I wanted, and we discussed the matter quickly and efficiently, and then I was on my way. It took about five minutes, which means we gained twenty-five minutes of our lives back that would've been lost in the meeting vortex.

It was an epiphany. I didn't know you were allowed to do that.

Applying this life lesson to writing, I learned to cut all the boring parts (or at least try to).

We've spent much time talking about brevity, removing clichés, and cutting anything that isn't thematically relevant. The quote at the beginning of this section is a pithy acknowledgment that cutting words takes extra time and energy—but that's part of revision—and it's worth it.

This also goes for emails. Don't send eight-paragraph emails. People won't read them. You know it. Yes, *some* people will read them. But the *right* people won't. They're too busy.

So keep it succinct—two, three sentences—and you may get a read.

The key to keeping the story flowing is to not be boring. In business, this is sometimes easier said than done, especially if you're reviewing Q3 financials, talking about new hiring guidelines, or communicating something equally mundane.

But that's what this entire book is about: learning how to not be boring by using *inventive language, suspense, tension, humor, empathy, story arcs*, and especially, as we discussed in Chapter 7, *originality*.

Unfortunately, it's easier to cut the obvious "fluff" than when you've written something you like. You wouldn't believe how many *Star Wars* references were in the first draft of this book.

And so we resort to murder.

Murder

Whenever you feel an impulse to perpetrate a piece of exceptionally fine writing, obey it—whole-heartedly—and delete it before sending your manuscript to press. Murder your darlings.
— Sir Arthur Quiller-Couch, *On the Art of Writing* (1916)

If you've ever read a book about writing, you've no doubt seen the phrase "murder (or kill) your darlings." It's been attributed to William Faulkner as well as Sir Quiller-Couch, but through the splendor of the internet, now nobody will ever be sure.

Regardless of who said it, this pithy aphorism means that when one is revising, one must inevitably remove words they like. This could be a line of dialogue that doesn't advance the story, a breathtaking but unnecessary scene in a movie, or a third face-melting guitar solo (see "November Rain" by Guns N' Roses).

Murdering your darlings is painful, sad, and difficult—but it distinguishes the professional writer from the wannabe. Like a real mobster, or even God himself, a professional writer is willing to let that which they love die for the betterment of the work.

Cutting cliché is easy because it's terrible and it needs to go. Cutting clutter is easy once you've been honest and identified it. Clutter sucks; it needs to go.

Finding passages without thematic resonance to cut is more difficult, because you have to identify your themes first. It's even harder if some of your off-theme points are interesting, funny, or if you wrote them in a snazzy or clever way.

Cutting all the boring parts is usually the most difficult—because this stuff isn't boring to *you*. If it was, it wouldn't have made it into whatever draft you're in. You would've cut it already.

So how do you ascertain what the reader will find boring, or what isn't thematically relevant? You need to be objective. Recall Chapter 11 on Point of View, and put yourself in the shoes of your audience: what do they *need* to know from your communication, and what will they not understand from the way you phrased it? What parts of your communication are extraneous, confusing, or a bit too clever? What is requiring their attention and time unnecessarily?

A tactic that really works is to take what you've written and put it in the drawer. For novelists, I recommend putting your first draft in the drawer for at least two weeks before looking at it again. Most people at work don't have that luxury, so put the current document away for at least a bathroom break or a cup of coffee so you have some time away to collect yourself before going in with the revision scalpel. Because emotion will get you every time.

WRITING EXERCISE: DREAMING

Part I: Write out an anecdote from your life that you enjoy telling people. It can be professional or personal, funny or sad, and from when you were young or old. Just start telling the story. Here's a short example of my own:

> *I once found an errant, leather-bound moleskin in the bathroom stall of a New York ad agency. Nowadays, I wouldn't dare touch it—not after COVID. But back then, I had no qualms about immediately picking up someone else's notebook in the toilet and flipping through it while my stomach and intestines fought over last night's tray of bodega sushi.*
>
> *To my horror, the pages contained song lyrics. If I were charitable I could call them "poems," in that they were written in verse (meaning line breaks), but the lines rhymed, and they contained nothing poetic. If I remember correctly, one narrative was about a small-town Midwesterner, Danny, who came to the big city to make it as a "rocker," but fell on hard times and had to sacrifice his dreams and get a job as a hotshot advertising copywriter.*
>
> *My face flushed with embarrassment for the anonymous songwriter, and also from whatever was coming out of me. But mostly with embarrassment for the writer, who I was pretty sure was our new HR manager, Donny. He hailed from Bloomington, Indiana, and once invited me to one of his gigs. It didn't feel weird because he wanted to be a rock star—we all did. It was because these songs were terrible and he'd*

clearly been writing one in the shitter. In any case, good guy that I am, I subtly left the notebook in reception so hopefully "someone" could claim it without shame.

Part II: When you're done, look at what you have. Are extraneous details interrupting the flow? Will any words or phrases cause confusion? Is every person that appears in the anecdote identifiable? Is the setting clear?

Take a second pass and fix anything you see that might relate to the questions above.

Part III: Take a moment away from your beautiful anecdote, and come back in a week or two. It's time for a third revision. Work on each sentence to ensure that it relates, specifically and exactly, to what happened. Add details to bring the story to life and cut words that aren't necessary. Your anecdote may or may not be any *longer*, but the writing should be much tighter and livelier. Every word should count.

Part IV: Finally, compare your first version—where you were just typing out thoughts—to your final version, where you really started *writing*. Give yourself 250 words on the difference: what have you learned?

PART III:

DEPTH AND LIFE

18: CRITICISM AND REJECTION

I go to extraordinary lengths not to hear what people are saying about me. But that is itself a form of ... self-protection because I know that all I have to do is hear one phrase—somebody will report to me all innocently, oh, somebody said such-and-such about me or about something I wrote, like I did this piece for the *New Yorker* a year-and-a-half ago where I made some, I thought, sensible points about the reality of climate change and the unavoidability of radical climate change, and people said, "Oh God, somebody called you a birdbrain. Somebody called you a climate change denier." And all it takes is one little phrase like that, and I will lie awake for hours at night constructing pithy, lacerating rejoinders to some idiotic ... truly, just a phrase is enough to keep me awake for hours.

— Jonathan Franzen[21]

THE MFA WORKSHOP

Jonathan Franzen, from the quote above, is one of the most successful authors of this century. His novel *The Corrections* (2001) won a National Book Award. And yet even he knows how dangerous it is to read his reviews on Goodreads.

So much can be said about criticism, but two aspects we'll focus on are:

1. How to take it.

2. How to ignore it.

MFA writing programs operate on the theory that writing, like any other discipline—such as carpentry or pottery or even statistics or chemistry—can be taught and learned through doing, an idea with which I wholly agree. If you practice the techniques discussed in Part II, you *will* become a better writer.

The *doing* is via the workshop, which functions like so: Every writer submits one to three times per semester (usually twice), and other class members have one week to read and respond to the piece. The type of submission—a short story, novel excerpt, handful of poems, a play (or scene from a play), or a creative nonfiction piece—is usually dictated by the focus of the workshop.

Submissions are in various stages of draft, from fairly polished to raw and full of typos. Personally, I edited mine extensively before submitting so my readers didn't waste time and attention on typos or other mistakes, such as a character having blue eyes on page one and brown eyes on page ten. Just as I would never submit a presentation full of typos to a client, I found it a bit discourteous of my peers who submitted something they threw together at the last second and didn't proofread (see Figure 30). That said, sometimes even Jedi Masters miss a semicolon.

After you email or pass around copies, the other members of the workshop spend the week reading your work, making

When you already know well what you've written, your eye sometimes unintentionally skips over typos and errors. Some people suggest reading your work backwards (by line, not by word) so you don't get lost in the meaning. I also recommend reading your work out loud, as it will force you to pay attention to your language differently and you hear your mistakes. Slow down. Print out a copy, if possible. Hand it to a friend or colleague to double-check.

Figure 30. Proofreading and Copyediting.

notations in the margins, and writing a one- to two-page feedback letter. The next week, during the workshop, the class discusses the piece.

Things have changed, but I gather it used to be somewhat sporting for people to invent the cruelest insults of each other's work. All in good fun, I suppose, but I imagine the secret thinking behind it was that there were only so many spots on the *New York Times* bestseller list, so if you could hideously and permanently disfigure another writer's ego they might perhaps quit the program altogether and never write again.

Ah, professional jealousy.

I tried to avoid doing this, but I'm sure my well-meaning comments and criticisms were bitter nonetheless. And I definitely got my share of it from others in the program on my work. It was often the most fragile egos who participated in this kind of savagery—one letter advised me to "bury this story in the ground," which I found unhelpful, though amusing—but nowadays people are being taught to be kinder and more respectful.

Surely you, too, have encountered folks in your career who seem especially and wantonly cruel. It's too bad for them to live that way. Ignore them.

On the other hand, some of your critics will be your friends, and may take it easy on you. This might feel good in the moment, but it too is unhelpful. You should ask and expect them to be honest with you, even if it'll hurt your feelings. You need to know what is and isn't working if you expect to improve.

Back to the workshop: when your submission is up for critique, your peers will tell you what they liked, what they thought was working in the piece, what they thought you were trying to do, and then they tell you what they thought was *not* working, what they didn't like, and what you need to fix. The majority of the time is spent on the latter half—the painful part—and not the ego-stroking part.

Oh, and if that isn't brutal enough, the entire time they are talking, you must remain silent. You must sit there and just take it. And while you *should* be listening and taking notes, it's hard not to start fuming, crying, and/or thinking of vicious comebacks and defenses.

Because you worked hard on that shit! And now they fucking hate it! And you're the worst writer and why did you even *apply* to an MFA program the admissions team was on *drugs* when they decided to let you in you should just throw your laptop in a swimming pool and never write again and why do you even wake up in the morning, you worthless piece of—

Then you recover and hopefully recognize such criticism does not reflect your worth as a person.

At best, it is objective and helpful, and at worst, it is mean and spiteful. Either way, the MFA workshop teaches you to recognize that everyone who criticizes you has their own agenda.

You'll also start to see that the cruelest critiques often come from those who have the most doubts about themselves, and they make themselves feel better by putting others down. On the other hand, you can also begin to tell when honest criticism—even if it's harsh or negative—comes from a kind and genuine place, because someone is really trying to help you become better.

Lastly, you *also* come to know when the feedback is lazy—as if someone didn't even read your piece at all—and they're just reciting the same clichés as everyone else. I once got a letter stating "I am so sick of reading stories about shitty men." Perhaps true, but not very helpful.

In one workshop, my teacher T. Geronimo Johnson talked about how every workshop could have the same wicker basket full of the same Post-it notes from which each writer could simply pick one and say the same thing each week, such as "This character needs more interiority," "Watch your POV shifts," or "What is at stake?"

His point was that these comments are trite, common, and as useless as commenting on one's choice of font. He was right.

In my years of workshops, those three comments were applied, by one writer or another, to almost every single story that was submitted. In this workshop, however, Johnson wanted our feedback to be more honest and deep, and that takes more effort. To do this, he allowed each writer only one submission per semester, which gave our group a full three hours—rather than the usual ninety minutes—to dissect each piece.

No matter what, though, criticism stings. Even if you can identify it as lazy, cruel, or honest. On a gut level, criticism makes you instinctively want to defend yourself, put up walls, or fight back. It makes you want to dismiss your critic altogether as a know-nothing hack.

After enough workshops, you will be able to identify what criticism to ignore. But to make use of helpful criticism, you must try to appreciate what the other person is saying, and objectively assess that they are working in good faith. Criticism—and accepting it gracefully—is necessary to improve.

This is doubly so in business. At some point in your career, you will need to learn how to take criticism without hating yourself.

One way is to remind yourself that criticism is a reflection of your work, and not of you as a human. This important distinction can help you separate your personal feelings from the matter at hand and give you enough distance to objectively fix what needs to be fixed in the work.

Now, it is true that some people are just assholes. It doesn't matter *what* you do—they'll find something to disagree with, or hate you for it. That's their problem, not yours. Other people will give you feedback that is so far from what you intend that you realize they just don't get what you're trying to do, and you can politely thank them for their words and move on.

However, if *nobody* in the room understands what you're trying to say, then the problem is more likely in what you wrote, or how you wrote it. This is an important time for you to distance yourself from your emotions and assess your work objectively: Are you being clear and direct, or are you obfuscating and using vague jargon? Is your work laden with unnecessary words or clichés? How can you communicate better what it is you need to say to this audience?

Returning to Jonathan Franzen, the thing is that the more famous you are, or the higher up you climb on the ladder, the more criticism you will receive. It's just a fact.

You can't please everyone all the time, so stop trying. But do stop to take in true, honest feedback, and adjust course—when you can.

No Disclaimers, No Explanations

Another insight of the MFA workshop that can help you become a better communicator and citizen in the workplace is that your work must speak for itself.

Recall how the writer sits in mortified silence while the room criticizes their piece. The other writers discuss theme, dialogue, character motivations, voice, tension, language, everything.

Sometimes people won't read your work "correctly." They'll think the main character, Sam, is a forty-year-old British woman on holiday when you intended him to be an eight-year-old boy on a playground at recess. You thought it was clear from the context, but what you intended and what the readers took from your story were completely different.

Maybe that reader is an imbecile—and fine. But just as likely, you might be failing in your job as a communicator.

Because you can't defend or explain your work in the actual workshop setting—you can't argue with them or tell them they're misreading—you are forced to confront your own communication skills with objective honesty as you hear them elucidate what they, as a reader, took from your work. Even if it's "wrong."

It is worthwhile, in the long run, to become comfortable with this. When you publish something or send an email, people will read it on their own time and you won't be there to explain it to them, either.

As an example, recall my anecdote in the section "The Sound of Language" in Chapter 5, in which I included the word "goddamn" in my character's interior monologue. Wow, my audience misread what I meant. Or, perhaps more truthfully, I made an error in choosing that word. My writing did not convey what I wanted it to.

The lesson is that your work must speak for itself.

It's not unlike when you press send on an email, or deliver a presentation and go home, or leave a meeting. The person to whom you were communicating is now on their own, with no more caveats and explanations and counterpoints from you.

Elsewhere in this book we discuss context and framing your narrative in more detail, but essentially it is about making sure you control how your words are perceived. You can't control everything—if your client had a fight with their spouse that morning and they're in a terrible mood, well, there's nothing you can do about that.

But you can control how long-winded and boring your slide presentation is.

You *can* control how vague your language is, or if it could be misinterpreted. "I need those deliverables soon" is vague and can lead to misunderstanding or missed deadlines, but "I need the sales report and call log by 3:30 p.m." is not.

Make sure you are explicit in what you mean. Don't be ambiguous (unless you aim to be), and don't be vague. Be direct. Be confident.

REJECTION

One tortuous part of being a professional writer is the sheer amount of rejection you face. Even the best writers are consistently and continually rejected by publishers, agents, and their readers. Even the best books are hated by people.

I personally get rejected by publishers for my work at least a couple of times a week, every single week. And I'm *good* at writing.

Salespeople know all about rejection and are probably better than most at letting it slide off their backs. We all know people who have no problem going up to strangers at bars or parties and starting conversations. I envy the shit out of those people because I have such a hard time doing that. I take rejection too personally.

But hell, even seasoned sales professionals get the blues sometimes. So go easy on yourself.

We can all learn something from the rejected writer. Getting rejected is okay. It doesn't make you a bad writer, nor a bad person.

In fact, if you suck at writing, you're a Bad Writer—whether or not you get rejected—so you may as well put yourself out there and try. Indeed, an *acceptance* won't change your skill level as a writer, either: if some magazine *does* decide to publish one of your stories, that doesn't mean you're a Good Writer, now. It just means they liked one thing you wrote.

Unfortunately, the fear of rejection cripples many.

They hate public speaking because they're afraid the audience won't laugh at their jokes or find them interesting. They don't ask for a raise because they're afraid that their boss will say no. They don't ask for a promotion because they're afraid people won't think they deserve it.

If you never send out your work for publication, you will never be rejected. This is true. But you will also never get published.

Similarly, every salesperson knows that unless you ask for a deal, you'll never get a "Yes." Sure, sometimes someone will call you and want to do business, but you can't sustain a career that way. Just as a weird happenstance might come along and some editor may solicit a story or article from a writer—but that's no way to sustain a writing career, either.

Maybe your company gives yearly raises. You should still ask for one—a higher one than you'd normally get—if you think you deserve it.

The short documentary *Jacob* (2019) is about this genius polymath Jacob Appel who has published hundreds of short stories and poems, as well as several books. But on his wall, Mr. Appel has a framed rejection letter from an asshole editor to remind him of the reality of publishing. The interviewer asks Appel how many times he's been rejected.

Twenty fucking thousand times.

And Appel is a *very* good, *very* accomplished writer.

The key is: don't let rejection stop you from continuing your work, and don't let fear of rejection stop you from getting started.

Stories of Rejection

In case you're not convinced, here is a list of some people who were rejected before they succeeded:

- Abraham Lincoln lost, like, over a thousand elections before winning the United States Presidency in 1860.

- Walt Disney was fired from the *Kansas City Star* because he "lacked imagination and had no good ideas."

- Stephen King's novel *Carrie* was rejected by dozens of publishers before it was accepted.

- Twelve major publishers rejected J. K. Rowling's *Harry Potter* until Bloomsbury accepted it with a modest advance (£1,500).

- Jerry Seinfeld got fired from a small role in a 1980 sitcom, *Benson.*

- Elvis Presley would never play the Grand Ole Opry in Nashville after he bombed in 1954, and the manager humiliated him by telling him to return to Memphis and be a truck driver.

Writing Exercise: Rejection

Part I: Think of a time you were rejected. Take 250 words to write a short narrative describing the experience.

Now think of a time you didn't do something in your life, or your career, because you were afraid of being rejected. Give us another 250 words describing *that* experience.

Now write another 250 words, describing what you imagine could've happened if you had done that thing you didn't do. What is the worst that could've happened? What is the best that could've come from it?

Finally, write 250 words about a time you were *afraid* of being rejected, but did it anyway. What was the outcome?

Part II: Look at everything you have—that's a bit of a story, isn't it? A mini essay? See if you can string these individual narratives together with a thematic arc, because I would be surprised if they aren't all related somehow. Here is an abbreviated example from my own life:

After my undergrad at Binghamton University, I was reject-ed from every MFA program in poetry to which I applied. I wanted to be a poet—but the world didn't want me to be one. So I moved to Manhattan and began working in the adver-tising industry. I played in punk bands and wrote creatively on the side.

While I was working in the advertising industry, I was too afraid to make a real go of it as a musician and writer. I was afraid I didn't have the skills or talent to make it, and I was afraid I wouldn't be able to pay rent. So I kept working in advertising and keeping my passions as side hobbies.

> *Had I quit my job in advertising, I could've dedicated more time and energy into writing and playing music. The best thing that could've happened is that I could've published books or been a successful musician. The worst thing that could've happened is that I would've lost all my money and had to move back in with my parents.*
>
> *In my thirties, I was afraid of being rejected by MFA Programs in Fiction writing—but I applied anyway. I was accepted into a program, but then I was afraid of quitting my secure job in advertising to be a writer—but I did it anyway. After the program, I was able to combine my writing and my business by starting my own ad agency and writing books.*
>
> *The "connective tissue" is that art, music, and writing have always been the most important pursuits in my life, and it wasn't until I took a chance on them that I was able to find satisfaction in my career.*

My example is only 300 words, but yours should be at least a thousand (four to five pages, double-spaced).

Part III: You're not done yet, unfortunately. The final step is to revise. This is a writing book, after all, and we want to take any chance we can to practice our writing skills. Look for extraneous words and irrelevant sentences to cut. Add details to bring the narrative alive and introduce characters from your life that were present during these decisions (or non-decisions). Find clichés and come up with new ways of phrasing what you're trying to say—perhaps with an interesting and original metaphor or two. Above all, make sure to tell the truth.

19: HONESTY

A writer—and, I believe, generally all persons—must think that whatever happens to him or her is a resource. All things have been given to us for a purpose, and an artist must feel this more intensely. All that happens to us, including our humiliations, our misfortunes, our embarrassments, all is given to us as raw material, as clay, so that we may shape our art.

— Jorge Luis Borges[22]

TELLING THE TRUTH

Fiction is fake, right? The author sits in their ivory tower making stuff up. That's fiction.

Yet somehow, good fiction tells the truth. Fairy tales and myths may not be factual, historically speaking, but the *rules*, the themes, the values, and the lessons taught therein are true to human experience.

Fantasy fiction works this way, too. In our world, there are no orcs, dwarves, elves, or hobbits, as far as I know. Yet *The Lord of the Rings* trilogy captured the imaginations and hearts of millions because the characters inside the story were living a true experience: friendship and camaraderie, resolve in the face of hardship, and the fight against evil.

You know when you read something that isn't true because it doesn't *feel* right. Sometimes you watch a terrible movie with a big budget and you can't quite pin down what's wrong with it—that movie isn't telling the truth.

Recall my beef with *The Last Jedi* in Chapter 17. As ludicrous as the *Star Wars* universe is, we audience members take it for granted as "true" in the world of the movies that on all the planets, everyone can breathe the air, they speak the same language, and people can do magic. But when someone floats through space without a spacesuit, well, even in the world of *Star Wars*, it doesn't feel *true*. Even if one argues the vacuum of space won't kill you instantaneously if you surround yourself with the Force and use it to pull the spaceship toward you, thereby (through Newton's second law of thermodynamics) pulling yourself back to the ship, that takes Earthbound science into the fake world of *Star Wars*, and as rule, any scene that requires endless nerdy "explainer" videos *probably* violates the truth rule.

However, expert and artful writers will strive and succeed in making the possible seem plausible. This is because the best art comes from truth. That doesn't mean art says exactly what it means at all times, but at the core of great art there is truth.

The same goes for business.

If you run a business, you can't go around telling everyone your trade secrets. You can't go up to a struggling employee and just say, "You suck," to their face. But at the same time, you can't lie. People will know if you lie, and they won't want to work for you; they won't want to do business with you. Even if it's difficult, you have to tell the truth.

And if this really speaks to you, the book *Radical Candor* (2017) by Kim Scott turns this idea into an entire business philosophy.

VULNERABILITY

Good art comes from truth, and the *best* art comes from vulnerability. It's easy to mask oneself through skill, but it's a lot harder to expose oneself through honesty.

When writing memoir or creative nonfiction, you are literally telling the truth of your life and are vulnerable to criticism, hatred, judgment. It is difficult to write your deepest darkest secrets, and even more difficult to show them to people.

Poets do this when they write the most sublime and effectual poetry. Many poets, however, shy away at the last second and cloak their truths in grandiose imagery or vague language—and these poems are not as effective.

We fictioneers always have this excuse: *It's fiction! That protagonist, Bill Mandrel, that's not me! Sure, he's a nerdy, forty-year-old Jewish writer from upstate New York, but he's not me! That guy's an asshole! I'm a nice guy!*

But even a *roman à clef* is cloaked in anonymity, and so-called autofiction has enough mud in the water to hide from the reader what is mostly true, completely true, and what is made up. (The term roman à clef literally means "novel with a key," and refers to a novel based on real-life events, with real people as characters, but whose names are changed—thus the "key" being the difference between fiction and nonfiction.)

Nevertheless, when a writer puts their work out there, the audience may wonder, *how much of this is real?* Even if none of it is. And even if some of it is, why should it matter?

Well, it definitely matters to the family of the writer. Yes, we writers are real people, and we have mothers and fathers and brothers and sisters and wives and husbands and friends and kids and all those other people who may read that funny bit about the autoerotic asphyxiation and wonder, "Shit, did Phil actually *do* that when he was thirteen?"

I didn't. But I bet, even with that line, you're wondering.

Writing memoir and creative nonfiction is famous for creating rifts in families.

And yet.

And yet, if you *don't* write from a vulnerable place, you will have a much harder time connecting with or evoking a strong response from your audience. If you are not vulnerable in making your art, the viewer will have difficulty caring about it.

This may seem obvious, but **song lyrics** are a special case and work differently from business writing. True, great song lyrics communicate universalities and vulnerability, but combined with their music, they are intended to appeal to and evoke emotion rather than communicate information.

The best song lyrics are poetic and memorable, but can be either specific or general. I think "The love you take is equal to the love you make" (from "The End" by The Beatles) is a beautiful line, and because it doesn't refer to anything specific, it can be interpreted and "owned" by each listener. The lyrics to "Born to Run" (Bruce Springsteen), however, tell a more specific story that evokes a time, place, and atmosphere, even for (and especially for, in fact) the millions of people who love the song but did not grow up in 1970s small-town America.

Also, clichés such as "cold as ice" can work as song lyrics, even though they won't be celebrated as "great." This doesn't matter to the vast majority of listeners who enjoy a song for its music. In fact, the generality and simplicity of a cliché can make some songs more universally appealing, as they doesn't require extra time or energy for interpretation that would take away from the music itself. All this is to say: song lyrics are great—but in general, don't use them as a model for business communication.

Figure 31. A note on song lyrics.

However, revealing personal things about yourself should be for a reason—not just to shock the audience. People are perceptive, and your audience will be smart enough to know when you're not being genuine or trying to pull one over on them.

Consider one of the greatest rap songs ever: "Juicy," by Notorious B.I.G. What makes this song so great? Well, the sample, from Mtume's "Juicy Fruit" (1983), provides a solid melody, beat, and bass line. But the lyrics are also great. They are... well...*vulnerable*:

I remember when I used to eat sardines for dinner...
Girls used to diss me...

Considered a fool 'cause I dropped out of high school...
We used to fuss when the landlord dissed us...
No heat, wonder why Christmas missed us...
Birthdays was the worst days...

Song lyrics and business writing are very different (Figure 31). But a case can be made for putting yourself out there in business. Care about what you make, about what you do, and about what you say. To use a cliché: have skin in the game. Be vulnerable, raw, and real, and the people with whom you are working—your clients, your colleagues, and your customers—will take note and match you. They, too, will put their skin in the game.

WRITE WHAT YOU KNOW?

"Write about what you know" is the most stupid thing I've heard. It encourages people to write a dull autobiography. It's the reverse of firing the imagination and potential of writers.
— Kazuo Ishiguro, on the worst piece of writing advice
he ever received.[23]

There is an oft-quoted dictum of writing that floats around the advice-world every now and again: "Write what you know." At its basest and most trite understanding, this means you should create art about things you yourself have experienced, as your lived experience will give you the truth about these things, and thus the authority to speak about them.

There is truth in this statement, but like all pithy, one-sentence aphorisms, the reality is much more complicated. Yes, you should write what you know.

John Grisham, for example, was a lawyer before he started writing novels about lawyers.

Michael Crichton got an M.D. from Harvard Medical

School (he was also almost seven feet tall and a climate change skeptic). But did he ever actually take a time machine and visit the Jurassic era, or clone a real dinosaur?

The novelist Adam Johnson visited North Korea and did a ton of research when writing *The Orphan Master's Son* (2014), for which he deservedly won a Pulitzer Prize. But he's not *from* North Korea. He's not even Korean.

Nevertheless, you should still try to write what you know. But that doesn't mean you should *only* write what you know, or that you can't—or shouldn't—write what you don't know. That, in fact, is the process of how fiction writers *make* fiction— we *make stuff up*. But we use grains of truth from our own lives.

Kevin Wilson wrote a book called *Nothing To See Here* (2019) with a twenty-something slacker chick as the protagonist. Wilson is not a woman, but the character, as he said in an interview, was still based on himself. He *made up* the character, but he used lived experience to ground it.

In business writing, however, you're not making up fictions (usually). Stick with what you know as factual, especially when writing something down, especially because your words can come back to haunt you later if you stretch the truth. If you're not sure of an answer or a topic is veering out of your professional bailiwick, you're better served by admitting ignorance to yourself and either doing some honest and thorough research to get the answers and information you need, or not writing anything at all. Here at the Institute of MFAs for MBAs, we do not condone bullshit.

But. (There's always a but.) I *do* think that research and learning are always valuable and worthy, so when you don't know something, it's a great opportunity to increase your knowledge. This will make you a better writer, a better businessperson, and a better human. Even the hour spent chasing a lead and getting nowhere is time well spent.

The same advice applies to your career. If you only perform

tasks that you already know how to do, you'll never advance. That's fine for a lot of people—but odds are if you're reading this book, that's not you.

Let's say an architect has only designed bathrooms, but never an apartment building. Should they *never* try to design an apartment building? Of course not. Or an accountant only has individuals as clients, but no businesses. If they want to expand into business accounting, they need to acquire the requisite knowledge and do it!

Some people say you should take a job and learn by doing—even if you're uncomfortable—though this can be risky. I can't tell you one way or the other what to do, because each situation will be different, but sure, if you get offered a promotion from Individual Contributor Salesperson to Sales Director, take it. Be ready to learn how to manage a team on the fly, and know the first few months will be rocky.

However if someone offers you the job of astronaut, you may want to decline, unless you know what all the bleepy-bloops mean and which buttons to press to make the ship go into space.

Writing Exercise: Embarrassment and Knowledge

Part I: This one is a classic from the MFA canon: think back to one of the most embarrassing moments of your entire life. Think hard. This should be the one thing you could never bring yourself to tell *anyone*, because it wasn't funny, it wasn't charming, it wasn't a good learning experience. It was excruciating. It was humiliating. It was walking in on your in-laws having sex. It was farting in an elevator with your boss. It was smashing yourself into a glass door at a party.

It made you want to die.

Now describe the scene in all its horrific detail.

Part II: Think of your job right now, and the job you want to have five or ten years from now. (Maybe it's the same job—and good for you!) In a long column, start listing everything you know about your current job—things you do and tasks you perform, words and jargon with which you're familiar, services you provide or products you sell.

In a second column, start listing everything with which you're *unfamiliar*. This may be more difficult because you're unfamiliar with them, but as an example: in my role as a marketing executive, I am very familiar with copywriting and paid search advertising. However, I've never shot a commercial and am unfamiliar with directing a video.

Do the same for the job you want. See how much you have to learn?

Part III: Take the story you wrote in Part I and revise, revise, revise.

20: INTENTION

Most companies don't understand the value of making space for community and creativity, of treating employees like the extraordinary humans they are.

— John S. Couch, The Art of Creative Rebellion

LIGHGHT

The business cliché I hate the most is "think outside the box." This is despite—or perhaps because—"out-of-the-box thinking" is held up as the "holy grail" (another cliché I despise) of business acumen. The idea of coming up with better, more creative solutions to common problems, however, is sound—even if the cliché itself is abominable.

But creative thinking in business is rare. Risk-averse managers follow scripts handed to them by their predecessors, and harried problem-solvers usually don't have time to find any solutions better than the first thing that comes to mind.

One benefit of the MFA program is that it gives the writer time—TIME, that most precious of commodities—to do all of this "outside-of-the-box" thinking. You don't *need* an MFA to get the time to write—plenty of people schedule their writing at 5 a.m. or after midnight, when the rest of the family is asleep, or on the bus to work or during lunch breaks—but a dedicated couple of years definitely helps. So whatever you need to do to get the time, do it.

One of my favorite poems—which I discovered in an MFA

course on Postmodernism and experimental literature—is "Lighght," written by Aram Saroyan in 1965 and published in *The Paris Review*. Though I'm not sure about copyrights, this is the poem in its entirety:

LIGHGHT

That's it.

Now, this poem either gets you very excited, or it gets you very angry. Maybe both. I choose to be very excited by this poem, because it breaks so many rules: it is simply one word, and a misspelled one, at that, and has no objective, denotative meeting. But it works.

It's what I mean when I talk about breaking the rules.

This poem, now *this* fucking poem, thinks outside of the box.

Maybe you hate this poem. You don't even think it's a poem. That's fine. It works for me.

But this isn't merely about breaking rules, because thinking outside of the box can—and in most instances *should*—remain within a certain reasonable set of constraints, such as the common business practices of your industry. You can't pay for new jeans with used coffee grinds, after all. Let's imagine the executive team of Boeing meeting to brainstorm a new product.

"Come on, people, let's think outside of the box!" the CEO says.

"I have an idea," an oleaginous lackey says, with a small, doltish smile playing about their chapped lips. "What about a cordoned-off area where a few select rich people sit comfortably, with plenty of room, and eat decent food and drink complimentary champagne while all the poor and/or cheap people sit behind them?"

"We already have that, Simpson! I said *outside* the box!"

A hand is raised.

"You don't need to raise your hand," the CEO says, by this point exasperated and ashamed of his idiotic team. "Just spit it out."

"What about a plane that doesn't fly?"

"How do you mean?"

Johnson, excited to have the attention of the entire boardroom for the first time, stands up. He's glad he chose his lucky orange paisley tie this morning. "I mean, a plane that doesn't fly."

He begins gesturing wildly. "A couple of hundred people board the plane," and now he looks at Simpson, who spoke up earlier. "And yes, Simpson, we'll have a First Class area on the plane. Once the doors are locked, the pilot drives the plane—but rather than to the runway, they drive it to the airport's exit road, where they then get on the highway and drive, rather than fly to their destination!"

"Do you mean a goddamn bus, Johnson?" screams the CEO.

"It's a plane!"

"You can't drive a plane on the fucking highway!" By this point, the CEO, who had been on a heavy daily dose of statins for decades now, has turned bright red and is going into cardiac arrest.

Cardiac arrest. All because someone tried to think too far outside of the box. It's dangerous, don't you see? Someone *died*.

So how do you do it the right way?

It comes back to time. That is what the MFA degree afforded me—and to be sure, I was lucky enough to *have* the time to dedicate to the MFA in return. I didn't have kids, I was unmarried, I had some bread stashed in the bank for a rainy day.

What *you* have, every day, is at least your lunch break, if not an hour or two to sit at your desk and think.

I mean, really think. The first few ideas will probably be rote, repetitive, already done a thousand times. But once you get past the initial turd-cloud of bad or unimaginative ideas, you'll start forming new ones.

And as we saw in the instructional example above, not all of the new ideas are good ones just because they're different.

This may seem obvious. *Of course you should take your time coming up with good ideas!*

I guarantee it's not obvious. One reason is that many people are lazy. I know I am. I just *love* when I'm able to accomplish a task at work or come up with a satisfactory solution to a problem without exerting much effort. Leaves me more time to scroll on social media or think about what I'm going to eat for lunch.

But the first and easiest solution is not always the best. As you know.

I've heard a possibly-apocryphal legend that Google allowed—nay, *encouraged*—employees to dedicate a full 20 percent of their time to explore projects they were interested in. This supposedly led to tremendous innovations like Gmail, Google News, and other products.

The idea was so successful that other companies followed suit.

Despite the question of how (or if) this policy was ever enacted, the idea behind it still stands: when you go out exploring, you sometimes find treasure.

Know the Rules Before Breaking Them

Recall E. L. Doctorow's famous analogy about writing, which introduces Chapter 13: it's "like driving at night in the fog." True, you can get from Point A to Point B even if you can only see a few yards ahead of you at a time. But you must also first know how to drive.

And yes, I suppose you can put a dog behind the wheel and drop a brick on the accelerator and the car would go somewhere (until it quickly crashed), but I wouldn't call that "driving."

Driving in fog is dangerous. You need to know how to drive, and you need to do it carefully, checking your mirrors and speed, remaining alert for other cars and pedestrians on the road. You need to follow the curves of the road, or else you will end up in a ditch. You need to obey the speed limit, or you will get pulled over.

In other words, there are rules.

But art making is not driving. And business is not driving. To be successful in art, as in business, you must break the rules. This does not mean you should break the *law*: no embezzling five million dollars, or collusion and price-fixing with competitors, or getting handsy with staff. It does mean that you can't stand *out* from the pack until you know what's *in* the pack.

So don't let yourself get carried away with rule-breaking, regardless of how fun it can be.

There's a famous and well-regarded group of literary artists in France called *Oulipo*, which stands for ***Ouvroir de littérature potentielle*** (or "workshop of potential literature"), and the writers tend to create works of art that are very much non-standard and rule-breaking. By now you should be familiar with Raymond Queneau's *Exercises in Style* (1947), which I've mentioned several times. He was a founder of Oulipo.

One of the greatest novels to come out of this group was *A Void* (1969) by Georges Perec. It is a lipogram, which is a word game where one letter is omitted. The entire three-hundred-page novel does not contain the letter *e*, the most common letter in English (nor in French, in which the novel was originally written, and called *La Disparition*, or "The Disappearance"). The Spanish-language version, *El secuestro* (The "kidnapping" or "hijacking"), does not contain the letter *a*, which is the second-most common letter in Spanish. And lest you think translating is merely switching words from one language into another, know that all twenty or so translators of *La Disparation* (into languages such as German, Russian, Italian, Japanese, and more) preserved the lipogram.

There is a thematic and metaphorical reason for not using this letter, but it's also a trick. The point is that a specific rule of writing (that is, you can and should use any and all letters you want and need) is broken, and it leads to a stronger and even more impactful work of art. This type of writing is called "constrained writing," where the author gives him or herself a specific "constraint."

In the business world, a great example of rule-breaking is the iPhone. Steve Jobs knew about telecommunications, in the form of cell phones, he knew about entertainment and music (in the form of his iPod), and he knew about nascent mobile internet. He broke the rules by combining all these into one device.

Henry Ford broke the rule that cars had to be expensive luxury items. He created a car that many in the middle class could—and did—afford.

Twitter broke the rules by allowing people to communicate with the outside world in short bursts, in real time. It revolutionized communication.

RULES SERVE A PURPOSE

There are many books that flout the rules. For example, *Dear American Airlines* (2009), by Jonathan Miles, is just as its title suggests: a novel in the shape of a complaint letter to American Airlines. It is unconventional, to say the least, in structure, yet there are the familiar elements of a novel: character, plot, suspense, and thematic resonance. (This also isn't entirely original, either, as *Letters to Wendy's* by Joe Wenderoth came out in 2000.)

But breaking rules for the sake of breaking rules doesn't

always work, and it can go too far, quickly. Another book to come out of Oulipo is *Alphabetical Africa* (1974) by Walter Abish. The constraint is that in the first chapter, all words must start with the letter *A*. In the second chapter, words can start with *A* or *B*, and in the third chapter, *A*, *B*, or *C*, and so on, until all the letters are available. Then, starting in Chapter 27, no words can start with the letter *Z*. In Chapter 28, no words can start with *Z* or *Y*. By the last chapter, words once again only start with *A*.

This book fucking sucks.

It is not fun to read and outside of the debatable "cleverness" of the conceit I don't think it has much meaning. But maybe I'm too stupid to "get" it. That's fine.

In business, you can apply this lesson in many ways. Yes, once you know the rules, you can break them—again, unless you're breaking the *law*, like Enron (which you should not do). But breaking them just for the sake of breaking them may not be to your best advantage. Consider one of the most iconic and profitable brands in history: Coca-Cola. They tried to re-formulate the recipe for this brand, thinking that people gave a shit about the *taste* of Coca-Cola, and not the brand, and released New Coke in 1985. It was a spectacular failure. (Not to be outdone, its main rival, Pepsi, did its own failure not long after, releasing a clear version of its flagship brand called Crystal Pepsi in the early 1990s.)

IMITATION AND PRACTICE

Jane: Thanks for the ride, Trent.

Trent: No problem. I needed a break anyway. I've been practicing for ten hours straight.

Jane: Daria, would you say sleeping with a guitar in your hands counts as practicing?

Trent: As long as you don't drop it.

— Daria, Episode 102 "The Invitation" (1997)

A time-honored writing exercise we did in the MFA program was finding a page or two from a book we loved and rewriting it, longhand, word for word. The idea was that we would be "writing" like the master—echoing them, not imitating or copying them—to see and feel how they did it. We would learn the "rules" and see the "style" in practice.

This idea goes back a long way: the old masters copied paintings that came before them, and supposedly Hemingway re-typed entire books as practice.

I don't think it's a bad idea to read case studies or find sales pitches that were successful and study them to see how they did it. If you see a résumé, a real estate listing, or a product description you really like, copy it. Then discard the copy and create your own.

Throughout this book we discuss the importance of *practice*, or writing every single day to get better. This is true in writing as it is in every other facet of life—the more you do something, the better you get at it. Writing and communicating well are not just God-given talents that people have or don't have—they're practiced.

And one of the most fundamental aspects of practicing is to practice *well*. You have to use good form. If you practice *bad* form, then you will cement bad form into your skill. Malcolm Gladwell has famously expounded on a "10,000-hour rule," which states that you must do something for 10,000 hours to become a master at it—but those hours must be spent working diligently and purposefully. There are a lot of takedowns of said rule, but either way, the idea of deliberate practice is a good one.

Imitation is one of those ways.

However, be forewarned: once you've mastered the technique you're trying out, you have to stop imitating, and start creating.

Framing

In the anthology of conceptual writing *Against Expression* (which we discuss in Chapter 6 on style), there is a selection of pages from a project that is, in its entirety, a collection of scribbles. There is a more comprehensive exegesis in the book, but, I mean, at first blush, they are just lines and scrawls—no letters, no text. The lines were placed there with intent, but unless you know that intent going in, the lines themselves would have no meaning to you.

If I splattered a bunch of paint on a canvas, would it be considered a great work of art? Jackson Pollock did this exact thing, many times, then put frames around the canvases, and now they are hanging in the most prestigious museums in the world.

Does the *frame* contain the meaning, then?

When Marcel Duchamp signed a urinal "R. Mutt" and placed it on a pedestal in 1917 (see Figure 32), was it suddenly "art" because Marcel Duchamp curated it?

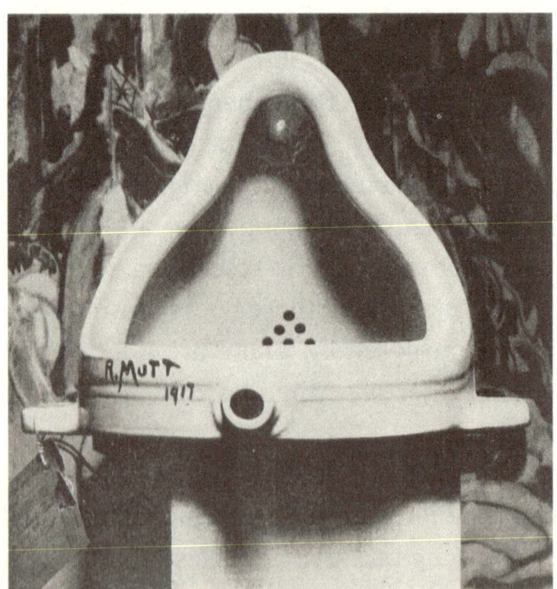

Figure 32. Marcel Duchamp, "Fountain" (1917). Photo by Arthur Stieglitz.

Banksy created a painting that was programmed to shred itself once it was sold at auction. Amazingly, not only are the shredded fragments of this painting still considered art, they're worth more now.[24] I love this, and not only for its anarchic, chaotic, and innovative playfulness—but also because it demonstrates plainly and inarguably that art has become wholly commoditized and the value of it is arbitrary. Also, you can only do this once because after that it's derivative.

It is the blending of performance and art, as well as the deliberate intention behind its creation, that makes the work meaningful. I could take the same amount of time and energy to splatter paint on a canvas as did Jackson Pollock and call it "art," though it wouldn't be any good, even if I put a frame around it. Because I can't account for Jackson Pollock's decades of experience, the way he thought about this art, and the mood and emotion *his* art expresses, in however abstract a way: a sense of movement, action, anxiety, detachment, and alienation.

Nevertheless, *despite* the merits of the artwork it contains, the frame is crucial. Some teenagers once placed a pair of eyeglasses on the floor of the SF MoMA with a placard describing it, and soon people were taking pictures of it and contemplating its merits and meaning.[25] I have no problem with this. People should always take time to contemplate the everyday mundane things in life. But it does show how the frame—in this case, the SF MoMA—affected people's reactions. Think how different the situation would have been if people were confronted with a pair of errant eyeglasses on the street—some would try to find the owner, some would avoid them altogether (not my business!), and some asshole would stomp them for fun.

Framing operates the same way in business, even if you don't see it every day, or in as obvious terms as a museum gallery.

Consider an email address: if you receive an email from someone whose email address looks sketchy, you'll probably delete it without reading the message.

Similarly, networking and referrals are types of framing. If you are given a warm introduction to a new prospect, they will most likely allow you more room to pitch than if you go in cold.

The style and professionalism of your résumé is also a frame, regardless of the contents therein.

In some ways, an education can be a frame—not *what* someone actually learned, but *where* they went to school. For better or worse, there's no question that if one's career is framed by the Ivy League, they'll find it easier to get interviews than someone who went to a community college or didn't get a degree. This doesn't mean an Ivy League grad is smarter, better, or more deserving in any way—it's just a fact of reality.

So be deliberate. Don't let someone else control the framing of your career, or of your project. Where possible, *you* should control the frame.

Context

In the book *What Artists Do* (2018), Leonard Koren discusses the artist Donald Judd (1928–1994), who, along with many of his peers, achieved the context for their work that they desired "by providing precise and consistent contexts for experiencing their artwork."[26]

Judd was considered a minimalist (among other things), and I saw a lot of his work on display in Marfa, Texas, an artsy, one-stoplight town near nothing else in the West Texas high desert. It's a beautiful and secluded oasis of profundity, pretentiousness, and inflated prices. I loved it.

But I found Judd's work tough to understand. It's a series of installations of metal boxes, plexiglass objects, forms made from sheet metal, plywood—that kind of stuff—all just sitting there. One room had every book and object specifically placed just so. It was confusing. Luckily my wife is an art historian and could explain it to me. Otherwise, it would've meant as much to me as the fart I was holding in during the tour.

The art was not only in the things themselves, but in how Judd arranged them, and the experience of all of it together, as Koren explains:

> Judd was determined that his art be viewed in well-lit, distraction-free spaces where it was placed just so in relation to adjacent art and/or non-art objects. His rationale made a lot of sense: When art and/or other objects and the environment come together in exactly the right way, a new "third something" is created. This precise placement of specific objects in a specific environment came to be known as an "installation."[27]

I'm not a visual artist, but this principle can be applied to writing. When creating a book of poetry or a collection of short stories, you don't just throw everything in willy-nilly; you put them in an order that creates a certain flow for the reader (even if they do decide to skip around).

Likewise, novel chapters are usually read sequentially, meaning the author has determined precisely how they flow for the reader. If you start a novel in the middle, it won't make sense. There are some notable exceptions, such as the novels *Hopscotch* (1963) by Julio Cortázar, which can be read in different sequences, and *Composition No. 1* (1963) by Marc Saporta, which is a stack of loose sheets that comes in a box and which the reader is supposed to shuffle like a deck of cards before reading. As with most exceptions, though, they too prove the rule.

Each story you tell—be it in a movie, short story, novel, or play—has an order, and it doesn't always have to be chronological, as noted in Chapter 13. A well-placed flashback can do wonders. But it will have a beginning, middle, and end, even if you don't present it that way (a masterful contemporary example of this is the movie *Pulp Fiction*).

But it's all about context. Once you've put your work out there, you can no longer make any disclaimers about it. Sure, you can try to explain what you mean in a follow-up email, just as an author or artist can do interviews...but those are ineffective and short-lived at best. The work will eventually stand (or fall) on its own merit.

Which means you need to control the context as best you can.

In business, this is called "branding." With advertising, public relations, corporate giving, logos, social media feeds, blog posts, interviews, and every other tool in the corporate communication arsenal, brands attempt to control how the public perceives them.

In your career, you have a personal brand, too. It reflects what you stand for and your values, as well as your work history and the skills you offer. If you don't control it, people will interpret your brand for you, and this can sometimes become negative.

So what are you known for? Be honest. Are you the person with great ideas? A master communicator? Funny but nonserious one-liners? Or are you known for nothing at all—meaning you are known as the person who is forgettable, or not worth knowing?

Historically, museums, art historians, gallerists, and curators have provided the context and interpretation for artists' work, but Judd and his contemporaries tried to pre-empt—or even elide entirely—these institutions by removing their work from those spaces and creating their own. Maybe they weren't *entirely* successful, but they certainly achieved part of their goal.

The corollary is, to whatever extent possible, control the context in which you and your work are seen. Otherwise, others will do it for you, and it may not be in the best light. And one of the reasons it is so important to get better at writing is to be able to do just that.

WRITING EXERCISE: TIME, EXPERIMENTATION, IMITATION, AND FRAME

Part I: Time. I am confident there are projects, emails, reports, or some other written material in your life and career that, due to time constraints, you started but haven't completed, or turned in before they were completely ready. In this exercise, carve out the time needed to complete one of them—however long it takes. It could mean you find three hours on a Saturday morning to do some research, or it could mean you carve out two hours every evening for six months to finish the first draft of a novel.

Remember, I'm only asking you to complete *one* thing. Surely you've got several "irons in the fire" (two for one special: metaphor *and* cliché!) at any given time—and to think about tackling all of them would most likely be paralyzing. Make time to do one. The finished product doesn't have to be brilliant or change the world. It just has to be complete.

Part II: Experimentation. I call this "work poetry:" find some of the worst emails you've ever gotten, then copy and paste them into a new document (know that "worst" is subjective, so whatever that means to you). Scrub out all identifying or confidential information. Reformat the content of the emails into a poem, with all appropriate line breaks, unintentional rhymes, and structure as you see fit.

Part III: Imitation. Find an email, report, pitch deck, or some other project you admire and copy it word for word. What did the original author do that worked so well?

Part IV: Frame. Write 500 words about the frame of your career, work, and personal brand. This should take you a while, so don't rush. How did this happen? Was it intentional? Is it still accurate to how you feel about yourself, or does it reflect

an earlier version of yourself, perhaps when you were first starting your career?

Now revise it, but not for language. Revise it to reflect what you *want* your frame to be. Did anything change? What, and why?

Now revise it for language.

21: PROCESS

All the other arts—as well as athletics, obviously—take the notion of practice and exercise very seriously. Too many writers make a fetish of the natural, untroubled writer who just breathes out a great story. Writing is hard work ...

> — Brian Kiteley, *The 3 A.M. Epiphany: Uncommon Writing Exercises That Transform Your Fiction* (2005)

The Magic of Shitty First Drafts

The term "shitty first drafts" comes from a well-loved craft book by Anne Lamott called *Bird by Bird* (1994). At least, that's the first place I encountered the phrase, though I'm sure the idea has been around since time immemorial. It means when you first get your ideas and thoughts and feelings onto paper—your "first draft," as it were—it may not be so great.

This might seem obvious, but it's not. No matter where you are in your career, shitty first drafts can be discouraging. The first draft of this book, you might like to know, was mostly puerile barf (and you might still think it is).

Sometimes the act of creation—art or work—can feel disheartening because all the great books, poems, movies, viral videos, social media posts, TV shows, songs, and other artwork seem so perfect, complete, and easy.

How did they make that, you think, *when my stuff is so terrible?*

Well, there were countless hours in the editing bay, reshoots, and dozens of paragraphs crossed out or deleted, perhaps even entire chapters and stanzas rewritten from word one. Photographers take countless shots of one subject because they know that only one of them will be perfect—the lighting, the framing, the composition, the color—and the rest will be okay at best. Painters create studies of work before they start on what will become the masterpiece. Social media influencers do twenty takes of their twelve-second video before posting it.

In addition, there are hundreds—thousands, perhaps millions—of unfinished works of art that you don't see.

The point is, everyone has to start somewhere. The finished product rarely looks like the first draft, and that's okay. In fact, it's more than okay: it's encouraged.

Some writers—very few, but some—are able to "write in their head." This means they go out for a walk and live their daily lives and are writing their work, word for word, in their mind, and then when they sit at the keyboard, it's all well-formed and not much needs to change.

Lucky them. There's a certain kind of brain that works this way, and these people are exceedingly rare.

Don't try to emulate this method, because you'll be missing a crucial step to making good work—the revision process. And yes, while you can be envious of these geniuses, the rest of us still need to spend hours in the muck and mire, searching for the apposite word, *just so*, whittling our phrases until they're exactly perfect, and rewriting dialogue to match a new verbal tic of one of our characters.

And besides, these "geniuses" are doing the same thing, they're just doing it in their heads instead of on the page. It's not like the first line they think of is perfect—their first line is just as shitty as everyone else's—it's just that they do mental revisions instead of digital ones. Their process might be spending three months thinking of a story and then only a week writing it, whereas *my* process is the reverse. I, personally, might have a dozen drafts of one story, each with its own file name, with characters taken out or put in, scenes added or deleted, POV changed from first to third and then back again.

Nevertheless, shitty first drafts are scary.

One thing I don't like seeing in business is when people are afraid to sound stupid or make mistakes. There is a lot of shame flying around the office, people gossiping about each other in the break room, using someone's mistakes against them.

This can prevent you from even getting started; from coming face to face with your own shitty first draft. If it's a novel, then fine—maybe the world doesn't need your novel (I don't agree, by the way). But if it's a great invention, a better process, or, hell, even a presentation about how to make more sales, then your company and your career—if not the world—do need it.

So whenever it's prudent and possible, permit yourself to say to hell with those people. You will not create your best work unless you start allowing yourself to create your worst work.

Successful entrepreneurs already know this. How many times did Thomas Edison fail before inventing the light bulb? How many times did Abraham Lincoln *lose* an election before winning one? Billions.

But you're not trying to be Thomas Edison, and you're not Abraham Lincoln. You're just a regular person who needs to write an email to the team about the new policy. Or you need to tell your client some bad news and your client tends to go crazy at the first sign of bad news.

Thus, the magic of shitty first drafts.

Just type it out. Write it, mistakes and all, knowing that you will go back and fix it.

Same goes for a prototype of an app, or a sketch of a business plan.

A lot of people might think this is obvious, but truly, it's not. The fear of making a mistake, seeming stupid, or creating something imperfect stops people from ever even trying in the first place.

Don't let this be you.

Embrace the magic of shitty first drafts.

Writing is Editing, Not Typing

So you've got your shitty first draft, and it is indeed quite shitty. Now what?

Revision, my friend.

This is the hard part.

Writing the shitty first draft was actually the easy part, I'm afraid. I spent many, *many* more hours revising this book than I did typing out the first draft. Which leads us to the inimitable and famously bitchy writer Truman Capote, who commented thusly on Jack Kerouac's *On the Road*:

That's not writing; that's typing.

He actually insulted several writers with this pithy epithet, denigrating their work as sub-par and unprofessional. In the context of Jack Kerouac, however, he was remarking on Kerouac's supposed technique of never rewriting his work. There's a famous scroll—a 120-foot roll of paper—that contains the contents of *On the Road*, which Kerouac said took him three weeks to write. It's not true. Kerouac did several rewrites, over many years, but the myth is grand.

The most important part of writing, the real *work* in writing, is the revision process.

Kerouac told people three weeks because it sounded good, but in reality, it was many *years*.

Editing is slow. It takes time.

You need to go back and re-read *every* word, every line, every page of your work and change what needs to be changed until you're satisfied. You must follow the craft principles outlined in Part II and ensure that every word earns its place (or else be cut); that there is a beginning, middle, and end; that you aren't dumping your reader from their inner tube on the lazy river (that is, interrupting their flow of reading).

And unfortunately, you'll probably have to do this a couple of times.

In business, however, the truth is that you probably will never have the luxury of spending an infinite amount of time editing and revising your work—there are deadlines, and you have to at some point turn something in. But when possible, try to keep the writing/editing dichotomy in mind, because working quickly and sloppily will hurt you more in the long run.

SPEECH

Writing and speaking are both forms of communication, obviously. The difference is writing gives you the opportunity to think your thoughts more carefully and deliberately, as well as revise and hone your language to express exactly what you want to say in the way you want to say it.

It *also* allows your reader to take their time comprehending what you mean, perhaps reading it two or three times, or coming back to it again and again for a refresher (something I hope you might do with this book).

Extemporaneous speech happens in real time, however, on the fly and off the cuff. (I'm not talking about speechwriting, as that is largely done ahead of time, with plenty of space for revision and deliberation.) This is why much leeway should be given to general conversation—you don't need to worry so much about using clichés or euphemisms, nor trying to come up with the most original phrase or witty anecdote. Just get to the point and make sure the person understands what you're telling them.

Now, while the lessons in this book are really meant for your business writing, the truth is all this practicing will *also* make your extemporaneous speech more sophisticated, polished, and deliberate. Just like working out a muscle, your vocabulary and creativity will grow over time. You'll begin noticing clichés before you say them, and you'll start using more interesting language in general.

But a word of caution: one memorable or original phrase goes a *long* way in a quick conversation that needs to get to the point, and nobody likes a showoff.

PRODUCTION

> If ninety-eight percent of our *medical* students were no longer practicing medicine five years after graduation, there would be a Senate investigation, yet that proportion of art majors are routinely consigned to an early professional death.
>
> — David Bayles and Ted Orland, *Art & Fear* (1994)

At some point you have to stop revising and turn something in. True, there are writers and artists who spend years—decades, even—working on their masterpieces, but if you're reading this book, then you probably have hard deadlines: an email needs to get sent by this afternoon, or a report has to be to the client by EOD Thursday, something like that.

So we also need to talk about *doing* ("shipping," as it were). About production. This is where you stop talking, thinking, ideating, strategizing, observing, planning, learning, seeing, finding, sharpening, and breaking through. This is where you start producing.

In Chapter 2, we talk about "permission," and how MFA programs treat creative writing and intentional reading as a job—as if it is *work* (which it is)—and how this is so liberating for many beginning writers, as it allows them to take their passion as seriously as they do their paying job.

But anything that you do seriously, with passion and intention, can feel like work, especially when you're under a deadline to produce a good product.

When I first started playing in bands, it was just for fun. We'd get together for rehearsal, drink some beers, hang out with friends. Sounds great. Doesn't sound like work. And if you get to do what you love, it doesn't *feel* like work. Lucky you.

Except it *is* work. Because when we were in a recording studio for fourteen hours a day, suddenly it *was* work. It wasn't data entry drudgery or waiting tables, but it was still work.

I love writing. But still, sometimes, writing is drudgery and suffering. Reading difficult books isn't fun all the time (for many people it's not fun at all). It gives you a headache. It takes time. The work isn't just going to a café and drinking cappuccinos and discussing poetry. It's sitting at the computer every day and typing, it's sitting with your manuscript and revising, over and over and over and over again. It's producing.

I learned in the MFA program that you had to write—you had to produce, you had to get those pages out—to be a writer. You didn't just talk about it.

Nevertheless, a common refrain from some MFA students is that they like workshops because it provides "structure." What they mean is that it forced them to write, because of a deadline.

I always wondered what they were doing with the rest of the time, being MFA students, if not writing. Maybe they were watching reruns of *Law & Order*, trying to hook up with poets, or drinking. Inevitably these people procrastinated until the day or two before the story was due, *then* finally got to work. Unfortunately, most of these people aren't *real* writers, but hobbyists.

To be fair, one of the ancillary benefits of being in an MFA program is that you can spend six hours at a bar with another writer getting wasted, and, as long as the first hour was spent arguing about books and writing, you can write off the entire affair as "working." But in reality, an MFA program does not *provide* structure. It's only what you make of it. If you spend three years drinking and watching reruns and graduate with only a handful of bad stories, that's on you. Personally, I wrote two novels, three plays, twenty or thirty short stories, dozens and dozens of unfinished exercises and vignettes, several academic essays about literature, and a couple of creative nonfiction pieces (most of which haven't been published). Oh, and a number of embarrassingly bad poems.

But I went into the program in my mid-thirties, after having spent much of my twenties lazing about, getting drunk, and seducing poets, so maybe it's good to get it out of your system first. In any case, the structure and deadlines of an MFA program are lax, at best. You can get by doing almost nothing if you really try. But in the end, what have you accomplished? Sadly, I knew one writer who spent three full years of an MFA—and all the tuition—working on the first two chapters of a novel, continually submitting the poor thing to workshops with a few words changed here and there, maybe a character excised then added back in, but now as a werewolf...

University administrators know MFA programs are cash cows, and that for every ten or fifteen people accepted, the majority won't go on to be professional writers. Many will stay as adjunct professors—a source of nearly free labor, if you're feeling cynical—or teach K-12 and publish a short story or poem once every couple of years until they stop writing altogether.

Tragic. Nevertheless, the lesson is that MFA programs *end*. And when they do, you must have the discipline to keep writing, every day, and revising, every day.

Just like when an MBA program ends, you have to go out and get a job and do the work.

Nobody is going to force you to write. In fact, some people might discourage it because they don't want to have to read your shit. But if you want to be successful, you have to do it yourself.

The semester-long workshops in MFA writing programs give a sort of validation and feedback loop for writers, as well as deadlines. But when it ends, and a year or two or four go by without publication, many of them stop altogether.

This principle applies to your career, too. There are people who've been in the same job for many years whose salary doesn't keep up with inflation, and they're satisfied. That's fine. Ambition is not for everyone, nor should it be.

But you're reading this book, so you want to improve. Which means you also already know nobody is going to do it for you.

You know the people who show up to work every day just to collect a paycheck. They don't care about the job, they take no pride in their work, and they require just enough money to pay their bills and afford a vacation once a year.

Don't let that be you.

Be a striver. Work hard. Be disciplined.

But it all has to come from within.

Nobody is going to do it for you.

Odds are those people didn't start out that way. Maybe some of them did, but many now-broken people had, at one point or another, some desire to succeed, to work hard, to take pleasure and pride in what they did every day.

But something happened. Something ate away at that.

Or, perhaps, they didn't care enough in the first place about what they were doing. This is a problem of motivation. If you are stuck doing something you hate every day, then you must find a way out and into something you *can* enjoy.

An MFA in Creative Writing is a voluntary degree. Sure, sometimes it helps to have one, as it burnishes your reputation (slightly), and it connotes an air of professionalism if you're trying to get an awful job as an underpaid and disposable adjunct professor of freshman composition, but otherwise, it's all and only what you make of it.

Your job, your career, and your business is the same. Nobody cares if you succeed in your job. Maybe your mom does, but nobody else.

You have to care. *You* have to have that inner fire to take charge of your day, to take charge of your career, and to set goals. *You* have to force yourself to want to work every day.

If this is impossible in your current job or career, then start the process of finding a new one. If *that*, for whatever reason, is impossible, then you have a very difficult task ahead of you: you either need to *find* meaning in your current job and career, or you need to find another outlet (art, for example, or family, or faith) that can give you that satisfaction and pride in achievement. *This* route, however, is not the purview of this book—you'll probably want to hire a good therapist for that.

WRITING EXERCISE: REVISION

Part I: Find an email, document, letter, presentation, white paper—anything you have written—and edit it. Edit the hell out of it.

Make at least four *significant* changes to the document, and five *minor* changes. This is subjective, but imagine that "significant" means altering an entire paragraph, while "minor" means changing a couple of words in a single sentence. This does *not* include fixing typos.

Then put it in a drawer.

Part II: In seven days, look at the document again. Make another handful of changes, both significant and minor. You don't have to send it out or use it, but this is good practice for looking at what you've made, then re-looking at it, and noticing the differences and the possibilities.

22: SHOW UP EVERY DAY

Do not believe those who try to persuade you that composition is only a cold exercise of the intellect. The only music capable of moving and touching us is that which flows from the depths of a composer's soul when he is stirred by inspiration. There is no doubt that even the greatest musical geniuses have sometimes worked without inspiration. The guest does not always respond to the first invitation. We must *always* work, and a self-respecting artist must not fold his hands on the pretext that he is not in the mood. If we wait for the mood, without endeavoring to meet it half-way, we easily become indolent and apathetic. We must be patient, and believe that inspiration will come to those who can master their *disinclination*. A few days ago I told you I was working every day without any real inspiration. Had I given into my disinclination, undoubtedly I should have drifted into a long period of idleness. But my patience and faith did not fail me, and today I felt that inexplicable glow of inspiration of which I told you...

— Pyotr Ilyich Tchaikovsky[28]

INSPIRATION, OR WRITE EVERY DAY

I could sum up the world's entire oeuvre of writing advice with three words: *write every day.*

That's it. You need to write, *with intention*, every day.

The second clause of that statement—the part about intention—is crucial. It means you need to think deeply about what you're trying to say, choose your words, language, and tone carefully, and edit your work mercilessly. It doesn't include writing a shitty email to your shitty intern Blake asking about their shitty weekend.

Avoiding cliché is the *second* most important lesson of this book. It is a specific admonition to keep in mind at all stages of the work and art life: whatever you are doing, try to not do it with cliché. But this lesson only applies if you are writing with intention in the first place. If you're just trying to make it through the day, trying to avoid discomfort or exerting any effort, then who cares if everything you write, say, and do is a cliché?

But you've read this book, and you've somehow navigated my logorrhea for some twenty-odd chapters, so that is certainly not you. So here's the really difficult, really important part of the book, the number one lesson that precedes all other advice: You have to show up every day.

Let me explain.

The quote that begins this chapter is copied and pasted all over the internet. It's a long quote, but I encourage you to read the entire thing, because usually only the first couple of lines are quoted:

> The only music capable of moving and touching us is that
> which flows from the depths of a composer's soul when he
> is stirred by inspiration.

But it's the *rest* of the quote that matters. Tchaikovsky, one of the greatest musical minds in human history, tells his friend that while one does, in fact, need inspiration to make great work, "the guest" (that is, inspiration) "does not always respond to the first invitation."

> We must *always* work, and a self-respecting artist must not
> fold his hands on the pretext that he is not in the mood.

I could just re-quote the whole damn thing, but essentially, he's saying that you need to work, even when you're not inspired, until you *become* inspired. And that's not just me saying it, that's PIT. And Mozart, too, who, in myth, took musical dictation from God—but in fact had an unbelievably rigorous work ethic. (Recall, too, Kerouac's myth of writing *On the Road* in three weeks, neglecting the years of rewrites because it made a better story to be, simply, a "genius.") These "geniuses" worked, and worked, and worked.

I remember a podcast episode of *WTF* wherein Marc Maron interviewed B. J. Novak, and they got on the topic of Novak's alma mater Harvard.[29] Maron went to Boston University and always seemed to have had a chip on his shoulder about not going to an Ivy League school, despite his obvious intellect. I sympathized because I, too, considered myself smart enough to get into the Ivy League, but didn't. In any case, Maron kind of gives Novak a hard time (out of jealousy, I'd guess), and Novak explains this about Harvard students:

Novak: It means you're very serious before you get there.

Maron: Which means what, you were constantly doing homework, compulsive, focused?

Novak: Yeah, you're just very intense, or anything you pursue, if you write for the school paper, you take it as life and death, which I did. If you're in a school play, you commit to your character in *Anything Goes*, the musical. So if it says anything it means you were very very serious before, and then you went to a place where there were other people exactly like that, that same level of focus and seriousness.

Maron: So would you call that healthy competition?

Novak: I don't think it's competition—it is for some people—for me it was intensity. And if you love comedy, you want to make *Dr. Strangelove*—you're not fucking around.

What Novak says isn't all that surprising—people who get into the Ivy League work really hard—harder than anyone else—to get there. But what struck me was realizing *I'm not, actually, that person.* I'd never been that person. I couldn't get myself to study or do my homework or put in much effort at school. I didn't even finish the books I was supposed to read, and I was an English major. I wasn't serious, and I didn't have focus—not then, at least.

Unfortunately, the world fetishizes geniuses and artists, holding them—in a different way than we do celebrities—as "above" the rest of us. There exists some fantasy about a prodigy who can just kick back and drink coffee and shoot whiskey and snort cocaine and get laid and travel around the world, waiting for "the muse to strike."

But the muse rarely "strikes."

In sports, we are regaled with legends of how much our favorite athletes train (and who have, admittedly, been born with talent and a genetic blessing). But the same goes for anyone who wants to master their field.

Successful writers and athletes and comedians and computer programmers and teachers and nurses and media planners and accountants and copywriters and architects and corporate recruiters and administrators work hard enough to go out and *grab* inspiration, to bring it down from Asgard and into their workspace, be it a home office or a cubicle or a classroom or a drafting table.

If you want to get better at writing, then make sure to write something with intention every damn day.

MORNING PAGES

But how do you sit and write with intention every day? Some days are busy as hell, and you're having meetings and firing off emails and doing your reports...

One option is called "morning pages." I don't know who invented the idea, though it's sometimes credited to Julia Cameron in *The Artist's Way* (1995), and it basically goes like this: every morning, write about three pages of material (or about 750 words). Doesn't matter what it is: a to-do list, a gratitude journal, or the next scene from that "pawsome" cozy puppy mystery you're writing, *The Hound & The Fury*.

The idea is that you simply write off the top of your head. Supposedly the ideal version of this is to write, by hand, in a notebook, but I mean, do whatever works.

Another important element for morning pages to really work is that you're not supposed to show it to anyone. This way, if you write real dreck, you don't have to be embarrassed by it. It really lets you be "free."

Truthfully, I don't know many people who do morning pages. I'm sure some people do, but what I find, in my own experience as well as anecdotally, is that people do morning pages for a few days, or a few weeks, then grow weary of it. There simply isn't that much to say every morning before you've had a cup of coffee, or before anything has happened yet.

The other problem with morning pages is that it gives you, as a writer, a false sense of accomplishment. In other words, you think, well, shit, I did my three pages today, I don't need to go work on my novel. I'll go dick off and watch *Law & Order*.

But if morning pages truly is top-of-the-head work, then it wasn't really *good*, or intentional, writing. Because as you've seen from everything I've written in this book, good writing takes a lot of time, and a lot of thinking and effort. If you could just toss off three pages, then everyone would be a famous novelist.

Also, for people who aren't professional writers, three pages is a *lot*.

So here's my take on morning pages: If it helps, go for it. If it doesn't, don't feel bad about not doing it, either. Just make sure you get in some kind of writing—a page, a paragraph, a poem, a scene from a play—every single day.

Revising is Writing

Another thing about morning pages is that it focuses on generating new words. But as we discuss throughout this book, *revising* is the bulk of the writing craft. Typing is only the first part.

So when I say, "show up every day," or "write with intention every day," you can be sure I include revision. Don't worry about word count. If you spend an hour revising a document—that's the work. That's the writing. It counts.

The Chain

Yes, "The Chain" is a great song by Fleetwood Mac. It's also a productivity tool I heard about that Jerry Seinfeld used for writing jokes: he got a large calendar and marked an "X" on each day he wrote a joke.[30]

When he saw enough days strung together with an "X" on them, he naturally didn't want to "break the chain," and this gave him the motivation to write jokes, even on the days he didn't feel like it. When it becomes a daily habit, like brushing your teeth, it gets that much easier.

I don't personally do this, but it's worth giving a shot. What have you got to lose?

Try Again. Fail Again. Fail Better.

The title of this section comes from a book by Samuel Beckett. I'm sure most of the people who have a poster of this motivational quote superimposed over a rock climber tacked to their cubicle wall have never read the actual source material, a novella called *Worstword Ho* (1983).

Well, I have. And it's fucking batshit impossible to understand. A lot of Samuel Beckett is. He wasn't known for beach reads, that's for sure. His (arguably) most famous work is *Waiting for Godot* (1953), a play about two dudes waiting for a guy named Godot who—spoiler alert—never shows up. It's hilarious, if you're super smart and well-read and you like the humor of *The New Yorker* or *McSweeney's*. Sorry, let me dismount this high horse. For many people, it's not funny at all.

Well, *Worstword Ho* is even more inscrutable. I'm sure it's a work of genius—I know it must be because I've been told it is—but I read it and was sort of baffled. It made me want to reread *A Game of Thrones* because that shit is *fun*.

Nevertheless, the quote *does* really apply to anyone making art, or making anything—a company, a sales pitch, a new app.

The idea is that you have to keep trying—and failing and getting better even when failing again—until you succeed.

Sounds simple, but most people concede after tasting their first bitter spoonful of humble pie.

Many of us were (unintentionally) shamed by our parents or society about our failings or faults: say something stupid, get a low grade in a class, go to the wrong college, strike out repeatedly in little league, fail to fit into the right dress, fall in love with the wrong person, and a million other things—so we retreat into our hidey-holes if something even remotely negative happens at work. It's one of the reasons people are afraid to ask questions.

I wish that just once, someone would let rip a huge stinky in a meeting. But it's never happened, not in my entire career. It would just be so funny.

But that person would probably run back to their office and hang themselves.

To be a good salesperson, you have to get used to rejection. People hang up on you when you cold call, they say unbelievably rude and unfriendly things to you when you go knocking on doors (things they would *never* say to a complete stranger but feel okay saying to you because you're "trying to sell them something"), and, most importantly, they say no to your pitch time and time again.

It's tough to be in sales, and you need to not take things personally.

But rejection is not the same as failure. Rejection is when someone else doesn't want what you're selling.

Failure, on the other hand, *is* personal. And that's a good thing. To improve, you must allow yourself to fail.

Most artists look at their best work and sometimes think, *This is a complete piece of shit.* You may think you can always do better. But the difference between a talented artist and a successful one is that the latter shows up to work every day.

WRITING EXERCISE: EXPECTATIONS AND INTENTIONS, PART II

Part I: Look back at the list you made in the first writing exercise of the book, "Expectations and Intentions," in the Introduction. How'd you do? Did you get out of this book what you wanted?

Now, rewrite this list answering these questions: *What do you want to get out of the rest of your life? What makes you happy? How much money do you want and how much do you really need? What would you like your tombstone to read?*

Part II: After you've written this list—in bullet points or in paragraph form—you know what I'm going to say: Reread it and revise it. Remove excess words. Make it more elegant. Punch up the language and add humor. Rewrite it in the third person, about a character with your name.

Cut all the boring parts.

23: WHY IT MATTERS

Texts, tweets, status updates, blogs, itineraries, instructions, lectures, permit forms, advertisements, primers, catalogs, comment cards, letters of recommendation and complaint, end-of-year reports, accidentally forwarded e-mail, traffic updates, greeting cards, insurance claims, and message board comments: each one of these categories represents a distinct space in which a particular type of communication event takes place; each one dictates that the language residing within must behave in particular ways and pre-scripted patterns. Thus, language becomes codified, confined, and restricted. And because whatever happens to language happens to us, we, too, become restrained.

> — David Shields and Matthew Vollmer, "Introduction:
> Learning How to Fake It," *Fakes* (2012)

LANGUAGE AND REALITY

Our reality and our experience living in the world is largely defined by the language we use to describe it to ourselves. This condition is only getting more pronounced as technology advances. People are communicating now more than ever, and people spend less and less time each day not engaged with some form of language—be it video feeds on social media, streaming television shows and movies, reading text messages and emails. When was the last time you spent an hour in silence, doing nothing, or waiting in line patiently and quietly, staring at the floor?

I'm not judging if this is good or bad, or if being bored is a tragically lost art. It simply is a fact of our modern lives, and we must contend with it. One consequence is a mass reduction in attention span, and our lessons on brevity, reducing clutter, and cutting anything that doesn't have thematic resonance will continue to be ever more vital to communication.

But another consequence is that, as Shields and Vollmer observed in the quote above, back in 2012, as language becomes codified and restricted, we too become codified and restricted. Twitter was a perfect example, as a Tweet originally only allowed 140 characters, or twenty to forty words in English. This is hardly enough space for a fully-formed thought, let alone a well-considered argument—about anything. Yet so much quasi-intellectual debate and popular culture is fielded in these terms.

Without getting too philosophical, let's consider how we think: it is, primarily, in language. We tell ourselves stories, we narrate our experience, we weigh options, we make decisions, we live through language.

A striking literary instance is Newspeak, the language in George Orwell's *1984* in which the totalitarian government of Oceania has warped English so they can criminalize words they consider subversive or dangerous. Even more insidiously, they continue to simplify words or extract them from the language altogether, so that people have a progressively simplistic vocabulary, and, perhaps, more simplistic thoughts.

Newspeak isn't real, but it isn't unthinkable, either. Language is a real and living thing, like a python wrapped around your neck.

Up until Kellyanne Conway invented the term in 2017, there had been no such thing as "alternative facts." The word "fact" referred to something that was true. If it was not true, it was a falsity, or an opinion, or a theory. It was not a fact. And lest you think I'm picking on Republicans, recall President Clinton's amazing prevarication from August 1998: "It depends on what the meaning of the word 'is' is."

Thus, ever more it is our imperative to control language, lest it control us.

To do this, you need to know how language works, the rules of language, and how to communicate effectively. Otherwise it will be controlled by other people, and your ability to communicate—your voice—will be rendered mute.

Ownership

Now let's return to the quote from the Introduction to this book. You can probably see how much of the writing advice in the pages between then and now involves thinking with intention—or, as Reeves and Fuller say, "reflection." Many of the writing exercises in this book involve reflecting on your own writing or your career, as well as taking some time to imagine new possibilities.

In one respect, it may seem obvious that people should take time out of their day to reflect—in fact, there are thousands of self-improvement books, as well as major religions, that teach this exact practice. But we all know it isn't that easy, and we all can admit that we fail to do so, especially when things get hectic, or, as it says in the quote, during times of "crisis." Paradoxically, that is probably the most important time to pause and reflect.

But one need not have a crisis to try reflecting on one's life and thinking harder. In fact, I'd argue it's a better practice to begin when things are calm, because it'll make your ability to do so in times of struggle that much easier.

In other words, if you picked up this book out of frustration because people aren't understanding what you're trying to say, then great—the exercises and techniques will help.

But if you are reading this book *proactively*, to develop your skills even if things aren't that bad, then you are also taking the right step, as it may prevent those problems from happening in the first place.

There are many other good reasons, too, for improving one's communication skills. Put simply, it's good for the world.

Why? Well, politics and media are all about communication. We all know it because we see it every day. And while this book is decidedly not about politics, our lives are infused with it whether we like it or not. True, it's gauche to talk about Roe v. Wade around the water cooler—but imprecise language can create miscommunications or misunderstanding that can lead to harassment, lawsuits, and workplace strife, let alone lost revenue and hurt feelings. While your stance on gender pronouns is none of my business, nor my concern, the proper use and employment of such pronouns in your business communication is.

In addition, improving your communication is not only good for your career, but for your entire workplace. Many folks I talk to in the generations born before 1980 seem not to "get" what Millennials or Gen Z want in their work life. They're just frustrated. Everybody knows people just want to feel satisfied with their lives and be happy. Nonetheless it is true that, more than ever, Millennials value "meaning" and "purpose" in their work over pure financial gain.[31]

But how can you understand what the words "meaning" and "purpose" signify to someone if you can't communicate with them? Or vice versa: how can you get someone to understand what *you* mean by it?

Improving your writing ability is better for your personal well-being, too. It will make you happier, because you will be able to express yourself more eloquently and more effectively. Not just at work, but with your friends and family. Your text messages will be more interesting and your love letters more memorable. You won't get as frustrated trying to get someone to understand what you mean.

You may also feel an urge to pursue more creative art outside of work. Albert Einstein sums this up, for me:

I was originally supposed to become an engineer, but the thought of having to expend my creative energy on things that make practical everyday life even more refined, with a loathsome capital gain as the goal, was unbearable to me.[32]

Perhaps you, unlike Einstein, don't have an aversion to utilizing your own creative energy to make money—though if you're reading this book, you most likely do have some artistic spirit burning inside you. But we all have bills to pay, and we're not all genius theoretical physicists who can revolutionize human understanding and science while punching the clock at the Swiss patent office.

The struggle we feel is *ownership*. We don't want to give our creative energy away, even for a fee. But what you've learned in this book—the lessons of a writing program and how to apply them to your work life—will give you that ownership. It's yours to take.

Writing Exercise: Now What?

Part I: Let's have some fun. First, think of one of the weirdest days you ever had at work, and write that scene in prose, as if beginning a short story. Try for 500-750 words, and add plenty of vivid details as well as dialogue. Describe each of the characters in the scene. If you like where you're going, then continue by fleshing out the scene with some backstory. The main character may or may not be based on your life, but at this point, you can make it up.

Part II: We're going to do some "erasure" or "blackout" poetry, which is where you take an existing text and remove (via whiting or blacking out) words to create a wholly new work. For this exercise, find some recent materials from work and create poetry from them. If you enjoy this, check out *A Humument* (1980) by Tom Phillips.

There's no better way to end this book than with my own example, taken from "The General Shoe Company" case study presented way back in Chapter 1 (Figure 33).

Figure 33. An erasure poem of "The General Shoe Company" case study.

NOTES

1From an interview with Simone Téry (March 24, 1945) as quoted by Alfred H. Barr, Jr., *Picasso: Fifty Years of His Art* (1946), also by Dr. Neil Cox, *An Interview with Pablo Picasso* (2014)

2https://hbr.org/2020/04/we-need-imagination-now-more-than-ever

3https://nces.ed.gov

4https://www.shrm.org/resourcesandtools/hr-topics/organizational-and-employee-development/pages/the-cost-of-poor-communication.aspx

5https://www.pbs.org/newshour/education/graduate-programs-become-cash-cow-struggling-colleges-mean-students

6Jonathan Franzen provides a nice summary here: https://www.newyorker .com/books/page-turner/the-birth-of-the-new-yorker-story

7"Adult Fiction Books Posted Highest Q1 Sales Since 2013, The NPD Group Says," https://www.npd.com/news/press-releases/2021/adult-fiction-books-posted-highest-q1-sales-since-2013--the-npd-group-says/

8Originally in "What Life Means to Einstein," *Saturday Evening Post*, October 26, 1929; reprinted in "On Science," *Cosmic Religion*, 97. (*Quotable Einstein*, Princeton University Press)

9Ngai, Sianne. "Stuplimity: Shock and Boredom in Twentieth-Century Aesthetics." Postmodern Culture, vol. 10 no. 2, 2000. Project MUSE, doi: 10.1353/pmc.2000.0013.

10https://www.theverge.com/2022/7/26/23279478/meta-apple-mark-zuckerberg-metaverse-competition

11Goldsmith, Kenneth. "Why Conceptual Writing? Why Now?" *Against Expression: An Anthology of Conceptual Writing*, edited by Craig Dworkin and Kenneth Goldsmith. (2011)

12https://www.fastcompany.com/1681562/how-to-tell-a-story-right-now-from-a-master-of-improv

13https://hbr.org/2017/02/why-sports-are-a-terrible-metaphor-for-business

[14]https://lithub.com/toni-morrison-is-more-hemingway-than-hemingway-himself/

[15]https://trumpwhitehouse.archives.gov/briefings-statements/remarks-president-trump-press-conference-september-7-2020/

[16]https://centerforfiction.org/fiction/travel-tips/

[17]https://www.forbes.com/sites/lindsaykohler/2022/02/14/the-rise-of-the-chief-purpose-officer/

[18]https://newsgeneration.com/2014/04/11/pr-case-study-dove-real-beauty/

[19]"Jessie's Song," Season 2, Episode 9. Originally aired November 3, 1990.

[20]Mendelsund, pg. 307

[21]In an interview with Isaac Chotiner at *Slate*, July 31, 2016 (http://www.slate.com/articles/arts/interrogation/2016/07/a_conversation_with_novelist_jonathan_franzen.html

[22]*Twenty Conversations with Borges, Including a Selection of Poems: Interviews by Roberto Alifano*, 1981–1983 (1984).

[23]https://www.shortlist.com/news/kazuo-ishiguro-talks-zuckerberg-game-of-thrones-and-his-new-novel

[24]https://www.cnn.com/style/article/banksy-shredded-painting-sale/index.html

[25]https://www.nytimes.com/2016/05/31/arts/sfmoma-glasses-prank.html

[26]Koren, pg. 57

[27]Koren, pg. 61

[28]Letter to N.F. von Meck., in Clarens, March 5th or 17th, 1878 (from *The Life and Letters of Peter Ilich Tchaikovsky*)

[29]*WTF with Marc Maron*, episode 185. June 20, 2011.

[30]https://lifehacker.com/jerry-seinfelds-productivity-secret-281626

[31]https://fortune.com/2022/07/18/best-workplaces-millennials-2022-purpose-meaning/

[32]Collected Papers of Albert Einstein, Vol. 8, Doc. 597, *The Quotable Einstein*, Princeton University Press.

ABOUT ATMOSPHERE PRESS

Founded in 2015, Atmosphere Press was built on the principles of Honesty, Transparency, Professionalism, Kindness, and Making Your Book Awesome. As an ethical and author-friendly hybrid press, we stay true to that founding mission today.

If you're a reader, enter our giveaway for a free book here:

SCAN TO ENTER
BOOK GIVEAWAY

If you're a writer, submit your manuscript for consideration here:

SCAN TO SUBMIT
MANUSCRIPT

And always feel free to visit Atmosphere Press and our authors online at atmospherepress.com. See you there soon!

ACKNOWLEDGMENTS

I would like to thank my wife, Catherine, for all her support and for reading early versions of this book. Thanks also to Maria Edwards for her crucial edits in later versions of this book and for murdering all of my darlings. Thanks to everyone at Atmosphere Press for making this book a reality, and to all of my professors and colleagues at Texas State University for teaching me how to write.

ABOUT THE AUTHOR

PHILLIP SCOTT MANDEL founded Mandel Marketing in 2019. He has an MFA in Fiction Writing from Texas State University and an MA in English Literature from NYU. His fiction, poetry, and nonfiction has appeared in numerous literary journals and anthologies. He launched *Abandon Journal* in 2021 and currently serves as the Managing Editor. Originally from New York, he now lives in Austin, Texas, with his wife and daughter.